ALSO BY GAIL BLANKE

Taking Control of Your Life: The Secrets
of Successful Enterprising Women

IN MY WILDEST DREAMS

LIVING THE LIFE YOU LONG FOR

GAIL BLANKE

SIMON & SCHUSTER

SIMON & SCHUSTER
Rockefeller Center
1230 Avenue of the Americas
New York, NY 10020

Copyright © 1998 by Gail Blanke Enterprises, LLC

Designed by Sam Potts
Manufactured in the United States of America

5   7   9   10   8   6   4

Library of Congress Cataloging-in-Publication Data
Blanke, Gail.
In my wildest dreams : living the life you long for /
Gail Blanke.
p.   cm.
Includes bibliographical references
1. Success—Psychological aspects.   I. Title.
BF637.S8B52   1998
158.1'082—dc21
98-6262
CIP

ISBN 0-684-84113-4

Acknowledgments

During the process of developing Lifedesigns, I was asked by a marketing consultant whether Lifedesigns was a business or a cause. The question provoked an enormous revelation in me, which was that I was desperate to combine my heart and my business sense. As a result, I created Lifedesigns to do both. It's a "business" in the sense that I make my living, and provide a living for all the Lifedesigns employees, from workshops, newsletters, books, and tapes—the Lifedesigns products. But it's also my "cause." The mission of Lifedesigns is to empower women, worldwide, to live the life of their dreams—to enable them to know, without a shadow of a doubt, that their lives are their own to create, design, delight in. Lifedesigns is my destiny, and my reason for being here. One reason I realized this as early as I did was that Fred Harmon asked me that crucial question.

I was given the resources to develop the business, and discover my destiny, by my former boss, Jim Preston, Avon's chairman and CEO. In its early days, when Lifedesigns was nothing more than a fledgling business unit that didn't "make its numbers," Jim not only encouraged the birth of Lifedesigns, but gave it room to grow and time to develop. After I had acquired the business from Avon, his encouragement stayed with me in my darkest, longest fraught-with-doubt nights. "I'll tell you one thing," he said. "If passion counts for anything at all, Lifedesigns will make it big."

Close to two thousand women have participated in Lifedesigns workshops. The early participants were our trailblazers and our inspiration. Even when the workshop was in its rough-draft form, they made us feel after each workshop that we'd "made it big"—that what we'd provided was crucial, even transformative, to their lives. Their input became part of the heart and soul of Lifedesigns.

The Generative Leadership Group has been our ongoing partner in developing much of the Lifedesigns workshop and content. Terry St. Pierre, in particular, has provided steady inspiration and support. Her touch, her insights, can be felt in almost every Lifedesigns conversation.

Our workshop leaders provided insight and input in the journey from rough draft to finished product. In particular, Hafeezah Basir, whose wisdom and love are evident throughout this book, is a pillar of what Lifedesigns stands for. It's in her bloodstream; she lives it daily. In addition, Amanda Morgan has dedicated meticulous attention to every element of the workshop and has helped set our standard for quality. Both Hafeezah and Amanda continue to empower other extraordinary women and men to join the growing ranks of Lifedesigns leaders.

Our workshop managers, Jennifer Short and Ireen Khan, are insightful beyond their years. Their political commitment to young women just beginning to navigate their lives challenged me to broaden Lifedesigns to include all age and economic groups. Jennifer and Ireen each have a unique vision of how to make the world a better place and an extraordinary dedication to bettering women's lives. I am grateful to provide the playing field, at least for now, on which they attempt to realize their dreams.

In My Wildest Dreams would still be a dream were it not for Joyce Hackett, my collaborator and partner in the writing of this book. No words can express (unless Joyce could find them) how grateful I am to Joyce for her art, her craft, her intellect, her humor, and extraordinary ability to "get it." She's a superb writer and a dear friend.

Becky Salatan provided sensitive and insightful editing that enabled our ideas to come through in their clearest form, and Laurie Chittenden championed this book in a way no one else could have.

Finally, it is to my family that I am most grateful. My mother and fa-

Acknowledgments

ther continue to remind me every day that I am the right person at the right place at the right time to make a difference. My husband and best friend, Jim, knew long before I did that this book would happen, that Lifedesigns (the cause and the business) was worthy and would work. And, of course, Kate and Abigail, our daughters, are the inspiration behind what I do. They are, quite simply, more than I could ever hope for.

FOR KATE AND ABIGAIL

whose lives, I know, will be
fuller, richer, and more fun
than I could possibly imagine.

Contents

Contents

IN MY
WILDEST
DREAMS

Introduction

The real voyage of discovery
consists not in seeking new landscapes,
but in having new eyes.

— MARCEL PROUST

R ecently I had breakfast with a woman who had come to talk with me about women. She was a high-powered executive recruiter, and someone had told me she had her hands on a ton of information about where women are now. I was in the first few months of starting my company, Lifedesigns, and was still chasing every fox down every hole as I tried to figure out what shape the company would take. As we ordered coffee, the woman began talking about the numbers pointing to women's lack of opportunities, the progress women haven't made, using familiar terms like backlash and glass ceiling. And she showed me the studies documenting the fact that women's pay scale really hasn't risen much since 1970.

As she spoke, I nodded, having no doubt that her facts were accurate.

She's the kind of person you'd trust to measure out explosive chemicals. At the same time, as I listened and nodded, I felt my throat tighten up. My mind wandered off, anxiously, to all the decisions I had to make as the head of my own company. Her facts seemed to spin a web of impossibility around me and my venture. Finally, I interrupted.

"You know what?"

She sat, her face expectant.

"I don't care," I said.

Considering I'd said about the rudest thing anyone could say in a business meeting, she took it pretty well. "What do you mean?" she asked.

"I don't care," I said again. I had absorbed her facts, and I was even willing to admit that her interpretations of these facts were valid. But I couldn't listen to any more of them.

Because while the facts were most likely true, her interpretations—though valid from where she stood—were not empowering me. The problem with research, of course, is that it's about the past. It's a description of what we already know about the state of things. Sometimes it surprises us with what's so. But most of the time, we use it to confirm and prove what we already know about how wrong things are. What her statistics were doing, powerfully, was entangling me back in the past. And what I needed, at that moment, was an interpretation that enabled me to move forward into possibility. We got the check.

Alone in my office, I searched for some sort of inspiration to pave over the pothole in my psyche she'd opened up. Suddenly I thought of Carolyn Stradley, the CEO of C&S Paving in Marietta, Georgia—the company that paved the track at the Olympic stadium in Atlanta—whom I'd heard speak, years before, when she'd won a Women of Enterprise award from Avon.

I had initiated these awards to honor women who overcame enormous personal obstacles to attain significant economic success, partly because I have been fascinated, for as long as I can remember, by breakthroughs. I wanted to hear stories about the moments when we transcend our past, our habits, our "character defects" and our limits of circumstance, which in Carolyn's case had been steep. Born into Appalachian mountain poverty, Carolyn was eleven when her mother died. Her alcoholic father abandoned the family, and for a few years she and her brother, living in a hut, ate wild berries and trapped rabbits to stay alive. Married at fifteen, pregnant in the eleventh grade, Carolyn started work as a secretary and continued to attend school. She had kept on with her studies in engineering construction even after her first husband died. As I sat in my office, I imagined Carolyn, sitting in her office after the bankers she'd approached for a loan to buy her first truck had laughed in her face. And I began to laugh at myself, thinking about how much more she had overcome.

Carolyn's astonishing journey had stuck in my mind for years. Or rather, the question of how was she able—how anyone is able—to remain undaunted in the face of overwhelming adversity. How had she created a terrific new life out of the remnants of a miserable one? How had she gone from living in the woods to landing the largest U.S. Air Force paving contract ever awarded to any female-owned business?

Then the obvious occurred to me: Being disadvantaged is a sort of advantage, because people who come from behind try harder. I started to get mad—not at the woman who'd served as the messenger of the bad news at breakfast, but at myself, for buying into the conclusions I thought those facts implied about my future.

It was an anger I remembered. I'd felt it once before, in a swimming race, when I was a kid. At twelve I had qualified for the semi-finals of the U.S. national freestyle competition. As we poised ourselves on the starting blocks for the next-to-last race, the girl beside me swayed back and forth in an odd way, and when I turned to look at her I lost my balance and fell into the water, feet first. A second later the judge shot the gun to start the race. Though I looked at the judge to rule it a false start, he shook his head no, telling me it wasn't. I was furious! But at that moment, I had to make a decision. I could either be right, and insist on my version of the facts, or I could start swimming.

I'm sure I swam the fastest I've ever swum in my life—though everybody else had taken a racing dive, I came in second in that heat. And ultimately I won the final.

What I needed, after that breakfast, was an interpretation that empowered me to swim. I could not ignore the facts the recruiter presented, the interpretation I chose, after our parting, was that women needed the Lifedesigns technology *exactly because* we have definitively proven that biases and obstacles exist. We've proven they exist, and we've also proven we can fight harder and work longer and give more, that we can compete and win—or at least place—in other people's races. The question now is, What race do we want to be swimming in? This is what the Lifedesigns program is about, and why, I decided, it was so desperately needed.

As we begin the twenty-first century, women—in the United States, at least—have significantly shifted their place in the world. Many of the struggles of the last hundred years have been about getting what men had that we didn't: the vote, the chance, the independence, the freedom, the partnerships, the salaries, the promotions, the board seats, and so on. Though the world still presents us with structures that are male-designed and -dominated—I know someone who has the facts to prove it—it is impossible to ignore the deep and significant gains we've made in access to opportunities. But even the women who *have* broken through, who have the partnerships, the salaries, the promotions, and the offices, are often wondering, *Is this all there is?* It was the question I had asked myself when, in the spring I turned forty, I got an office overlooking Central Park as part of a promotion. As I sat down on my gorgeous white couch on my first day, a sinking feeling overtook the luxurious atmosphere of corporate privilege. The fabulous office with the breathtaking view, I knew, wasn't "it." I had achieved the trappings of success that many people spend their lives trying to get. But, like many women, I had been so busy fighting to get there I hadn't allowed myself to question whether "there" was where I wanted to be. I'd been afraid, with my nose to the grindstone, to look up.

I think I was feeling what Gloria Steinem talks about in *Revolution from Within:* that like many women who have achieved "success," satisfaction was eluding me, because the "success" I'd achieved was preordained, predefined, prepackaged. And the question of why—of what it's for—remained obscure, because the demands of my daily life discouraged the sort of long-term thinking that would clarify or refine a higher vision.

Sometimes, by the way, we never even develop a vision of what "it" is! Women are taught from an early age to fit in, to be nice, not to stand out, to be pleasing. Often, they're waiting to be recognized or rewarded—or rescued—by others, before they acknowledge their dreams to themselves. They're waiting for the "right" answer to appear from outside, never knowing that they get to—and have to—make up what that right answer is for themselves. Women have the children, and are increasingly responsible for aging parents; we're *taught* to be responsible, and responsive, and to wait until those responsibilities ease up before we define and pursue our dreams. We're waiting to be married, or divorced; waiting until the children are a little older, until things calm down at work. And while we're waiting, while we're looking the other way, another window of opportunity to move nearer to the life of our dreams quietly closes. Until, if we wait long enough, we have a moment when we realize that something fundamental that we wanted in life has passed us by.

Now, in my office that day, I hadn't yet missed the boat—at that point I still hadn't defined what my boat was. All I knew was that my definition of great wasn't all the things I'd thought it was. It wasn't about having everybody think I was drop-dead gorgeous, or marrying the greatest guy, or having a bunch of stuff, or fitting in well enough to earn the great promotion that merited the office.

A few years later, I listened to Women of Enterprise winner Judy Bliss describe how she developed her $1.4-million business, Mindplay. Because her family had little money—her mother took in ironing to make a living while her father was in prison—Judy had grown up making cardboard cutout toys for her two younger sisters, to entertain them. Much later in life, as a computer programmer and the mother of a six-year-old son, Judy had decided to quit her job because her boss refused to listen to her predictions about the coming popularity of the personal computer. Judy's son had been diagnosed with attention deficit disorder, or ADD, and was having difficulty learning to read. Judy herself had always had difficulty reading, and had read very slowly; for years, her strategy for staying ahead had been to wake herself up at four A.M. each day and read for a few hours before going back to sleep. Now, having quit her job, and working at her dining table, Judy began to see clearly that her son was not learning to read. She began to design programs to teach him to read. But kids being kids, whenever her son knew he was supposed to be learning, he refused to execute Judy's programs. So Judy began to invent games—as she had for her sisters, years before—to get her son to learn. These games became the products that Mindplay sells.

As I listened to Judy's story, something occurred to me—again, something so obvious I almost missed it. The women I'd been listening to all these years, I realized, didn't set out to create astoundingly successful businesses. Carolyn Stradley didn't say to herself, while living in the woods, "You know what? I think I'll start my own firm, become a renowned woman entrepreneur, and be honored by whoever is elected president of the United States in 1992. It'll be *fabulous*." None of them, in fact, had ever mentioned setting out to make a lot of money, to be recognized, to smash the glass ceiling, or to become powerful. What they'd done was to develop a vision of what they wanted their life to be, a vision so compelling that they'd created resources where there were none, surmounted insurmountable odds, even re-created themselves. Not because they'd hit bottom, or because they'd set goals, but because what they were going after mattered to them more than anything else in their life. Judy cared more about creating a world in which her son would learn to read than about anything else. Her extraordinary success came in the pursuit of something very simple: how she wanted her life to go.

This held true, I realized, on whatever scale women were operating. I'm on the board of Trickle UP, an organization that helps people start businesses in third-world countries with an initial investment of about $50. At the three-year mark, these entrepreneurs, the vast majority of whom are women, have an extraordinary business success rate of over 85 percent. These women have fewer children, and they achieve literacy rates far higher than women who are urged by governments to do things that are good for them. They succeed not because the industrialized world says they're supposed to, but because they need to in order to chase their dream of economic independence.

When you develop a vision that matters—a statement of what's already most important to you—you can achieve breakthroughs. You don't necessarily need to work harder, or expend more effort, but simply to identify what it is you're working *for*.

My own moment of vision came on a plane after working for corporate America for twenty years, after a conference during which I'd announced, without permission, that the huge corporation I worked for could actually sell women's empowerment and self-fulfillment. Unfortunately, they'd seen the program I was developing as a marketing tool, or a human resource tool to inspire salespeople, not as a product in itself. "What does that have to do with anything?" the other corporate officers had asked me later. "We have to make our numbers!" The listening they offered, and the responses they gave to my ideas, were skeptical and lukewarm at best. On the plane home, the words of the high-powered marketing consultant I'd retained as I was designing the Lifedesigns program echoed in my mind: *Is this a business or a cause?* When I'd replied that it was both, he'd corrected me. No, he'd said, you have to choose. As I drifted in and out of sleep, I think I subconsciously recognized that like so many corporate women, I'd earned success at the expense of being fully female. You can ride in the front seat where we make the money, the men seemed to be saying, but only if you put your values and your causes and your caring about the world in the trunk. When I woke up I had acknowledged to myself that I would never be able to realize my vision within a corporation—any corporation—that hadn't been designed to my specifications.

On the back of a tattered envelope I pulled from my purse, I wrote down: M.O.B. These initials stood for My Own Business. I jotted down notes of what I pictured: myself as a motivational speaker who would do appearances, create seminars, and produce books and tapes that made a difference in other women's lives. On this envelope I made a small, quiet declaration of my future. I decided that I could design Lifedesigns to help women who wanted to make a difference, make it. That I would challenge the notion that the stock price and the bottom line were incompatible by creating good, and joy. And—dare I say it—money.

I left everything I knew, and had succeeded at, to create Lifedesigns. The program was developed with the input of consultants, employees, colleagues, friends, husbands, daughters, the workshop leaders, and, of course, the participants. Transforming that initial seed of a declaration into a profitable motivational company took three years. During that time I experimented with many ideas that partly worked—and partly didn't—all the while defining and refining the way I was going to make my vision a reality. The experience shifted how I thought. Radically. It convinced me that we're not just here to survive, to get through, to function impressively, or to support someone else's dreams, that none of us is here to settle, to compromise, to allow life to happen and hope it's not too bad. We're here to live fully and passionately, to allow ourselves to be fully who we are. Not to have it all, but to spend it all, to use it all up. I love this quote from Shaw's play *Man and Superman:*

> This is the true joy in life, the being used for a purpose recognized by yourself as a mighty one; the being thoroughly worn out before you are thrown on the scrap heap; the being a force of Nature instead of a feverish selfish little clod of ailments and grievances complaining that the world will not devote itself to making you happy.*

What I want on my tombstone is not: SHE COPED, but rather SHE WAS HERE . . . AND IT WAS NEVER THE SAME.

The Lifedesigns program is designed to provoke profound shifts in thinking. My mission is to provide you with the skills, confidence, and capability to create *your* version of a fabulous life. I'm out to explode your sense of personal and professional possibility, to give you a method for designing and creating a life you love, to support you, and help you support yourself during your transition. And I'm committed to your knowing that you're not alone in pursuing your goals.

One of the skills you'll develop, in the course of this book, is reaching out to others, and especially other women—either in informal groups, formal professional organizations, or larger networks. Perhaps one reason some women now hesitate to identify themselves with such a valuable movement as feminism is that it's picked up such negative vibes in the popular mind-set. A feminist is often now perceived to be a woman who's angrily fighting *against* something. The image of the women's movement that seems to be floating around in the culture these days is of a bunch of women coming up over a hill with pith helmets, with picks and axes! But when you define and then declare your precise vision of what you want in life, you blame no one. Making a commitment to design and create your dream life is a stance that is not *against* anybody or

---

*George Bernard Shaw, *Man and Superman*, Act III, "Don Juan in Hell." London, Penguin Books, 1946.

anything, but *for* joy and self-satisfaction. And declaring your dreams creates an almost instant community of supporters. Declaring what you want, rather than attacking what is, creates a positive force that brings others, including the men, along. The model of being chosen makes martyrs and victims of women in all kinds of little ways, all the time, whereas the model of choosing, and continuing to take responsibility for those choices, creates an inclusive space that says: *This is my journey, to my dream, and I want you to come. There's plenty of room, and anyway, I need your help.* It's a stance that's too loving to resist.

Since you're not creating a practice life—since this is the only life we're *sure* of having—I invite you to make your life burn brightly: to look past the frustrations, to dump the old beliefs that aren't working, to create and refine a vision for your life you can stand in—and stand for—now. Whether you're at the point of wanting to reconnect with your dreams and passions, or you're pursuing them tentatively; whether you're "successful" but dissatisfied or you're satisfied and happy, yet seeking to make a greater contribution—wherever you are in your life, my goal in this book is to convince you that the life of your dreams is a matter of your design, your power, your control, and not something that "happens to you." Scary as it may be, I'm inviting you to chuck the idea that it's any harder for women. To shed your belief in—your conviction in— what holds you back. To peel off the fear that you're too old or too young; a little too big, a little too small; that you're too enthusiastic, or too emotional; that you're "too black" or "too white"—or just a little too female. To quit having to be right about how wrong it is, and was, and how wrong it is around here. To abandon the desire to be provided for, to stop waiting for the world to serve up the perfect environment in which to develop and express yourself. To design and create that environment yourself. To declare your passions to others, and to reach out to support other women's dreams. Most of all, to consider the power of your own possibilities, the power of one individual—a single woman— to make a difference in the world.

Thousands of women have participated in Lifedesigns. Whether they're CEOs or homemakers, actors or artists, students or mothers, entrepreneurs or athletes—we've even had a Rockette!—they all had in common a dream of making a greater difference in the world. Over and over, I'll be asking what "great" looks like to you. The exercises will encourage, beg, and badger you to define success in your own terms; to define, refine, and then declare a vision that matters to you. Once you've put what you want out into the world, the book will walk you through the process of making your dream real, a process that will serve as a template for change in any area. If this sounds grandiose, keep in mind: I am now living the declaration I made on the back of an envelope.

So I will begin by declaring, again, that my vision is to empower women, worldwide, to design and live the life of their dreams. This book is a catalyst to enable you to do just that.

PART ONE

BREAKING THE GRIP OF THE PAST

The Lifedesigns program is not based in its content. It does not offer a slew of new information or ideas. Many of us know what to do—we've got the books, we've ordered the tapes—yet we don't do it. And it's not exactly a process workshop either: You don't do activities X, Y, and Z until finally you master a field. What this book will do is enable you to take many ideas you've already been exposed to and place them in a new framework, or context. The breakthroughs women achieve in our workshops happen not because they work harder, or expend more effort, but because they begin to see their lives from different perspectives. When you begin to see the outrageous possibilities in your careers and relationships, you'll stop dousing your own fires and harness the natural heat of your passions. In other words, you'll use the commitments you already hold, the desires that already are the most important to you, to motivate the actions that yield breakthrough results.

That's why Chapter 1 begins by asking you what your commitments are. Knowing yourself by your commitments, and knowing other people by theirs, can cut through the past like an egg slicer. One genuine commitment—even one as small as the commitment to read this book and do the exercises in it—can begin to shift the outward situations of your life. You may find, once you glimpse the possibilities of a great life and the energy that comes from focusing on your commitments, that your current, "okay" life is no longer okay. You may find yourself taking new risks in a job situation or in a relationship. The focus is: What would make your life worth living? What do you stand for? What is your idea of a great life?

Now, as Tom Robbins writes in *Jitterbug Perfume*, "The price of self-destiny is never cheap, and in certain situations it is unthinkable. But to achieve the marvelous, it is precisely the unthinkable that must be thought." What I want to know is, completely apart from the limitations you now see on yourself, what is your ideal life? What does "great" look like to you?

Much of this book is about shifting your attention from the obstacles to the possibilities. To do that, you'll need to scrutinize, closely, what you think your obstacles are.

Once participants explore their individuality and think the unthinkable, we encourage them to declare what they've discovered to as many listeners as possible. Declaring can feel like jumping off the diving board and inventing the water on the way down. But often just the act of speaking turns up the "noise" in our heads about why we can't do what we want to do. It's stunning, when we stop to look at how we think, how many paralyzing assumptions we've bought into, usually without even realizing it! When we look at these old beliefs from a neutral space, we get to decide. Some rules for living may serve us, and these we may decide to keep as beliefs. But those that disempower we may want to abandon. Especially the notion that it—whatever "it" is—is too hard.

In declaring the dreams we're committed to, we make them real, which is why speaking these sorts of declarations, without the resources or plans to make them come true, can be terrifying. Who wants to hear people say "You're nuts!" Who wants to say "I'm going to get a Ph.D." when you don't even have a high school diploma? Who wants to acknowledge a desire so powerful and compelling that you know in your heart you can't live without it—without the means to get there?

Most of us live in a box that keeps us where we are. Though the box is in some ways a coffin that buries us alive, it's usually comfortable. We know it. It protects us from all sorts of dangers. It's like a house we inherit from our parents and grandparents, constructed from ideas about how the world is. The walls in this house are decorated with the status quo. We inherit murals of our culture, and pictures of the world. The problem is that we look at them for so long that we begin to view them as the world itself. After a while we're looking at old, outdated landscapes—outdated interpretations of the world—and seeing them as real.

The rest of Part I will do two things. First, it will focus on what it is you want out of this book—what you're out for. It will also look closely at the beliefs that have rooted you in your past.

Chapter 2 looks at how our automatic listening keeps us walled in and limits change. In it you will learn to listen not through the filters of your limiting beliefs and assumptions, but *for* possibilities and opportunities for change.

Chapter 3 diagnoses the incompletions, the unresolved areas in your life that keep you from moving forward. You'll get some immediate energy by beginning to resolve the grip that the past has on the present. It provides a strategy for identifying what's incomplete and examining the possibilities for how to resolve the situation by choosing the action or perspective that will enable you to leave it behind, and move forward.

Chapter 4 addresses the fundamental beliefs that structure any box—beliefs that assert that reality is fixed, and that we already know about it. When you crack open your box, you'll find yourself in a "clearing"—a wide open, empty space in which you can see the view on all sides, and decide where you want to go. I am committed, in these next few chapters, to helping you reach that clearing.

Chapter 5 engages in an almost microscopic scrutiny of the rules you've identified in Chapter 4. Examining your tendency to meld fact and interpretation, and separating the two, is the most profound way to pry apart the crack you'll introduce into your box. It demonstrates how much of what we think of as fact is actually interpretation. It can be startling to realize that the fixed reality that holds you back is actually somebody else's idea of reality, and that it doesn't happen to be—or have to be—yours! At the end of the chapter, I hope to have broken through a lot of your convictions about why you need to stay where you are, to take you to a clearing that, while scary, will contain much more possibility.

I ask only that you *make two commitments.*

First, try it on. Have you ever been in a store and known what you wanted, gotten it off the rack, then had someone suggest that you'd look great in that yellow mini-dress with the aluminum foil belt? "Trust me," the salesperson says. "Try it on." You want to kill her—you're fussing and fuming—and then you come out and everybody in the store does a double take and says you look fabulous! Aluminum foil, they say, is your fabric! You were looking for that blouse with the Peter Pan collar to go with your plaid skirt, and now you're bewildered. "Well, maybe," you're forced to say.

What I'm requesting, with the ideas in this book, is that you use a "Well, maybe," when you want to respond "No way!" I'm hoping that you can at least consider that it might be possible to think differently from the way you do. That you start to see your worldview as just that, only one view, rather than seeing it as the way things are. As a landscape painting, rather than reality itself. You don't have to buy the dress, just try it on.

The book follows fifteen participants, whom you will come to know intimately. Though most names and some details have been changed to preserve anonymity, each participant is a real woman who took the Lifedesigns workshop, and none of the dialogue is made up. As you watch these women model the process of redesign, you will get to know them, and their commitments, as you get to know yourself. Each chapter contains exercises that will enable you to "participate" with them. If you do them carefully, they'll coax your dream out of your head and put it "in your face." The exercises transform skills you already have—speaking and listening—into tools that will make the impossible possible. My second request, then, is that you commit yourself to doing them. Buy yourself a blank notebook, now. If you skip the exercises, you'll gain insight and knowledge about your old world, but you won't develop the skills to break into a new one. The exercises aren't extra credit for the eager. They are the program itself.

Chapter One

Commitments

In the external world, we tend to know each other by our titles, our economic class, our degrees, our position in the family, our neighborhoods, our race. I'm managing director of a chemical manufacturer, you say, but what you want to add is: I'm not really as much of a geek as that sounds. I'm a real estate broker, you say, knowing in your heart that you're a jewelry designer. You tell people how much you love being a stay-at-home mom, and it's true, but you find yourself wanting to add that you were accepted to a master's program ten years ago, even though you didn't go!

Quick categories help people locate us, and they help us locate them. Unfortunately, they were all defined before any of us stepped into the box labeled "mother" or "oldest daughter" or "executive vice president." Boxes that are designed by others—our parents, our colleagues, or simply our culture—pinch and cramp us because they're never tailored to fit our unique soul. Yet we all want to know, quickly, who's the boss, and who's the guy we need to bribe in the supply room. And so we pigeonhole each other, even though when someone asks, "What do you do?" the question makes us cringe.

So the first questions we like to ask the participants of our workshop are: What are you committed to? What are you out for? What do you love?

Often, though, when our leaders ask these questions, they hear comments like that made by Lauren, a stunning Italian beauty with long auburn hair who, after thirteen years, quit her job as an executive in a cosmetics company. Unemployed for a year, Lauren has come to the workshop looking for what her next life will be. She wants to find something she can be passionate about.

> "I hate that word," says Lauren. "It gives me a scary, suffocating feeling. It's funny, because when I worked for my cosmetics company, I was totally rah-rah! Now 'commitment' gives me the creeps."

Why Commitments Threaten

One of the definitions of the word *committed* is being trapped in a mental institution, by others, against your will—no wonder it drags a lot of baggage behind it! Commitments are scary, I think, for two reasons: We're scared we won't fulfill them, or we're scared they won't fulfill us. The first issue, I'll deal with later. It's the second one I want to discuss here.

We have all, at one time or another, felt that suffocating panic Lauren expressed. Often we shy away from commitments *exactly because* most of us already know how awful it feels to be committed to organizations we no longer respect; projects we didn't design and don't believe in; relationships we've outgrown; and inherited ways of thinking about the world that box us in.

Often, in groups of people—especially in corporations—commitments you've made can be used against you, to get you to do something you don't want to do. This happens because the word *commitment* is often heard—or misheard—as a promise to take a specific action.

What's the difference? you might ask.

A commitment is a looser framework than a promise. It's a steady, unwavering intention to go in a certain direction, rather than a specific set of steps to get there. If you have a commitment to learn to dance, for example, you could do it in a variety of ways—by going to a class, by watching ballet, by hiring a private teacher, by going to a folk-dance weekend workshop. A promise, on the other hand, is a way of speaking that generates action. It says: I'm going to register for that folk-dance weekend by Friday at five P.M. Now, you don't promise the predictable: You don't promise that you'll get up in the morning, or go to the bathroom, because that's simply stating the obvious. What you promise is the unpredictable. But because it's unpredictable, and because we live in an unpredictable world, it's not 100 percent sure. The truth is, we make promises not because we always know we can keep them. *We make promises to help us stretch into the unknown.*

I may promise to be in a nurturing relationship with someone, to marry him, for life. But though I made the promise with integrity, I might not have known that, at twenty-two, committing for life might not have been an appropriate promise to make. My fundamental commitment may be to be in a nurturing relationship, but at forty-five, "nurturing relationship" might not mean what it meant at seventeen. In this case it's possible to authentically say: I need to revoke this promise. There are, as we all know, consequences to revoking a promise.* But there are also many consequences to keeping promises that we can no longer authentically accept.

> "My ex-husband is gay," interrupted Jenny, a banker who looks
> like a bigger and more exuberant version of Jodie Foster.
> "When he finally admitted that to me I insisted we stay married

---

*See Searle, J. R., "The Background of Meaning." In J. R. Searle, F. Kiefer, and M. Bierwisch (eds.), *Speech Act Theory and Pragmatics* (Dordrecht, Holland: Reidel, 1980).

because I couldn't stand that he'd broken his promise to be my husband. It went on like that for three years! It was a farce! And I couldn't speak to him for two years after that, even though he really wanted my friendship, because even though I was remarried, I was still angry that he broke his promise. Even my parents were, like, Get over it! And I'm still, you know, fuming. I made a mess."

"Haven't we all," said Hafeezah, the workshop leader.

Sometimes, though we haven't made a promise, our commitments are *interpreted* as demanding a particular action. Say you tell your boss you're committed to doing a great job, and you are. You do above and beyond the work your job entails, and you achieve results. But if the corporate culture interprets "being committed to your job" as a promise to work from eight in the morning to eight at night, then no matter how spectacular your performance is, if you're leaving in the afternoon to pick up your kids from day care, your boss may ask you why you're not committed. The men in the office may get pretty resentful if they assume that a mother of two is going to demonstrate her commitment the same way they do, which is to live, sleep, and shower at her desk. In a culture like that, it's no wonder we fear committing ourselves!

THE LONG-TERM POWER OF COMMITMENTS

Often when we're doing things we don't want to do because someone (or something, like the corporate culture) is "making" us, we're actually honoring commitments *we decided to make* to ourselves. We may not remember what our commitments are, because we made them so long ago that we forgot having made them. How many of us work with someone who's always martyring herself? You know, that person who constantly complains about her workload and swears she won't take on another project, and then does? She may say she's committed to balancing her life, but if what she's really committed to is proving that she's the hardest-working camper, then she'll continue to overcommit and overextend.

And what about when no one's asking you to do anything? How often have you eaten something you didn't want to eat, or said something you knew you shouldn't say, feeling almost as if it was happening against your will? With deeply ingrained behaviors, which we feel forced to engage in even after we've recognized they don't work for us, the place to look for change is not at the level of will. Ultimately, we need to look back at the deep commitments these patterns reflect, commitments we made to ourselves long ago. We may not even know we hold these commitments, or remember that we made them. But if you think about it, we must be deeply committed if we persist, even in the face of repeated pain, in engaging in these patterns!

So we may have a commitment to get thin, but at the moment we're eating, we're honoring a deeper, older commitment: I must get my share of pleasure, which won't come to me in any other way. Sometimes it can be as primal as: I must keep myself from starving. Or: we can desperately want to get married, and we can know that to do that, it would probably be a good idea to keep this relationship going more than six dates. But if we hold a deeper, prior commitment to not being trapped by somebody else's limitations, we'll do something to sabotage the relationship no matter how hard we think we're trying to sustain it.

Whether or not we admit it, we *already have* commitments. We chose them, and now we're honoring them. Our commitments nearly always have consequences in the realm of action. And because commitments are broader than promises, and the pathways by which we can fulfill them are so many, the consequences of holding on to old ones can be enormous. The consequences of keeping one promise are minuscule compared to the huge, long-term consequences of honoring old commitments. Over the course of a lifetime it's like the difference between a shower and the water falling from Hoover Dam.

Most of us intuitively understand the long-term power of commitments. We hesitate not because we're afraid of the unknown places where our new commitments might take us, but because we already know what it feels like to be imprisoned by commitments that don't give us joy. Sometimes we know the fit is bad; these old commitments become like that uncomfortable suit your mother gave you for graduation. But most of the time we've had that old suit so long, we don't even realize we're wearing it!

Lauren, initially, did not feel she was committed to anything. But staying in a job you don't like for thirteen years reflects a profound commitment: to safety, to financial stability, to providing for your children, to maintaining respectability in your parents' eyes—to something!

> "My father always told me I didn't need an education," Lauren added, "because I'd just get married. He was the typical Italian patriarch. He said, 'No man likes a woman who's too strong.' I guess all these years, everybody's always said what a great job I had, and how I should be so grateful. I've been just thinking I should go with the program, and not make waves. Now what I'm committed to is losing my makeup case, and everything that went with it."

Thus, even though for six years Lauren has wanted to look for a new job, her prior commitment was not to become the kind of woman—the empowered job-seeker—who might threaten her father. Her commitment, as she finally put it, had been "to stay connected to her family."

CHOOSING THE COMMITMENTS THAT MATTER

When you look at your commitments actively, you will begin to recognize that you're choosing them, and not the other way around. Accepting that you're not "committed" by others, but only by yourself, frees you to revise your list of commitments to reflect who you are and who want to be now. Some you will choose to reaffirm, others to reinterpret. In Lauren's case, she decided that staying connected to her family didn't have to mean believing what they believed all the time. She reinterpreted her commitment to mean that she had to start letting them know where she was and who she was.

> "But not all commitments are so negative!" Elinor cried. Elinor is a telecommunications executive who, in spite of her young, freckly face and mounds of curly hair, practically radiates competency. She is married with two children. "I'm committed to my husband, who's terrifically supportive. We've been married nine years, and I think it's the thing I'm the most proud of in my life!"

Elinor's point is important. The idea is to look at *all* of your commitments from a neutral place. Even if you're stuck in your life, it doesn't mean you necessarily ought to abandon all the commitments you currently hold. The goal is simply to identify what past commitments you're actually honoring. Then you can decide whether they still matter to you as much as they used to. In a later section of the book we deal with throwing away things: One of our leaders, when faced with this assignment, found that she still had on her key ring the keys to the first apartment she'd bought, which she had been able to afford when she was only twenty-three years old. Amanda was proud of her achievement—for her, that little studio represented economic independence. Holding on to the keys was asserting a positive aspect of her maturity: the fact that she had taken charge of her financial life very early on. She'd long since sold the apartment, but holding on to those keys was a way of holding on to that achievement.

When she heard about the keys, another participant, Helene, a soft-spoken African-American professor of anthropology, tentatively raised her hand.

"You know," Helene whispered, "on my key ring I still have the keys to a truck I bought years ago, when I had a sort of carefree life and would go off into the mountains. A few years ago I got breast cancer. My two sisters had already died of it, and when I got it in my early forties, like they did, I was sure I'd die, too. I shut down, waiting and ready to die. But I survived."

"Could you speak up?" asked Alane, a software designer in her late twenties with short platinum hair and bright red lipstick, who was sitting next to Helene. Helene was speaking so quietly that no one could hear her.

"I survived the breast cancer," Helene said again. "But then, a year later, I developed lymphoma in my eye. And that just about crushed me. I thought, how can this be happening to me? I guess . . . I guess I started living to die," she said quietly, and began to weep. "I separated from my husband because I just withdrew into myself. I'm sitting here realizing that I'm living in a commitment to die gracefully. But"—Helene's tears turned to giggles—"it's not working. I'm alive!"

"So," said Hafeezah, "I'd like you to write down what you're committed to in this world. You don't have to know, at all, how you're going to fulfill your commitments. Just spend a little time writing down what you stand for, what matters to you. What are your reasons for living? What are you committed to see happening, in the world and in your life?"

"I don't know how to say this, but I want more passion in my life," said Page, a blonde in her early sixties who has enough accomplishments to fill three résumés.

"Page—it must be hard when you're so inarticulate," quipped Amy Jo, a sparky forty-six-year-old who runs her family's business.

"Really," said Page, "if you looked at my life from the outside, everyone thinks it's fabulous. I wear my wedding rings on the right hand, because I'm left handed, and they get in the way. A few weeks ago a colleague whom I've known for years found out that I've been married for thirty years, and said, 'I can't believe you're married! You seem so . . . happy.' And it's true, my life is terrific. But on the inside, you know, it just feels, well, drab."

"I want to be at complete inner peace," said Debra. "I want to get my life back. And I want a home that's a refuge where I can go to get some quiet time alone."

"I want to unpack the load that makes it foggy to see ahead," said Mary Scott, an African-American community activist who is associate director of a youth service project that creates programs for over three thousand kids. "And I want to create something for girls. But I'm very shy; I feel like a little girl in a grown-up body. I've only had a small vision. Told myself I couldn't do things. I'd like to write stories for young African-American girls and teach everybody to live in a multiracial world."

"I want to learn to receive," said Jenny, "and to be able to make progress, and anticipate good in my personal life, not just my professional life. I want a better relationship with my husband and my body."

"I want my work to be closely aligned with my values," said Julie, a thin, petite, late-forties brunette with strong, chiseled features and a serious look of integrity. Julie has worked at the same nonprofit for over twenty years, and she speaks almost plaintively, as if searching for a place in the world to do good.

"I was an M.S.W., a social worker, and spent eleven years in counseling," said Sara, a therapist with huge, brown, empathetic eyes and a gentle midwestern accent. "Then I went to work for an HMO. I didn't know I was transitioning into workaholism! I want to free myself of my fears. I find myself apologizing for my lack of credentials when recruiters call me. I want to get off of this treadmill. And . . . there's something else I want to say, but I feel like I've been complaining so long I just had to stop talking about it. So it's hard to say, because if I say I want it, and then don't get it, it'll just make my current life unbearable."

"And that is?" asked Hafeezah, smiling. Hafeezah has the presence and smile of Jessye Norman, and a way of making each woman in the room feel safe.

"I want to be married and have a child," Sara concluded.

"We're pretty much hitting the big categories," joked Hafeezah.

What I'm asking you to do, in the following exercise, is to dare to stop dismissing your wildest dreams—even if you have a million reasons why they can never happen.

....

EXERCISE: IDENTIFYING YOUR COMMITMENTS

1. Write down *I'm committed to . . .* at the top of a page in your notebook.
2. Now jot down, quickly, what you're committed to. What are you out for? What are you passionate about? What matters to you? What do you love?

   One note: For the purpose of this exercise, the word *commitment* simply means an important wish, one that gets you up in the morning even if you've never done anything about it.

   You may want to add to the list over the next few days, but try to get the most important commitments on paper in the next few minutes. Set aside any judgments of whether the commitment is frivolous. Set aside the question of whether fulfilling it would force you to promise the impossible. And set aside what you think it might say about you—for example, if you think that, as a mother of three, wanting solitude makes you self-centered, or greedy, or complaining, that's okay. For now, the idea is simply to say it.

Once you've identified your major commitments, the next step is to home in, specifically, on why you want what you want. One way of doing this to ask yourself: What would that allow for?

Asking this question helps you find the straightest path to what you want. Say, for example, that you're committed to getting married. Do you want to be married so you can have children? Or because you think being married would mean you are finally allowed to affirm your body, and let your hair go naturally gray? Is it because you want a companion to go to the opera with? Or simply because you want the intimacy inherent in that relationship? If, for example, you wrote down that you're committed to financial security: Do you want it because it will finally gain your father's respect? Or do you want it because it will enable you to fulfill your dream of living on a sailboat? Because it would make you feel successful enough to quit your job and work in an animal shelter?

If you're stuck wondering what it is you're supposed to want, keep in mind that none of these commitments is inherently better, or holier, or more valid, than any other one. *The scale on which to evaluate your commitments is simply how close or how far away they are from who you want to be, for now.*

> "What if you have a commitment you've had forever, but it doesn't really excite you anymore, but you don't feel you can let it go?" asked Shelly, a soft, slim southern belle in her mid-fifties. "I dropped out three semesters short of finishing my B.A. to marry Mr. Wonderful, and now, I'm not married to Mr. Wonderful anymore. Part of me wants to go back to school; part of me feels like, Forget it, it's too late."

There are three possible ways you can address an old commitment: You can reaffirm it, reinterpret it, or replace it.

Suppose you want to go back to school. And when you ask yourself what that commitment would allow for, your answer is pretty much as you expressed it. Nothing excites you more than sitting in a classroom learning about medieval castles. In this case you'll want to *reaffirm* your commitment.

Perhaps you're not sure you can go through with the whole degree, and you don't want to start if you're not sure you'll finish. Reaffirming can be frightening, even when you're sure it's what you want to do. Often we don't want to identify or declare or try to honor a commitment because we worry we won't be good enough, smart enough, dedicated or energetic enough to make good. Another version of this is that your friends won't be supportive enough, the world won't compensate you enough, the critics won't be appreciative enough, and so on. If these are your fears, you're on the right track. Read on.

Suppose you think you should have a B.A. You want to be exposed to other cultures and perspectives. But the idea of going back to school with a bunch of eighteen-year-olds nauseates you. In this case, you may decide that what you really want is to take a yearlong trip around the world to expose yourself to the cultures and landscapes you've never seen. In this case you are choosing to *reinterpret* the commitment to educate yourself through a pathway that excites you.

Say you want to go back to college because you work in a field where everybody has a degree. You now manage a staff of 153 people, all of whom have more advanced degrees than you, and you feel like a fraud. At the same time, you love what you do and don't want to take time off. In this case you may decide that though, all these years, you thought you needed that B.A., you've now decided that the greatest joy is learning to live without artificial certificates of self-worth. In this case you may decide to discard your commitment entirely, and *replace* that outdated need for a degree with a commitment to enjoy your own natural gifts and to help others live without needing artificial, outside validation. You may want to start, or join, a mentoring program. Or you may want to learn to grow organic tomatoes!

> "I'm having trouble," says Page, "because I want to say I'm committed to solitude, you know, to find a higher purpose. But that would mean quitting my job, and my husband's unemployed right now, so I can't really affirm that. I'm stuck."

One belief that can keep us from homing in on our passionate commitments is that often we think that if we affirm and lock ourselves into one thing, it can't include something else. When you look at them closely, you see that these either/or dichotomies or sets of opposing choices (healthy kids vs. high-powered career, entrepreneurial freedom vs. health benefits and perks, structure vs. freedom, artistic expression vs. financial security, etc.) are often choices other people had to make at some point in their lives. They then say, "That's the way it is in life."

The more specific you get about what you're committed to, the more you *expand* the possibilities of what actions you can take to get there. One participant had a vague idea that she'd like to work for UNICEF, but given her economics, it wasn't feasible. So she was stuck. Yet when her workshop leader asked what going to work for UNICEF would allow for, Nancy identified that she had a commitment to fight hunger in the world. Immediately, the possibilities for how she might do that expanded. One woman suggested she donate money to a charity that feeds children; another, that she take in a stray dog, another, that she become a vegetarian; another, that she choose to give her leftovers to a shelter on a regular basis. All these were ideas she'd never thought of, because she'd fixated on how she wanted to, but could not, work for UNICEF! When you stop thinking that your commitment forces you to promise a specific course of action, you increase the possibilities for how you can do what you're passionate about.

Chasing your heart's desire can sometimes feel like opening those Russian nest dolls that fit one inside the other. Each time you ask yourself "What's it for?" or "What would that allow for?" you look further inside yourself to see if there's a commitment you care about even more than the one you just expressed. On a fundamental level, when you're sure of what you committed to, you know who you are. I'll get into this more in Part II, but for now, I want to say that often your greatest contribution comes not from doing what you think is helpful, but from being the joyous person you were meant to be. Asking these questions helps you access that person and that joy.

REFINING YOUR COMMITMENTS

Three sisters I know from a big family of siblings illustrate how asking "What's it for?" can radically increase happiness. Though they grew up in the same family, each developed different techniques that helped them survive; the commitments they carried into adulthood were based on these survival strategies.

The oldest sister, Barbara, who was put in charge of the younger siblings, developed into a ultraresponsible person. She was full of advice, and worry, for everyone. Now that Barbara's own children are settled in college, she has realized that she's outgrown the commitment to ensure that everyone else is taken care of. Barbara decided that this was a commitment she was ready to set aside in favor of one that would get her her own share of joy. Last I heard, she had stopped baking bread for her neighbor's kids' lunches in order to become a master silk painter.

As a middle child, Vicki learned early on that more than one point of view exists on every issue. To keep peace, she developed a commitment, in dealing with her family, to recognizing others' points of view. As an adult, though, Vicki has now recognized that playing the diplomat has kept her stuck for over a decade in a job where she's been placating a difficult, unfair, and demanding boss. Currently, Vicki is assessing her finances and considering her choices. If she decides she needs her job, she may replace her commitment to keep the peace with a commitment to honestly assert herself at work. Or perhaps she'll redefine—reinterpret—her commitment as one to diffuse violence in the world: In this case, Vicki could decide to train to become a family therapist for violent parents. Maybe she'll decide that her commitment is still fundamental to who she is, and that she wants to reaffirm it by working in a field that promotes cross-cultural relations.

The youngest sister, Margaret, always got the hand-me-downs and the leftovers. Not surprisingly, Maggie developed a commitment to vigilantly protecting her share—to getting her due and helping others get theirs. She became a litigating lawyer, a job she loves. She has, she says, her dream job and house and life. But a few years ago Maggie realized that she was bickering over "portions" in every area of her personal life. At the holidays, Maggie was driving Barbara and Vicki nuts, insisting that they each contribute the same amount of cooking, of money, and even of the time required to make the phone calls to organize the event. Even her conversations with the checkout clerk at her grocery store seemed to end in a debate about whether Maggie would get what she fairly deserved! When Maggie heard Vicki talk about her commitments, and the struggle she was going through, Maggie decided to reinterpret her own commitment to get her share. What she wasn't getting her share of, Maggie realized, was peace of mind! Maggie adopted a new commitment: to recognize other people's points of view.

Each sister, you will notice, uncovered commitments she'd previously rejected. In the process, they learned more about each other and deepened the bonds among them. Maggie gained new respect for Vicki, whom she'd always thought of as a wimp. And Barbara, who used to treat Maggie as if she couldn't live without the advice of her older sister, has even started to call Maggie for advice on how to negotiate with galleries on the sale of her silk paintings!

When we find ourselves on a regular basis tangling with the people in our lives, it's often because we think we know—but don't—what their commitments are. Or we take a defensive position and put down our loved one's commitment to save whales, because we assume that it conflicts with our commitment to care for our aging parents. We take the defensive position that our own commitments are morally superior. Or we chide ourselves and put off pursuing our joy, because while everybody else's commitments seem valid, ours seem trivial. I'll go into this more in the chapter on paradigms, but again, I want to reiterate that though we're all pros at putting all kinds of spin on the commitments we and others hold, none of them is morally superior.

> "What about the rest of you?" asked Hafeezah. "Those of you who haven't spoken? What are you out for? What are you committed to?"

After a few more minutes, Zully Alvarado, a designer with a disability who owns her own corporation in Chicago, threw her huge red scarf over her shoulder. Zully is from Ecuador; she was raised by an American family in Chicago after a priest, who had taken an interest in her, brought her to the States for medical care. She has blackberry-colored eyes, a dazzling smile, long black hair pulled back into an elegant knot, and an elegant, stylish outfit that I—sitting in the back of the room in my dark, tailored suit—envy. Ten years ago Zully quit her job and went back to school for fashion design, eventually starting a company that creates stylish, one-of-a-kind shoes for people with hard-to-fit feet. She has come to Lifedesigns because she's looking to widen her world even further.

"I want to share myself totally," said Zully. "Just to share myself and be fully self-expressed. I want to get rid of the belief that I shouldn't let people get to know me, because they'll use what they learn against me."

"That's an assumption we'll be looking at," Hafeezah said.

"I work at the Women's Self-Employment Project," said Josie. "I'm a successful trainer of other women—WSEP got the first presidential award for microenterprise. But I haven't yet achieved personal success. My grandmother said, 'Don't put your shoes on the top shelf of the closet.' I know I'm not achieving, because I'm waiting for approval. I want to do what I want without needing approval."

"I'm having trouble," says Mary Scott. "I know there is a story inside me I want to tell, but I don't know what it is, or how I'd go about it."

"Sometimes identifying your passion is a totally new discovery," said Hafeezah. "Sometimes it's more like remembering what the world taught you to forget, taught you that you couldn't have."

"I want to move to Italy, create design software for a fashion company, and marry a fabulous Italian man," said Alane.

At this, even the most serious and self-important woman in the room roared with delight. Alane blushed and threw her face over her hands as she laughed. But Zully, who was sitting next to her, grabbed her elbow.

"No, you know, that's great," Zully cried. "I love that! Ten years ago I left my job, and went to school to become a fashion designer," Zully continued. "And I'm a success. But what I want is to be more self-expressed."

"I've known Zully for ten years," Mary Scott said. "We came here together. Whatever she does, it's with style. Look at her gorgeous cane with the ivory handle, how it matches her outfit! I had meningitis when I was ten, and got a stunted leg. I've always been in hiding, because I didn't want people to see that I have two legs that are different sizes. The message I got was stay in hiding. But seeing Zully, who's elegant and created this beautiful life, I realized why I'm overweight wearing flowing clothes. I thought if . . . if you're not perfect, people won't like you. I've been committed, all these years, to not letting people see I'm not perfect!"

"Maybe a commitment you want to replace," said Hafeezah.

Whenever I'm sitting in a workshop, the question of what *I'm* committed to gets me right in the gut. And my answer varies from week to week and from day to day. Right now, as I write this book, what I'm out for is to interrupt traditional thinking, to interrupt any limiting assumptions about what you're capable of, and how the world works. Each time I force myself to write it down my answer varies slightly, but the act of answering the question recharges me as quickly as a bolt of lightning.

Identifying your true commitments—as opposed to the old ones that have been running you—frees up enormous amounts of blocked energy. It enables you to redirect your natural energy, enthusiasm, and determination in the direction where *you* want it to go. Once you know what you want, and what you're working for, your commitment becomes a jet forward, rather than the ball and chain around your ankle that keeps you where you are. It's easier to get into shape to fulfill a dream to compete in the fifty-five-and-over National Figure Skating Championships than because your doctor told you to fix your cholesterol ratio. It's a lot easier to make partner in your law firm because the idea of being the first woman in the partners' portrait gallery lights you up than because your father always wanted to make partner in his law firm.

EXERCISE: WHAT'S IT FOR?
With each commitment you wrote down, do the following test to discover what it's for.

1. Close your eyes and imagine it's already happened. Imagine it fully, in as much detail as possible. The question is: Are you content? Or is your goal really a vehicle to something else that you want more profoundly?
2. If there's something else you want, a deeper commitment that you think the initial one would make possible, write it down now. Don't cross out what you wrote before, just add to it.

As we'll see more in Part II, focusing on commitments also frees up energy in our dealings with others. Knowing others by their commitments enables us to respect, or at least understand, their actions when they do things that seem a little nuts. In addition, people who are communicating in a mode we call "complaining," who repeatedly vocalize dissatisfaction and frustration at a situation, experience a profound shift when they're listened to with the acknowledgment that they probably hold an important commitment that isn't being honored. When someone asks what the commitment beneath the complaint is, they feel respected rather than dismissed, and often cease complaining. In the work arena, too, getting to know the commitments others have made helps distribute responsibilities according to what people are actually interested in doing, and willing to do.

"I'm jealous of other people who have a dream," said Shelly. She fidgets a bit at the neck of her prim flowered blouse, which is buttoned all the way up. "I want a dream."

"As Helene was talking about her sisters dying of breast cancer," says Julie, "I realized that one thing I'm out for is communicating with my sister better. We're in our sixties, and we spend hours on the phone, yet all we do is talk about boring, impersonal things. Our relationship stays superficial because we don't talk about the real stuff!"

"Great," said Hafeezah. "Who else? Leslie?"

"My company works with corporations developing multicultural marketing plans," said Leslie, a mother of two whose overalls somehow emphasize her Whitney Houston looks. "And it's going well. But I can't keep working this way. I bought a

new home, started a new consulting firm, and separated from
my husband all within two years. I guess I'm here to complete
that, and figure out how to spend more time with my kids. You
know it's scary when you realize that people might not be
around. When I was nineteen my best friend died. And I went
to the funeral home to style her hair for the viewing. You just
don't know when people you love will be gone. I'm committed
to letting my loved ones know I love them, while there's still
time."

"That's crucial," Hafeezah said. "Time becomes a crucial issue when we're not living by our commitments! Because when
we're not living by our commitments, we never have enough of
it! What about you, Elinor? What are you committed to?"

"I'm committed to finding a structure that's balanced!" Elinor
sputters. Her face shows her exasperation. "I have a great husband, who makes me laugh, and I'm a mother. I want to not get
crushed by work."

"I'd like the courage to demand space, and experience solitude, without feeling the responsibility for husband, parents,
children. To paint, to eat, to sleep, but to not see people. To
lose structure in my life," said Page.

"Know that one," said Debra. An African-American graphics
designer, Debra owns a company that designs corporate give-
aways for Fortune 500 companies. She is dressed from head to
toe in leopard print fabrics. Now, she pulls down her chic, leop-
ard-print glasses to look the entire workshop straight in the eye.
"Ever heard, 'You better be careful of what you ask for, 'cause
you might get it?' Well, I wanted to be married. My brother
had been killed, my grandmother murdered, and my mother
died of cancer. I met my husband in my twenties, and that was
that. Well, now it's almost twenty years later, and though I
never had a problem with people or being successful with
things, I'm on this totally self-destructive path! My husband
came into my company, people were calling him by my maiden
name, so I allowed him to take financial control. But that wasn't
enough. He had to start his own business. So then we had two
businesses that we each owned fifty-fifty. Then he wanted to di-
vest me, to have his own. My husband always demands more:

more employees, more computers, etcetera. And I just went along with his demands because I wanted the marriage. But at what cost do you have a marriage? At the cost of yourself? At this point, I feel like, I don't hate him, I just feel sorry for him. But I need out. Two years ago his company went Chapter Eleven, and my company was in such financial straits that it almost went bankrupt. And, as my grandfather would say, 'When you have your head in a lion's mouth, you ease it out.' So I did—I saved my business for my two small children. I downsized from twenty-two to five employees. I was about to turn forty, and I said to myself, I don't want all this stress. What emerged after all the emotional abuse was that I realized that I have some good qualities. But now I need to know what it feels like to get free. I need some time alone."

"Wow," said Mary Scott.

"What I really want to do is restructure the nature of capitalism," said Julie. "I'd like to restructure the tax laws that control how corporations do business to motivate them to improve the communities within which they exist."

Everyone sat silent for a minute, awed by the power of Julie's vision. Then Lynda, an at-home mother for eighteen years, spoke a dream that was equally moving, though in a completely opposite vein.

"I thought I came here to learn how to go back to work," Lynda said quietly. "But as I'm listening, I realize that what I'm most committed to is to finding a better relationship with my daughter. We're in shambles. She has ADD, and I'm really worried about her. I nag her constantly."

Shelly, who, until now, had been nodding quietly with her hands folded on the table, spoke up. "As I hear everyone else speak I keep writing down more and more! When I started, what I wanted was intangible, like to become assertive, take risks, lose my conservative demeanor. I want to learn how to stand my ground. I'm not confident in knowing what my ground is! I'm a peacemaker, always take the middle ground, and so on. I work at an organization that hires Harvard M.B.A.s. It's a gas broker. I've been with them twenty-nine years and I'm totally miscast in my job. I want to get my college degree. I relate to Lauren and her dad: I'll never forget my dad saying, 'You girls don't need to go to college. You'll just be a teacher or a nurse, and then you'll quit.'"

"What a prescription for how your life would go!" exclaimed Hafeezah.

"So this is my embarrassing secret," Shelly continued, "and a goal of mine, to get my college degree. I went to a counselor, said I want to get my college degree, and we talked about what I'd do when my son's out of school—I have to be realistic—"

"We're going to be looking at just what 'reality' and 'realistic' are," Hafeezah interrupted.

"I guess I'm waiting for self-esteem, or . . ."

"What I see is waiting for certainty," Hafeezah said.

"Why do you really want this degree?" Debra asked. "Because you think others judge you, or because you want it?"

"I'm not even sure what I'd get a degree in," Shelly said.

"Do you see it as a validation?" asked Amy Jo. "I was in the second class that accepted women at my business school, in 1969, when there were six women in a class of a four hundred. And I finished a four-year program in two years and four months. But even after that, when I wanted to go to law school—my goal was either to be a lawyer or an airline stewardess!—my dad said that I should just become a prostitute. To him, being a lawyer was exactly the same thing! So even the achievement of business school didn't get the validation I needed. I'm forty-six now, and though I was accepted to law school in '72, it took me twenty years to let myself enroll!"

"On the other hand," interjected Alane, "my mother went back to school, and we graduated the same year. She really explored, and she loved it!"

The lively discussion continued for a while longer, as participants dug into trying to help Shelly get at the "What's it for?" behind her desire to go to college.

EXERCISE: HAVING COMMITTED CONVERSATIONS

1. Look over the commitments you've written down, and your refinements of them.
2. In the next two days, initiate conversations with three or four people you love. In these talks, tell them what you discovered about what matters most to you.
3. In these conversations, begin to practice the habit of asking the person with whom you're talking what they're committed to—in school, in their job, in their community service, in their family. This is a habit that drastically shifts the way you see those around you, and enables them to give you information about themselves that they may never before have revealed. You may discover that people you think you know—including yourself—drastically surprise you!

Chapter Two

A Different Kind of Listening

*It is not possible to solve a problem
within the same consciousness that produced it.*

—ALBERT EINSTEIN

When my daughter Kate was ten, she began studying at the American Ballet Theatre. In the next few years Kate performed in several ballets at Lincoln Center. My husband, Jim, and I delighted in every performance; we were thrilled to watch Kate stoke the cannon in *The Nutcracker*, or leap across the stage in *The Firebird*. And we loved knowing the back routes to get the good seats at Lincoln Center.

Only a third of the girls were invited to continue for the final year of the program. Kate was one of the privileged few. "That's wonderful!" Jim and I said, congratulating her. "But I don't want to go back!" Kate said. "Why not?" we asked. "It's such an honor," I argued. "How many young girls do you think get an opportunity like that?" I asked, thinking Kate didn't quite know what she wanted. Jim and I loved watching her so much that in the lobby of our building—I'm even ashamed to admit it—we even offered Kate a puppy if she'd just go back for one more year.

"Doesn't anybody get it?" Kate finally shouted at my husband and me, bursting into tears. *"I don't want to be a ballerina!"*

"She *doesn't want* to be a ballerina," reiterated Danny, our doorman.

"I got it," I said.

Jim and I were stunned. We'd been thinking about the great opportunity, about how Kate's success would look on the outside world, about how pleased we'd be, about how much we thought she'd love it. What we hadn't been doing, very well, was listening.

Whether in a family or a company, we all know what it's like to be in a nonlistening environment. Companies can be even harder on allowing change than families: Anyone who's worked in a big corporation knows what it feels like to watch her brilliant idea slip away, to work toward a breakthrough we and others were committed to, only to watch it fizzle. And the consequences can be disastrous.

In the late sixties, the CEO of Xerox, which was the first company in history to reach a billion dollars in sales in less than ten years, funded the legendary Palo Alto Research Center (or PARC). PARC was a think tank whose scientists were encouraged simply *to research what they thought was interesting.* It seemed the perfect open medium for breakthroughs. And in fact, PARC researchers invented computer mice, the prototype for windows software, the first laser printer, local area networks, and the first personal computer!

But although Xerox had a CEO who had declared a commitment, and though he'd dedicated enormous resources to that vision, Xerox management was only listening for the perfect copier. As a result, their radical new discoveries slipped through their fingers. Xerox had made its money leasing copiers; management couldn't see how they'd make money selling the personal computer. The idea of trying to market a home computer was dismissed on the grounds that people would never bother to learn how to use it. Xerox so discounted the gold it had mined that it gave the frustrated PARC scientists permission to show their inventions at a worldwide conference—the start of these inventions being "discovered" and exploited by other companies!*

The Xerox example illustrates, in a corporate context, the irony of the fact that planning, circumstance, and even luck are not enough to create breakthroughs.

THE CULTURE EMBEDDED IN LANGUAGE

When breakthroughs happen, it's because a medium exists to support their growth—a medium that nurtures innovation the way pond water "grows" microorganisms. I would define this invisible medium as an organization's culture.

The culture of any organization—and I'm using "organization" to mean either a company or a family, any group of people who function and survive interdependently—is often hard to locate. Now the organizations themselves are easy to locate: a family exists within a race, a religion, an economic class, on a street in a neighborhood; a company operates within an industry, as a type of business, in a specific state or region, as profitable or unprofitable. But though the culture of an organization enables its existence, in the way that air enables us to breathe, it's hard to see. Because it's as pervasive as air, it's less obvious.

Where the culture of any organization is located, is in language.

What air is to our bodies, language is to our identity. Human beings exist in a medium of language; what "grows" our sense of identity are the interpretations language allows us to have about ourselves. The same is true for organizations. The culture of any organization, then, lives in conversation—that is, in speaking and listening. More specifically, you can find it in the assumptions embedded in that speaking and listening. Whether visible or invisible, it is assumptions, rather than stated commitments, that hold an organization's culture together and enable business to continue as usual.

---

*The PARC scientists set up a demonstration of the personal computer and its functions, one of which was word processing; but the only people who "got it" were the executives' wives, who, of course, had been secretaries and understood how much labor was being saved.

Thus, when people speak and listen assuming that change is impossible, it doesn't happen.

A famous example of this was studied by the American linguist Benjamin Whorf. Whorf worked as a fire safety engineer, an insurance inspector whose job was to go out and investigate fires in the workplace. He began by analyzing purely physical conditions— "facts" like defective wiring, presence or lack of air spaces, and so on. Again and again, Whorf was surprised to note that fires were caused not only by the physical situations but also by the *language* with which those situations were being described. The term *gasoline drums* generated careful behavior, whereas *empty gasoline drums* generated carelessly thrown cigarette butts, even though workers knew that "empty" drums contain vapors that were more explosive than gas itself. Thus, if the language used to describe the workplace neutralized the possibility of fire, workers were unable to anticipate the possibility of fires, until it was too late.

If you think of fires as breakthroughs, the problem becomes clear.

In retrospect, the Xerox story sounds as absurd as a billionaire walking away from her investments. But at the time, of course, the assumptions its management was operating under were invisible to them—the way water is invisible to fish. They saw a fixed reality in which you made money leasing, not selling, machines. The Xerox management's actions—to ignore their pot of gold—were perfectly consistent with how the world was occurring for them, which was that their gold bricks looked like lead.

Ironically, ten years before, Xerox had disregarded the "wisdom" they'd received from consultants, which was that the copier would never catch on because we all loved our carbon paper too much to change. In just a decade, Xerox went from groundbreaking to arteriosclerotic because its management had acquired, in that decade, a fixed vision of what succeeded and failed. In some ways it doesn't even matter what the assumptions are; when they become embedded, they become invisible. And when they're invisible, they start to limit the ability to change.

Invisible assumptions limit our listening by filtering what's being said through what we think we already know. We're hearing something we're scared of hearing, or we don't hear what we don't want to hear. So rather than wondering why we're in a nonlistening environment, the obvious questions to ask are: What assumptions are people listening from? What, in other words, is their, and our, listening already about?

Anyone who's sat through a corporate meeting in which twelve people each addressed only their own agenda, intuitively knows the answer to that question. Most of the time, what we and others are listening to is the noise in our own heads. In the most basic sense, these skeptical questions, or noise, arise from rules from the past that somebody made up. "How are you going to open a health club for overweight women?" your husband asks. The implied rule here is: Fat women don't exercise. Or, "Where are we going to get the money to pay for child care for our employees?" your boss will ask. The underlying assumption behind this question being, This expense does not impact the bottom line. Your brother asks, "What credentials do you have to think you could negotiate the sale of Dad's business?" The implied assumption being that one needs a fixed set of credentials—past experience—in order to sell a business.

These rules about how the world works, of course, were made up by somebody in the past. Usually they were made up to minimize risk. When people say, "You can't do that because . . ." they're usually trying to protect something or to avoid the risk of losing what they currently have. In some ways, past-based listening is *designed* to minimize risk, the way the preventive instructions Whorf looked at were designed to minimize fires. When we operate under invisible assumptions like Fat women don't exercise, or Child care will cost money without increasing productivity, or Xerox makes money with things that copy, what we get is listening that hinders the possibility of change, and automatic questions that keep the past in place by producing resignation. How will you produce these new results, people ask, without threatening the current set of conditions I define as reality?

"If anything were possible, what would you like to see happen?" is a question designed to elicit radical new ideas. Yet many workshop participants, when they look at the answers they've written down, find that their radical new ideas—opening a spa for overweight women, or writing a children's book, or whatever—are ones they came up with twenty years ago that somebody shot down. Then they tell the story of how, after someone told them it was a stupid idea or asked them what their credentials were, they stopped talking about it—and eventually forgot what they wanted! In a nonlistening culture, we get the idea that we shouldn't speak our ideas, to avoid getting them shot down (or, in my daughter Kate's case, to avoid letting someone *else* down). Because in the past we've been listened to in a way that boxes us in and minimizes risk, we react by speaking in a way that minimizes risk. We're happy to share pleasant modifications, but we keep the really radical, risky ideas to ourselves. We begin planning conversations in our heads, and second guessing ourselves, and by the end we become so careful and so self-editing that we start making decisions for other people about what they want to hear. The old-timer at your new job tells you, "Joe's a guy who loves target practice. Don't bother taking your ideas to him." And from then on, even though Joe is desperate for new ideas, you never share yours with him. Or your husband starts a business, and you have a wild idea for how you might participate. But you think he'll think you're criticizing what he *is* doing, or you think he'll think it's silly. So you keep your great idea to yourself.

In a business, what "old-timers" learn to do is use language to describe and label "the way things are." Resignation—with a capital R—becomes embedded in description. This is a paradigm so fundamental that often we can barely see it. Language exists in order to label; there is no power in talking, except to label things accurately or inaccurately. One of your children becomes "the difficult one." Your boss becomes "a person who promotes men," and that's that. We start describing love, a feeling, and suddenly it gets defined as, he's got to bring you flowers on a certain day, and if he doesn't fit that description, he doesn't love you.

In this context, everything occurs as a thing that can be described. There's you, and there's the other stuff—work, the future, a project, other people—that gets represented in language as being already a certain way. The thing, then, gets fixed in our description, which starts to appear to us as fact, as truth. Whether we describe it right or wrong, there's no real possibility for new thinking, because we're busy fixing things as they are—in whatever pigeonhole we put them—rather than creating a field for new possibilities. If we decide someone's a rude, abrupt person who lacks common courtesy, then even when they do something that's kind or polite, it's so out of our fixed description of them that we dismiss it!

> "That's so true!" cried Elinor. "At my old job I had a personality conflict with my boss, who ran the whole state in which I was working. He had all the managers in the state in a conference call every Monday morning, in which he would just rake us across the coals. I started getting physically ill when I got up for

work in the morning. I thought this guy was a tyrant; he used to embarrass me and my peers unmercifully, and after three months I began to think he was picking on me in particular. I approached him, and said I didn't like his style. His response was to hire his own personal coach, to work with me.

"I asked the consultant why I should trust him if he was hired, you know, by this boss? The consultant asked me some questions back. 'Why do you think he hired me? Why would he invest in you if he didn't believe in you?' He said that the training was mine to use, and that I might find that I was so empowered by the end of it, that I didn't want my current job anymore. That blew my mind. So we started working, trying to separate what the boss is, what he trains people on, from his gruff delivery. The coach focused on all my insecurities, all the baggage, etcetera, that said, this is the way he is, and our relationship will always be this way. He asked, 'If we separate him from his delivery, what does that look like?' And I created in my mind the idea that my boss is brilliant, that he would be my mentor, and that I would learn more from him than from any other person in business. I stopped listening to his tone and started listening to the words. Behind his back, I would talk about him in a very positive light and hold him in high regard. Conversations he could never have heard—but somehow they got back to him. I started listening to him as somebody other than an ogre. That wasn't the truth; in fact, there *was* no truth. And you know, within the month, I was never picked on in a conference call again.

"The day I went in and resigned—and I had seen this boss cut the legs off people if they mentioned they might want to leave—I told him about the opportunity. I said I was telling him first because he was my mentor, and I knew he'd be excited for me. And though he didn't really want me to leave, he was really excited for me! He did everything in his power to help me leave smoothly."

Now, the worst part of descriptive resignation is that because human beings are efficient—we all learn to do everything quicker and faster—ultimately we don't even need to speak to get shot down: To save time, we shoot ourselves down, inside our own heads! The skeptical noise in our heads chimes in about one nanosecond after a new idea pops up. By far the most devastating consequence a nonlistening culture produces is that people internalize the censorship. When resignation's internalized, it becomes invisible. We don't see ourselves fixed in past ideas like the old-timer. We see ourselves as being realistic, or appropriately cynical, or worldly. Or experienced. Or knowledgeable.

To realize how pervasive the internal resignation is, all you have to do is think back to the last time you approached a conversation with someone you know well—too well—thinking, I'm *not* going to react. I'm just going to be open and neutral. I'm going to hear whatever it is that moron has to say. But of course, because we're human beings, we're not empty vessels listening for possibilities. Before five minutes are up you're most likely reacting the way you always do. Their words get filtered; the only ones you hear are the ones that confirm what you're expecting. Even if the person you're talking to is gently suggesting that you may be having trouble seeing because you're wearing sunglasses in a shady forest, if what you're listening for is evidence that they're narrow-minded, you'll conclude that they're trying to tell you there's no such thing as night. Take the story Jane, an education specialist who works at a huge technology company, told in the workshop:

> "Last year," Jane said, "I got another offer out of the blue. And
> I went to my boss and told her about it, with a list of all the things
> I wanted, to get me to stay, including wanting to take a month off
> to teach a class. To my surprise, my boss said, 'Okay, we'll see
> what we can do. We're flexible.' We ended up negotiating all the
> things I wanted. But at the end, my boss said, 'I'm glad we
> worked this all out, but I have to say, you were a little belliger-
> ent.' And I was floored! I realized I had been expecting a harsh
> reaction on her part, so I approached her that way, expecting her
> to say no."

If you're lucky, your listener, like Jane's boss, will tell you that you're not quite hearing what they're saying. But because internal conversation remains unspoken, it's harder to notice when we use these automatic filters that prevent us from listening to ourselves. The innovative, creative genius inside us comes up with an idea, and what does our listening filter respond with? You never finish things, says the voice. That's unreasonable to want. Or, You don't deserve that—you're not good enough yet! "I'm not good at taking initiative," you say, though there are a dozen things you'd like to do differently. We assimilate that nonlistening culture inside ourselves so efficiently that we are capable of reproducing inside our own heads, upon command, all the negative, discouraging voices we've ever heard.

Because humans exist primarily in language, even in our own heads, that mode of listening is there all the time, without our needing to do anything to put it there or turn it on. That little voice becomes our own worst enemy, worse than all the sexist, unreasonable bosses and competitive spouses and repressive parents rolled into one. These assumptions in our listening "box out" information. Our box of "reality" —though it's as uncomfortable and awkward and limiting as wearing a refrigerator box on a hot summer day—becomes invisible to us. Unlike a home, which we can leave and come back to, our mental box is one we carry with us, all the time! There are holes—openings—where information can enter, but only if the information fits into the slot or hole in the box allowed for by our invisible assumptions. Thus, even if the information is that there's a red convertible car running outside to take you to your dream house out West, if the hole we have is the size of a quarter, we'll see the chip in the paint, the spot of rust on the handle, and declare it a flawed means of transportation.

Because so many assumptions are embedded in our internal mental language, there is a design to the way we listen to ourselves and to others. Focused listening is very useful—it's crucial, in fact, to any sort of efficiency. But from focused listening, while we get what we're looking for quickly, we don't know what we missed, because we missed it! Our listening can be as finely tuned as radar, but while radar picks up fighter jets, it misses wind. This is a problem if your dream is to become a hang glider!

THE SOURCE OF RESULTS

You may be wondering, then, what exactly is responsible for the results you're getting? We all know, in the most basic sense, that the results we get depend on the actions we take. The question is, what is the source of our actions that determines which actions we take?

Often we think that it's will: If we just want badly enough to lose weight, or make up with our spouse, or get a new job, it will happen.

$$\boxed{?} \longrightarrow \boxed{Actions} \longrightarrow \boxed{Results}$$

But our actions are not determined by what we want, or even what we're committed to.

As obvious as it may sound, actions are determined by what we think is the right thing to do in that moment. That is to say, they're a function of how we view the world, our "reality."

Everyone's actions are perfectly consistent, at all times, with what they perceive to be reality, with how the world is occurring to them at that moment. A baseball coming at 100 miles an hour is a fact. It's measurable. But for different people, it's a different reality. To me, a 100-mile-an-hour baseball is a weapon. In my reality, the thing to do is duck. But to an umpire, it's a pitch. Though he's standing right in front of that weapon, what he does is call a strike or a ball. To a homeowner, that same baseball is a window breaker; the appropriate action for her may be to scream a tirade. To a major league baseball player, it occurs as a two-million-dollar bonus. He leans into it, and swings.

FACT:

100-mile-an-hour pitch

Occurring as:	→	Appropriate action
weapon	→	duck
pitch (to umpire)	→	call a ball or strike
window breaker	→	yell
$2-million bonus	→	swing!

The chart of cause and effect, then, starts to look like this:

Each person's actions are so appropriate to how their reality is occurring to them in the moment that it's probably fair to say that, from this perspective, nobody's ever made a mistake. However we might judge them later, our actions are perfectly consistent with what we define as reality; our results follow those actions. Thus, because our actions, in that moment, will always seem perfectly appropriate to us, the place to interfere with the results we've been getting is not via will, in the realm of actions. It's in the realm of how the world is occurring to us.

But because our listening determines what information gets into our world, it actually determines how the world is occurring to us—that is, what it is we define as "reality." Thus, the place to affect the results we get in the world is way back in how we listen.

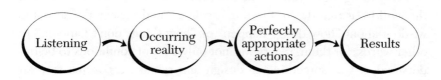

On the most basic level, reading is a form of listening. So, your getting the most of this book will depend—crucially—on how you take in the ideas it offers. Keep in mind, even if you're not recoiling consciously, or arguing out loud, you may still be listening automatically. Even when our filters to listening are more subtle and internalized, they still limit, enormously, the information we take in! The best way to widen the range of what you think is possible will be to observe, and become conscious of, the filters behind which you commonly listen. So try to "catch yourself" listening from within your box.

FIVE FILTERS TO LISTENING

What follows are five common filters to listening. In reading the book and in your daily life, try to catch yourself employing them. The goal is not to eradicate your filters, which, if you belong to the human race, is virtually impossible to do. The power of the exercise lies simply in becoming *aware* that you are actively imposing a filter.

CATCH YOURSELF THINKING "IT'S NOT POSSIBLE" OR "THAT NEVER HAPPENS"

This is the most obvious form of resignation, and it reflects a belief in a fixed reality.

Often, if we say we want something outrageous, people tell us to "Get real." In Lifedesigns we call that being resigned. There's a cliché that if you always do what you always did, you'll always get what you always got. It's likely, however, that this book may persuade you to seek out a challenge you formerly thought impossible. Many of the women profiled in this book have done things that the world said were impossible. One thing these women had in common with the great inventors of the world was that they refused to assimilate and believe the accepted wisdom about "how things happen" or "how things don't happen." In other words, for them, reality was not only a set of conditions to be understood, it was something to design and remake according to their own specifications. Until Roger Bannister ran a four-minute mile, everyone said it was impossible for the human body to run that fast. After he did it, though, other runners quickly broke the record as well. What had been broken was the mental block.

The same is true organizationally. The head of the Xerox PARC scientists once admitted that the biggest mistake they ever made was showing the personal computer to other computer scientists, like Apple founder Steve Jobs. Because once those other scientists had seen it, the possibility cat was out of the bag. When they knew it was possible, they ran with the possibility.

Thus, beware of investing in a fixed reality with statements like "That'll never happen."

CATCH YOURSELF VOTING, JUDGING, OR ASSESSING

We all have expectations—scripts—for how life should go. At the same time, the mental energy it takes to constantly assess whether a certain experience is happening the way we think it should impedes the flow of information. One participant in our workshop, when asked what she was committed to, said that she was committed to exploring death in a new way. Ruby said she wanted to create new rituals around death; that she wanted to work with morticians as a death coach; she wanted to revolutionize the way funerals are conducted; and she wanted to help people celebrate in this moment. When she was finished, a "deadly" silence came over the workshop. Hafeezah asked how many of the participants were having a reaction to what Ruby had said. No one spoke. Hafeezah put her hands on her hips and waited. Finally, one after another, women raised their hands, until the entire group burst into laughter. What they were doing, Hafeezah realized, was judging and assessing what Ruby had said. Later, on the second day, Ruby revealed that her twenty-six-year-old son had been murdered and that she had healed herself by learning to celebrate, and be grateful for, his life. Ruby's commitment took on depth and resonance within the group. Once they'd listened to the whole story, what had seemed a morbid and depressing interest became an inspiring and profoundly moving story of self-healing.

Voting and assessing includes the moment when your mind produces the word *should*. This book *should* be written X way, Gail *should* get to the point more quickly; I *ought* to be reading faster; I *should* be able understand this more quickly; I *should* be able to change my life without reading a book; my husband *should* anticipate what I want, without my having to explain it! Having standards is part of being human. The "shoulds" that drive us to distraction, though, usually grow out of inherited values and standards that we absorbed early on but didn't necessarily choose. We need to look at values and standards, to see where they came from—parents, religion, culture, TV. Once we examine them, we can decide whether or not we want to adopt them actively. I have a friend who believes marriage is a three-year renewable contract and wrote that into her vows with her husband! She and her husband wouldn't have been able to do that if they'd listened to other people's idea of what marriage *should* be.

The point, here, is to catch yourself shouldering too many "shoulds."

Catch Yourself Seeking Confirmation and Approval — That Is, "Looking Good"

How many of us, as the other person in the conversation is talking, find ourselves thinking, "Should I say that? Will it come off OK? If I wear that, what will people think?" We spend an extraordinary amount of time and energy seeking approval or trying to conform.

> "I know what you mean," said Lauren. "Even though I'm unemployed, I bought myself this silver and diamond necklace, for sixteen hundred dollars, at Tiffany's. I love it, and every time I go on interviews I touch it, and it makes me feel terrific and confident. But realistically, I can't afford it. I have to take it back. I think I have a month to return it, and the month's almost up—I've been avoiding returning it because I'm afraid of what the sales clerk at Tiffany's will think!"
>
> "That salesperson will probably think how undeserving and cheap you are, for the next five years, don't you think?" joked Hafeezah, as she wrote "Looking Good" on her flip chart.
>
> Lauren burst out laughing.
>
> "'Cause how you appear to her is how you are, right?"
>
> "Stop," Lauren said, shaking her head in recognition.
>
> "And you know for sure," Hafeezah said, "—sorry, I can't write straight—what that girl is talking about, on her break, in the fancy employee lounge at Tiffany's."
>
> "I haven't returned it because I can't think of how to explain it!" Lauren cried out.
>
> "I guess we're going to have to design a reality where you get to keep the necklace," said Hafeezah.

After a coffee break, Ireen Khan, one of our two operations managers, asked Hafeezah if she could interrupt the workshop to offer a thought. Hafeezah nodded, because in Hafeezah's world, she accepts help and input from any source. When the group reconvened, Ireen asked, "Hafeezah, why did you apologize three times for your writing, when it's completely legible?" Ireen is a bright, and impatient, member of our team, a Bengali-American with dark skin and startlingly white eyes and teeth. She is the most empowered twenty-three-year-old that any of us know. When Ireen suspects that any of us at Lifedesigns aren't living the technology, she does not hesitate to speak up.

"My father was a mechanical draftsman," Hafeezah said, smiling almost ruefully. "For him, this handwriting would be totally unacceptable. Ireen caught me trying to be perfect."

"I wondered why you were doing that," Amy Jo said. "When I saw it I thought, 'What's she talking about? She writes so perfectly!'"

"What I thought was, 'Why does that paper have to be so perfect? What's she going to do with that damn paper anyway?'" cried Elinor.

"I also see it as a need to take care of us," said Mary Scott.

Julie, an older sister, is nodding furiously. "You need to take care of us and make sure we can all read it."

"As if there's never going to be another moment for anyone to walk up and look at a word they can't see clearly!" Hafeezah exclaimed. "Thanks, Ireen. By the way, it doesn't go away. I'm still in training."

CATCH YOURSELF TAKING EVERYTHING PERSONALLY

"What happens if you work with Elinor," asked Hafeezah, "and one morning you pass her in the hall and she says 'Grumble grumble grumble.' What does that make you think?"

"She's in a bad mood," said Alane.

"She's under pressure," said Page.

"She thinks I'm dumb," said Josie.

"It took her two and a half hours to get to work today instead of her usual hour," said Lynda sympathetically.

"She's forgotten me," said Jane.

"Fascinating," said Hafeezah.

"Well," Jane added, "I'm going through empty-nest syndrome with my only son, and one of the things I seem to be thinking a lot is wondering if people will just forget about me."

"Lots of interpretations," said Hafeezah. "'Course, three weeks later you're avoiding Elinor, and all you want to do is get out of the coffee room when she comes in it, because that woman is a you-know-what, and she doesn't like you. And you're making your coffee and Elinor tells you how she's having problems with her contact lenses, and about the awful oral surgery she had last week, and how it got infected, and how she couldn't *eat* for three days."

How much suffering have we gone through thinking things are about us? That our husbands are sloppy because they don't care enough *about us*? That someone doesn't call back because they *don't like us*? I could go on forever with examples, because we all have them, every single day. Taking things personally is what we sometimes do when we assume that the world is organized just the way our mind is. It's thinking everything is *about* us. We can decide to take anything personally—circumstances, behavior, and even thoughts. I'll look at circumstances first.

We want to go to dance class, but every time we get ready, the phone rings with a crisis. Our company decides to dissolve our division, and though we had a million dollars in sales last year, we subtly start negating our achievement. The subway's running late, we think, because the white mayor doesn't care enough about African-American people to invest in public transportation. In a community development workshop Lifedesigns offered for homeless single mothers living in shelters, a thin twenty-four-year-old beauty named Anjanette recounted the following tale. Like the other women in that pro bono workshop, she had come because she wanted a better life for herself and her children. When Anjanette began to talk about going for job interviews, she remarked that it always rained when she had an interview. In fact, she *knew* it was going to rain every time she got dressed up or got her kids dressed up to go out. "I don't even need to look at a forecast! If any of you needs the weather . . ." she offered.

Anjanette was laughing at her tendency to take the circumstance of rain personally; she had some distance on it. In general, though, we need to be very careful about listening to events and circumstances in the world with the mind-set that these things are only happening to *us*, that we're the only person on earth who is suffering in this way—that the suffering is being inflicted intentionally, to get us down!

> "But where do you distinguish between taking political action and taking things personally?" asked Josie. "'Cause, like, I come from Alabama, where poor people in cities—who are mostly black—can't get to their great welfare-to-work job because there are no buses. Because only highways are funded, and not buses. That's a circumstance, but it's a racist circumstance! Am I not supposed to take it personally, even though I'm black and it means I can't get to work?"
>
> "No," said Hafeezah. "You know, not taking it personally doesn't mean you pretend there's no racism. It doesn't mean: Don't take action on equality if you're committed to equality. It just means that even if your limitation is due to racism, you have many more possibilities for actions to address it if you in-terpret it as cultural and not personal. The people who set up those bus schedules didn't know anything about you or your life. I bet they were probably taught to ignore blacks a little while before you went out to the bus stop."

A second variation on taking everything personally is that we take re-sponsibility for behavior that isn't ours. As I said, women are pros at this! We find ourselves taking ownership for whether our children mis-behave, whether our husbands succeed, whether our family holidays go well, whether our friends fix their lives. Someone offers us information on how to prevent our dog from leaping on the counter to gobble up the Swiss cheese, and what do we think? She's criticizing my style of dog training. She thinks I run a sloppy house.

We can even take our thoughts too personally! We think that we have control over our thoughts. Of course, anyone who's ever had insomnia knows that often it's not we who are having thoughts, but rather the thoughts that are having us. It may be that the thoughts we're thinking aren't even original thoughts. We had a woman in one workshop whom everyone agreed was the most attractive woman in the room—she was

fit, stylish, had gorgeous chestnut hair, and was an enormously successful executive. Yet as she approached forty, she was unhappily single.
She had come to the workshop to make a breakthrough in her personal
life.

Throughout the workshop, Joelle recounted how she kept asking her
male friends what she was doing wrong. She was trying to learn what to
do differently. But Joelle said they'd laugh in her face, and say, Nothing!
You're intelligent, and you're gorgeous. Joelle found this enormously
frustrating, because she couldn't figure out why she wasn't married.
When the leader probed a little deeper, though, Joelle told us why: She
was dead certain she wasn't attractive. Her paradigm was that her sister,
the tall blond former model, was the attractive one. So no matter how
much will she exerted, no matter how many great clothes she bought,
no matter how much she exercised, no matter how many times she re-
decorated her house, no relationship lasted.

The problem, of course, was not one of *doing something differently,*
but of *being* different. Which is why Lifedesigns is about being who you
are rather than about doing things somebody tells you to do.

Joelle was packing up in the middle of the second day, on the verge of
tears, ready to leave the workshop early because we had suggested it
was within her power, and no one else's power, to think herself lovable.
After she left, the workshop manager for that day, Jennifer, chased after
her in the lobby of the hotel. Jennifer has an insight that comes from
the ability to empathize with every person in the world; she wanted
Joelle to consider that the idea that her sister was the pretty one, and
that there could only be one pretty one in the family, might not be her
own idea. The rule that only blond and tall was pretty was a cultural
norm that *Joelle had taken as a personal assessment.* Because she was
choosing to take authorship of these negative thoughts, they lived for
her as reality. And she couldn't imagine that there would be a man out
there who thought differently.

Jennifer hoped to at least open up the possibility to Joelle that these
were someone else's interpretations of the world, that Joelle did not
need to take others' interpretations personally or validate them as her
"reality." Joelle left anyway, because she felt too emotional to continue;
but months later, Joelle says she is slowly building a relationship with
someone who thinks she's gorgeous and treats her well.

A last note: A variation on this third category is to take positive thoughts personally. If you find you're always wanting to say, "That was my idea!" or "I worked on that!" you may still be in the mode of thinking that everything "out there" happens because of you. Because looking for immediate recognition can be a form of taking it personally, the next time you're sitting in the space of "you stole my idea," you may want to consider the concept that there are thoughts out there in the world with which we (and others) interact. Not only do we not author everything bad, we don't author everything good, either.

When we take circumstances, behavior, or thoughts too personally, we can't listen.

CATCH YOURSELF THINKING, "I KNOW THAT" OR "I ALREADY KNOW"

Already knowing takes many insidious forms. The first is the most obvious.

Even if we're not what's commonly called a know-it-all, we need to be careful about dismissing new information by saying, "I know. I know. I know," before we've heard, and carefully considered, the information that is being offered. How often do we find ourselves finishing other people's sentences? We need to be wary of tuning out if someone doesn't say something significant in the first few seconds. "Quick" listening assumes a sameness that often misses nuance and assumes that the information being offered fits in exactly with what we already know. Sometimes, even when we're not judging or assessing, but are just simply trying to relate or empathize, we rush in too quickly and flatten the content of what the other person is saying. If you can think back to the last time someone interrupted you to say "I know *just* how you feel!" and then launched into a story of their own that wasn't quite related, you can remember the feeling that "quick" listening gives us, which is that it often leaves us feeling unheard. Thus, as a listener, the goal is simply to ask a question and listen thoroughly rather than speeding out to what we already think we know.

In addition to making people feel unheard, already knowing makes us deaf to information. The assumption that *knowledge is power* is so powerful and unexamined that it has become a cliché. But the fact is, as I pointed out, knowledge doesn't always get results. You may know how to look for a new job, or lose weight, but that doesn't mean you'll do it.

Even in cases where we think we do know, we need to ask ourselves, How much do we really know? Of the knowledge that's out there in the world, how much of it do we know? If this circle is all the knowledge that exists in the world, how much of it do you know? How much does any one person, even someone with multiple expertise, know?

Even for the most knowledgeable among us, I think the answer is "not very much." Perhaps we think we know one percent. So say this wedge represents how much we know of what's out there.

Now, how often do you run across something that completely blows you away, that doesn't fit into anything that you know? That you come across something that you can't process at all? That makes you feel thunderstruck and in awe? It may happen, but not often. If we're not often truly surprised or made aware of something that we'd assumed didn't exist, yet we actually only know about one percent of what's out there to know, what this means is that we're taking the 99 percent of the unknown and shoving it into the one percent that we do know.

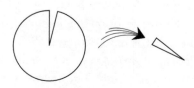

By making information conform to what we do know, we shut down extraordinary amounts of input!

The idea of a "learning curve" is that, as we know more about a topic, our learning speeds up. Quick learning, then, involves placing new information on preexisting scaffolding. But that implies that the scaffolding, or current structure, remains in place! So fast learning, or confident learning, is often conservative learning, which leaves less room for change. Fitting something in too quickly, even if we're agreeing with the supposed content, collapses the actual content of the new information another person may be trying to offer us into old information we already have.

Other cultures, incidentally, don't always hold the American paradigm of quick certainty. One of our workshop leaders, Amanda, who for years lived in India, reports that if you answer a question quickly and confidently there, it's an insult. Because you haven't really thought about the question.

In the words of theologian James Carse, "Knowledge lifts the veil. But can also become the veil."

Thus, embedded in ideas like "knowledge is power" and "credentials qualify you" is the assumption that you *already know* what knowledge or skills will be required to do something you've never done before!

And who made up what the credentials are, anyway? How many stories have we heard like the one told by the movie *Lorenzo's Oil*, which is a true story about two parents, neither of them doctors, who researched their son's esoteric joint disease themselves. They ended up discovering what is now a widely accepted treatment, and being awarded an honorary degree, because they didn't think like the experts.

So, if we want to make breakthroughs—as Gloria Steinem talks about in *Revolution from Within*—then we need to *un*learn some of what we already know.

> "What Elinor said, you know, about making somebody be a certain way, is really true," said Alane. "I worked for this woman who was very capable and dynamic, but whom we all hated because she was a credit hog. Then she left our company to become the head of a cable network. And I saw this interview of her, where they interviewed her employees? And all the employees raved about how generous and inclusive she was! And

she said in the interview that it was so great to be in a new place where people saw you totally differently. It was so awful to realize that it wasn't her all those years—or at least, it was as much her as how we'd dismissed her!"

"I study all forms of healing," said Hafeezah. "Once, I went to a Yoga workshop that was teaching the five principles of Yoga: proper nutrition, proper meditation, proper exercise, proper relaxation, and proper breathing. The teacher explained that all of these were forms of bodily cleansing and toning, and he mentioned some other techniques. He used a little teapot to pour salt water so it ran into one nostril and out the other. Now, I was already resisting pouring water up my nose, when he mentioned, in passing, a technique that involved drinking your own urine. And I was like—" Hafeezah's eyes now popped out of her head, her face a cartoon of fright. "You have GOT to be kidding! The information was so scary," Hafeezah said, "that even though he said the technique had been around for five thousand years, I couldn't process it at all. I already knew that that one was outta here!"

"My daughter's always saying that about me," said Lynda. "And my husband gets furious at me because I'm nodding, saying, 'I know. I know.' And I'm not listening! Sometimes my daughter takes my chin and turns it to her face and says, 'Mom! Listen to me now!'"

"That works," Hafeezah said. "Lynda, do you think you're listening in those moments?"

Lynda shook her head. "I guess I don't want to have to get in a fight," she said. "If I don't listen, I don't have to disagree with anything."

"Lynda already knows!" added Amy Jo.

Even habitual disagreement, by the way—the inverse of too-quick agreement and knowing—is another form of this same dismissive listening.

We all have a career debater in our lives: that person who reflexively takes the contrary, no matter what is said; who needs to skeptically disagree with, or at least reformat, any new idea they encounter; who needs, before you've finished summarizing the argument of an article you're reading, to start arguing with its premise. Career debaters demand, and offer, proof of their opinions. My favorite example of a family of debaters is the classic dinner-table scene from the Woody Allen movie *Radio Days,* in which the family gets into an argument about which is the better ocean, the Atlantic or the Pacific.

The debating reflex is part of another paradigm that's so deeply embedded in Western culture that it's almost invisible: We ought to believe only what's been proved. Thus skepticism is the right, the mature, the smart stance in the face of new information. Give me statistics, we say, not experience or anecdote. Western culture values scientific data, which is about certainty. Could you prove to me that the sun will come up tomorrow? we ask, when someone tries to cheer us up. Valuing skepticism is a form of I-already-knowism: not with regard to the *content* of the new information someone else is offering but of the *format* in which it's offered. Thus, you can't just suggest that perhaps someone who coughs a lot might try quitting smoking. You'll need to cite five studies from the *New England Journal of Medicine* before you suggest that smoking and coughing may be related.

The habit of already knowing collapses new information by too quickly categorizing it as some you already have. The habit of debating dismisses information by critiquing and taking apart the wagon on which the new information arrives. Both habits try to take the uncertainty out of learning, to move toward and stay in what's definitive. This usually means the past.

Yet because learning something new involves wading into uncertainty, if your sources of information have to be dead certain, the information they'll offer is usually dead.

Now, it's not that what I've called automatic questions and focused listening do not have a purpose. They do. Their purpose is to keep us learning quickly. Being highly focused has worked for a lot of us; it's taken us far. In corporate environments it's highly rewarded. Yet the idea of efficiency as a dominator is based in a nineteenth-century industrial era in which the new machine was seen as a messiah that would revolutionize the world. All we had to do, it was thought, was keep these machines running efficiently, make more and more efficient machines, and manage ourselves until we become efficient machines. In the twentieth century, though, it's worth considering that the notion of efficiency can also stifle. Just as the economy of the Industrial Revolution has been replaced by a service and creative economy, the dominant value of efficiency, while important, may be replaced by a value that could be best described as creativity.

If the value is invention and creativity—and by the way, the U.S.'s biggest export is not widgets but culture—then automatic, efficient listening may not be the most productive kind. Nuts-and-bolts questions like "How?" and "With what resources?" are great questions to ask, but not first.

On the other hand, if we don't have a plan for *how* to listen, we're left in a place that feels like a "free for all" in which everything is possible. Thus I would offer the following questions as the ones to ask first, with the goal of creating breakthroughs in your life and the lives of those around you. These are questions that generate speech and ideas rather than shutting them down. Since we're already so good at asking the "how" questions, I would suggest that these are the ones we need to practice. Generative questions help you maintain the Zen concept of the "beginner's mind," in which your radar is tuned to possibilities, not limitations. In the simplest terms, these questions move us from a stance of already knowing—in which we listen automatically and cancel possibility—to a stance of not knowing at all, which allows us to sit in a stance of discovery and wonder.

Automatic vs. Generative Questions

Automatic	*Generative*
(Listening About)	(Listening For)
How will that occur?	What's the possibility in that?
Why do it?	What could that provide for?
Does this make sense to me?	If that were so, what would
Do I agree/disagree?	that allow for?
Do I like it/not like it?	What could I build with that?
Do I believe it/not believe it?	What commitment would
Is this right/wrong?	that fulfill?
Is this good/bad?	

Generative questions allow for things to become possible that weren't previously. The idea is to open up huge playing fields. You may not choose to play on that entire field; you may choose to focus and play on a small part of it. But the idea is choosing, rather than allowing your assumptions to choose for you.

What generative questions enable us to do is to listen "for" ourselves. And to help others listen for breakthroughs in themselves.

....

EXERCISE: NOTICING YOUR FILTERS

1. Make a copy of the previous page and post it somewhere where you can see it and use it as a reference.
2. For two days, check in with yourself, intensively, each time you respond to information somebody is offering to you. Are you generating possibility with your questions and comments? Or are you responding under one of the five filters and shutting possibility down?

....

LISTENING TO YOUR WILDEST DREAMS

"So if anything were possible," asked Hafeezah, "what would you like to see happen?"

"I'd like to cease obsessing about my body, to achieve a healthy body without working hard at it constantly, but, rather, through activities of joy," said Jenny.

"I want to learn how to support myself without needing to have a nine-to-five corporate type of job. I want time for international travel and romantic relationships, to meet a best friend to be my husband and start a family. I want to own a business where I can combine computers, marketing, kids, flexibility, and education," said Alane.

"I work in my family's business," said Amy Jo. "It's a furniture store. We have an adding machine from 1947. I just passed the Illinois bar—twenty-five years after graduating college. My son is sixteen, grown, and I feel like, What am I going to do when I grow up? I have a dream of doing divorce coaching, but I'm afraid to just open a business. I lied to my brother about coming to this workshop—and called in sick! It was pathetic!"

"I'd like to work on campaign finance reform," said Julie, "and to refigure the rules of American-style capitalism to generate investment in a different kind of society. I'd like to create a society without guns."

"I want a life without perpetual drama!" said Debra.

"I want drama," cried Alane. "I want a dream or a guiding-light vision that would be so compelling that my life would fall into place. I want definition and focus for my international dreams. How am I going to get to Italy, marry a wonderful Italian man, and work for a fashion company?"

"I'd like to do something really outrageous, like be a pianist in a bar. A smoke-free bar," Elinor said.

"I need a direction for my next life," said Lauren.

"I want to own the bar," said Leslie.

"I want to design the costume for that performance," said Zully. "And I want to make a difference for people with disabilities all over the world in a creative way."

EXERCISE: LISTENING TO YOUR WILDEST DREAMS

Part I

1. Open your notebook so that you have two blank sheets of paper—one on the left and one on the right.
2. On the top of the left-hand page write down this question: *If anything were possible, what would you like to see happen?*
3. Now answer the question. Helen Keller said that life is either a daring adventure or it is nothing. What I'm looking for, here, are adventures—outcomes that sit somewhere between highly unlikely and almost impossible! So imagine that you have infinite time and money to create what you want to create. And start writing.

DECLARATION

"As you were writing your outrageous dreams, did you notice some noise coming up?" asked Hafeezah. "Did you catch yourself?"

"I thought, 'How can you give up something you're already successful at to do something you know nothing about?'" said Leslie.

"How am I going to go off to Italy by myself?" Alane asked.

"Typical noise," Hafeezah said.

"How am I going to get the energy?" asked Lynda.

"When I wrote down that I wanted to see my art in the Chicago Art Institute, I heard all the people who'd said to me, 'Boy, that's a long shot,'" said Page.

"What if my passion consumes me and I burn up like a star?" asked Jenny. "I'll be overtaken by my passion."

"Just the word, 'Ha!' came into my mind," said Amy Jo.

"To be a good mother, I have to cook dinner every night," said Elinor.

The participants in that workshop were starting to notice, as they began to declare what they wanted, the voices that came up. "This is trivial," you may hear yourself thinking. "Be realistic." I like to lump these voices together as "noise." Very often, as you begin to dare to think in the realm of the outrageous, the volume on that noise goes up. Voices in your head will put you down, call you ridiculous, unqualified, or selfish. The volume going up is a sign that you're up to something *big*. I'd even go so far as to say that if you don't hear any noise, you might not be up to something worthy of who you already are. Thus, Part II of the above listening exercise involves becoming present to the noise. We ask participants to write down on a separate sheet in their notebooks the obstacles they think could get in their way.

"I feel like I have no dreams," said Josie. "And I can't get started because there are too many things to do already, and I'm too tired."

"My own ambivalence," said Julie. "Needing to be reasonable and to be seen as reasonable."

"Fear of the chaos in my family getting even worse than it already is," said Debra.

"I don't deserve a husband," said Sara.

"You just can't go off and do something without knowing you'll earn money at it," said Page.

"I'll make the wrong choice," said Alane.

"My family will sabotage me," said Amy Jo.

"Waiting for something to happen," said Shelly.

"If I lose weight I'll intimidate my mother. And she'll attack me," said Jenny.

EXERCISE: LISTENING TO YOUR NOISE
Part II

1. On the right sheet in your notebook, write down the following question: *What do you think could get in the way of your accomplishing that?*
2. Now answer it, writing down all the things you think could stop you or stand in your way.
3. Over the next few days, ask people around you the first question, and listen to their responses. Notice that as you hear other people's dreams, you may want to steal them. In the next few days feel free, as you're reading and thinking about this, to keep scribbling and to be outrageous. Keep alternating, writing in whichever category comes to mind. In both categories, you will want to add all sorts of ideas from the sublime to the ridiculous. Just make sure you keep the dreams and the noise on two separate pages.

By the way, declaration is one of those areas that is especially important for women.

A lot of people asked us, as we were working on this book, why the program is only for women. The answer is: It isn't. Automatic listening happens in both men and women; defensiveness and rigidity are universal. But because men and women face different expectations, and to some degree live in different cultures, so their resistance to change can show up differently. Because women are taught to serve others and to sacrifice, we often think that what we want is trivial, superficial, inappropriate, or unreasonable. We're taught not to out-and-out state what we want. Further, because it's only been a recent development that women have the opportunity—and necessity—to be financially independent, in a way our minds haven't caught up with our checkbooks; it's not surprising that many, many women fear that they'll become a "bag lady." So women still learn in all kinds of ways that they can't take care of themselves, or that if they do state and go after what they want, they're being selfish. For these reasons they're often less comfortable than men declaring what they want.

As women, when we exist in a reactive and resistant mode—waiting for someone to fix us up with the man, or tell us the job of our dreams already exists—we're still placing in someone else's hands the permission to stand in what we want. They promote us, they reward us, they help us, their structure gets in our way. But if you think about a moment when you really made a true breakthrough in your life, as often as not it had less to do with reacting to somebody else than with deciding that you'd reached your limit of having things go a certain way. So you decided—you stated and declared, without evidence—that it wasn't going to go like that anymore. Usually, in these cases, you gather so much commitment around the issue that you don't care whether people shoot you down. Often it's the speaking of it, and the standing in it, that creates the breakthrough.

> Zully piped up. "That's very true," she said. "When I started out as a fashion designer, I didn't know anything about shoes. But I just got so tired of people telling me I couldn't have the kinds of shoes I wanted because my legs are different lengths and my feet are different sizes. I quit my job, hired a crafter, bought the equipment, and started drawing the shoes I wanted to wear to Seventh on Sixth, the annual New York runway show. When I went in to buy my shoe supplies, it was a totally male industry—rough talk, you know. But I just ignored them; I was com-

mitted to removing disability as an issue, for people like myself, who are exploring their dreams."

EXERCISE: PRACTICING DECLARATION

The phrase "If anything were possible" creates noise. Tell these people what you'd want in your life if anything were possible. Let them know how it would be in your wildest dreams. At the same time, listen for—and also declare to them—your noise about how impossible what you want is. When your listening partner responds, listen with your new, dedicated listening, with a commitment to hear the possibility in what they say.

Chapter Three

Incompletions

You jump out of bed, ready for a great day.

You walk into the bathroom and notice (again) that one of your lightbulbs is burned out and needs to be replaced.

While you're brushing your teeth, your dog wanders in, sits down, and begins scratching. You remind yourself, as you have every day for the past two months, that summer is here, and she needs a flea collar.

You stand at the closet, deciding what to wear. This takes a while, because you have three sizes of clothing mixed together because of your recent weight fluctuations.

You walk into the kitchen, make coffee, and notice the fish you bought last week and never cooked needs to be thrown away.

At breakfast, as you're opening yesterday's mail, you get the four-teenth bill from a doctor your insurance company has failed to reim-burse. You decide (again) to do something about it, but since your insurance company isn't open yet, you set it aside for later.

As you leave you look in the full-length mirror at the purple dress you're wearing. If you smile, you look like Barney the dinosaur. It's the wrong dress for your big meeting today, anyway. But the time it took to get dressed has made you late, so you go out to the car and try to forget how you feel.

In the garage, you step over the camping equipment you bought three years ago, for a trip with your daughters you haven't yet had time for. You get into the car and start the engine, hoping that familiar rattle won't mean anything—today.

At work, you go to retrieve a file for a meeting, but can't find it. So at the meeting you improvise; later, when you find the file, you realize that the information you gave was a little off. You spend two hours writing a memo to convey the facts.

Before lunch, your coworker tells you she's pregnant. You're thrilled for her, but then you remember it's been nearly a year since her wed-ding, and you still haven't gotten her a present.

An associate comments that you've lost weight. You nod; it's true that a few weeks ago you had lost a few pounds. But you didn't tell anyone then, because you were afraid you might gain it back. And now, sure enough, you've been cheating on your diet for weeks.

Then you go to another floor of your company and run into an old friend you went to school with. You've known him for over a decade. He stopped calling, or returning your phone calls, three years ago. Each time you see him, you feel hurt. Last weekend he had yet another party where he invited all your mutual friends, but left you out. You in-vite him to lunch, intending to ask if it was something you did. But at lunch you lose your nerve and chat about business.

Later, at work, you pitch a new project to your boss. You're on a roll—you know you have a terrific idea—but your boss interrupts you and asks whether you ever finished that project you started six months ago.

At the end of the day, you take home enough work to keep you busy for three days.

At home, you collapse into the ugly maroon chair your favorite aunt gave you as a gift. The chair is hideous, and it drives you nuts. But you can't throw it out, because if she decides to visit next year, she might be hurt.

You know you need to do your taxes—the extension on the extension is almost up. But you're tired, so instead of facing that pile of receipts, you turn on the TV to relax.

Any of this sound familiar?

Each of these little situations describes an incompletion.

Incompletions are areas of our past that remain present for us. They validate an old view of ourselves that we may no longer want to affirm; they distract us from concentrating on present goals, boyfriends, jobs, or projects; and they drain our energy for new initiatives. They nudge us, and keep nudging us, like whispers in ourselves that we're not listening to closely enough. When we don't resolve them, they keep us stuck as janitors of our dreams. Without completing the past, we can't move on.

> "Tell me about it," said Leslie. "My marriage is over, but I'm not over it."
>
> "In other words the marriage is finished," said Hafeezah. "But you're incomplete about it."
>
> "I guess so," said Leslie.

FINISHED VS. COMPLETE

Leslie's divorce, and her feelings toward it, is a good example of the difference between being finished and being complete. Finishing things is, as everybody knows, a challenge. The visionaries among us are terrific at inventing, or creating, vision, and they may even be good at firing people up. The doers among us plan and initiate; they love to be assigned tasks, which they usually execute marvelously. Some of those doers are even good at taking *all* the actions necessary to finish the task. Yet even though the outside reality may be finished—the degree is earned, the divorce papers signed, the marathon is run—we're not necessarily in a place where we can move forward.

Ironically, what prevents people from moving on is not so much not being finished as a state of mind or *stance* with regard to that reality. When you're what I'd call "complete," you are interpreting the facts in a way that gives you a feeling of resolution that allows you to move on. While being finished has to do with taking a set of *actions* in the outside world of fact, feeling "complete" enough to move on has to do with how you interpret your situation in the domain of language.

Often, I think, we tend to confuse the realm of action with the realm of interpretation. We tend to think we need to finish something in order to move on, when in fact what we need to do is achieve completion. The irony is, you can have taken all the actions to finish an activity, but if you're incomplete about it, you're still stuck.

The ideal, of course, is to be both *Finished and Complete.* In this case, the end result satisfies the original idea: you earned the degree, you got the promotion, you saved up the money and bought the car. The simple act of finishing a crossword puzzle, on the way to work, makes us feel a little smarter, a little more energized, a little more empowered to go out and face the world. Even completion on a less-than-triumphant finish, like quitting a job you hate or emotionally moving on from someone who treated you badly, leaves you with a feeling of closure, of satisfaction, and a readiness to move on.

On the other hand, on the days when you don't finish the crossword puzzle, you probably go to work and basically forget about it. You're not obsessing.

And at the end of the day, you're not finished with everything you have to do, but you're able to go home and sleep at night, being complete with the fact that all your work isn't done.

You may occasionally think about the fact that you dropped out of that training program in Competitive Spelunking. But then you realize that you never really wanted to explore caves; you signed up in the first place because the instructor was cute.

This combination of *Not Finished but Complete*, then, while it's not as energizing as being both finished and complete, does yield a feeling of peace—and an ability to move on.

Keep in mind, you don't have to like everything about reality to be complete. The dictionary definition of complete is being whole, lacking no component part. If part of the whole situation is "I don't like the way it is," that's okay, because that's part of the whole. You can have an acceptance of the fact that a certain opportunity, or relationship, is lost to you. But if you're complete about it, while there may be things you'd do differently, you're able to work with that knowledge and move on.

This is why it's the lack of completion, rather than the lack of finishing, that keeps us tethered to the past. A friend of mine told me a story about a woman who'd published a scholarly book she'd worked on for twelve years. By some mistake, the first page of the book contained four typos. For years afterward, although this writer had gotten terrific reviews, she stewed about those four typos. She wasn't complete, and she couldn't write another book because she hadn't really acknowledged to herself what was so—that the first edition of her book would always have four typos on the first page. The combination of *Finished but Not Complete,* leaves us disappointed and dissatisfied. It's the feeling Leslie had about her divorce, and it's the feeling you have when you accomplish something but don't get—or give yourself—recognition.

In an organization, *Finished but Not Complete* is a dangerous place for employees. Because it makes people feel undervalued, this state can be even worse, motivationally, than *Not Finished and Not Complete.* When employees' efforts don't get acknowledged, when we are deprived of recognition for what we've done, we start to feel as if we don't matter. And when people stop caring about whether they do a good job because they feel nobody notices if they do, results inevitably suffer. The Xerox PARC scientists who had invented the personal computer and the local area network, for example, were sitting in *Finished but Not Complete* for quite some time—until finally, when they were given the chance to show off their inventions to computer people outside Xerox, they gave away their secrets—to get complete!*

Ultimately, dissatisfied people stop finishing things, and end up *Not*

---

*One of those people was Steve Jobs, who, once he saw the possibility at Xerox, went back to his garage and built the first Apple p.c. This happened in more than one area, until the joke became that Xerox was an organization that was great at developing brilliant ideas for other companies. The second and third companies in the world to reach one billion dollars in sales, in under ten years, were Apple and Compaq—selling variations of Xerox PARC inventions!

Finished and Not Complete. This is the state that yields anxiety, migraines, stress, a feeling of being burned out and overwhelmed.

The suggested activities to complete this chapter are designed to help you identify incompletions (and unacknowledged accomplishments) by practicing your new listening on yourself. They will also open up possibilities for completion by asking you to make some decisions about what, if any, actions you want to take. At the same time, you'll start to notice areas where you're resisting completion. Once you can be fully present, you'll begin to be able to invent a future that is not necessarily based on, or shaped by, a continuation of the past.

AN INVENTORY OF INCOMPLETIONS

Since making any change requires acknowledging what's so, the first step is to begin to unobscure the shroud of incompletions under which many of us operate. Most of us have already been unconsciously keeping track—for years—of our incompletions: We daydream, while doing our laundry, about a boyfriend who broke up with us for reasons we don't understand. We feel queasy, each time we give out a résumé, about a degree we didn't finish. Instead of enjoying the spray of our shower each morning, we're practicing what we'll say to a coworker who let us down. A coat sits in the hallway closet for years, but we can't return it, because it belongs to a family member to whom we need to apologize. So rather than trying to "discover," the suggestion behind this first exercise is simply to use writing as a tool to help you remember what you already know and haven't been able to forget. For our purposes, an incompletion is not a failure; it's something that keeps you distracted from being in the present.

Becoming attuned to how incompletions rob you of energy and initiative will enable you to get into the habit of noticing them as they come up. The goal is to notice, to define what it is you need to come to closure. My goal for you is to give you a *process of completion* you can duplicate over and over to create an energy boost for yourself. Armed with the steps in this process, you'll be able to steer your life based on the road in front of you, instead of with your eyes on the rearview mirror.

What you'll be doing, in the next exercise, is taking an inventory using the following categories, which are designed to provoke you to consider all the aspects of your life, and to consider the gaps between where you are now and how you want things to be.

1. Things I Want to Start and Am Not Starting

This is a basic category to get you started in the process of identifying some basic directions for yourself.

"I want to start working less, and being more open with men," said Alane.

"I want to start an aggressive savings plan," said Debra. "After all this junk with my husband, I want to start planning, financially. I want an education fund for the kids. And I need to decorate the master bedroom and complete the wall treatments in the house."

"I want to clear out my corporate wardrobe now that I'm out of that world," said Lauren.

"I want to follow up on my overseas contacts," said Alane.

"I want to start going places by myself, and not be afraid or ashamed to be there alone," said Shelly.

"I want to start taking care of me," said Jenny.

"I want to start my divorce coaching business," said Amy Jo. "And to get a master's in clinical counseling."

2. Things I Want to Change That I Am Not Changing

This category often brings up commitments that you want to reinterpret.

"I want to be more spontaneous and less hesitant," said Zully.

"I want to change my relationship with my family," said Mary Scott. "To be more responsible to them and less responsible in relationships that get in the way of relating to them."

"I want to treat my body better," said Jenny. "And respect myself from inside."

"I want to stop doing the busywork first," said Jane.

3. THINGS I WANT TO STOP AND AM NOT STOPPING

This is a great category for instantly identifying old commitments you want to throw out.

> "I want to stop working on other people's goals," said Mary Scott. "To get off all those boards that drain me."
> "Pretending I'm satisfied when I'm not," said Leslie.
> "Talking about my marital problems with my friends and family," said Debra.
> "I want to stop hoping my ex-husband will turn straight," said Jenny. "It's crushing me."
> "I want to stop using self-deprecating talk," said Alane. "And I want to stop interrupting others and being impatient."
> "I want to stop apologizing for my opinion," said Shelly.

4. THINGS I STARTED AND WANT TO FINISH

This category concerns commitments you may want to reaffirm.

A big one for me here is that when I moved East from Ohio decades ago, I never transferred my driver's license. My stock explanation is that I haven't taken the test because I would have to study for it, and that would take time. But the truth is, after twenty-five years of avoiding it, I did go to take the test. But in Connecticut the test was more sophisticated than it had been twenty-five years earlier in Ohio. I saw this big bank of computers, and suddenly it was me against the Deep Blue chess computer. My automatic technophobia kicked in, and my mind went blank, and I left. That was two years ago! And still, each time I drive to the country with my family, my kids tease me in the way that only kids can. My husband gently pokes fun by saying things like "When you get your license (*ha ha*), remember that this is the place where the cops hang out." This is an incompletion I want to deal with!

> "I started an idea for a fashion magazine for and about people with disabilities," said Zully.
> "I want to give up on the money I wasted because I haven't been to the gym in ten months," said Jenny. "I want to just go

back there and use up the rest of the membership. And I want to lose weight."

"I want to get my college degree," said Shelly.

"I want a new wardrobe," said Julie.

"Me too," said Lauren.

"Painting the kitchen wall, redecorating my office, and cleaning out the garage," said Debra.

5. THINGS I WANT TO HAVE AND DO NOT HAVE

Besides things, which are not trivial material wants but often expressions of self, this category also includes kinds of relationships you've wanted—a mentor, for example, or a child you sponsor in a foreign country, or a friend of a particular age or race, or a yoga partner. It also includes states of mind and regular habits.

"Increase my revenue and financial security," said Zully.

"I want financial freedom," said Debra. "I want a loving spouse and a great marriage."

"I want nice underwear," said Alane, "and a pair of leather pants to go with my new look. I used to be a brunette!" she cries proudly, showing off the short, stylish way her platinum-colored hair was cut.

"I want to own my own home," said Mary Scott.

"I want to have a consistent spiritual practice," said Julie.

"Peace of mind," said Sara. "And I want a child."

6. THINGS I WANT TO DO AND NEVER HAVE DONE

This includes things you want to do on your own, things you want to do with people you have relationships with, technical or professional societies you've wanted to join, places you've wanted to live, areas of your house you've always wanted to develop. And anything else you want. This category is wide open for your dreams.

"I want to write a children's book," said Lynda.

"Study belly dancing," said Zully.

"Let's see it," Hafeezah dared.

"Go to Italy and marry an Italian stallion!" said Alane.

"Take a course in computers," Debra said. "And art direct a movie."

"I want to go on an African safari and write it off," said Leslie.

"I want to ride a motorcycle," said Shelly, as a few jaws dropped.

"I want to spend time in a Tibetan Buddhist temple," said Sara, "or some other culture."

"Take a parachute leap," said Helene.

7. Things I Want to Be and Never Have Been

Part of this is recognizing the areas of our lives in which our dreams have been purged, in which we feel we're not allowed to dream. The trick here is not to force some invented goal on yourself but to notice whether you've stifled your dreaming, whether it's difficult to allow yourself to want anything. For example, you may think wanting to be something you can't be will feel unbearable, and so are pushing out everything you want. Or you may think that pursuing what you want— whatever that is—is trivial.

"An internationally famous antiracism expert," said Mary Scott. "And I want to be debt-free."

"I want to be accomplished at something," said Julie. "And I want to be unconcerned about others' opinions."

"Comfortable around sexuality," said Jenny. "A sort of Miss Kitty. I'd like to be a madam in a very elite brothel."

"I can't think of anything," said Josie. "I feel as if I've lost the ability to dream. I had answers for all the things I didn't want to do, but when you ask me what is it I want, I don't know."

"I want to be a secure, nondefensive person," said Alane.

8. Things I Want to Say and Have Not Said

You may not want to drive two hours this weekend, but you are doing it because you feel you should to see an old friend. There are things you may be embarrassed to say, such as that you prefer mates of a type different from the ones you've been dating. You may want to decide that a particular friend is no longer appropriate for you. You may want to tell a parent "I love you, but I don't respect you." Or you may need to tell a loved one that he or she hurt you, and explain to him just how important he and his words are to you.

"I want to tell my boss I'm working fewer hours," said Alane.

"Please say my name correctly," said Zully. "My name is not Sue."

"I don't want to listen to you right now," said Julie.

"I guess I've never really said what a disappointment this marriage has been to me," said Debra, "and why."

"I want to tell my friend Jeanine that though I enjoy spending time with her, she treats me poorly," said Shelly.

9. Anger I've Had and Have Not Expressed

Not all angers are that simple to resolve; at the same time, simply cataloging why you've been angry starts to shift the knot to one you have the choice to unravel. I've done this exercise many times, so I did not have many big knots of unexpressed anger, but even writing this section reminded me of something I was harboring that was keeping me tied to the past. So I had a drink with a guy I used to work for, and told him that I was still angry that he always seemed to think of me the way I was when he first met me, and that he never gave me credit for how much I'd grown. And to my utter surprise, he apologized, and told me he'd had no idea that I'd grown so much!

"I'm angry at my dad for not ever really knowing us," said Mary Scott, "and making us step to his tune. And I'm mad at those kids who teased me because of my legs. And I'm mad at all those who think I'm not smart because I don't speak."

"I'm angry at my brother for minimizing my contribution to the family business," said Amy Jo.

"My mom doesn't listen when I have problems: She measures success by money, and by that standard I'm the most successful, so when I call with a problem I need help on, she dismisses it," said Alane. "And I'm angry at God for the way my father died."

"I'm angry at the way my husband's ego jeopardized the welfare of our family," said Debra.

10. Things I Want to Learn and Never Have Learned

This includes all the subjects you think are too big for this lifetime, all the areas—physical, intellectual, or spiritual—that you feel intimidated by or think you don't have the head for or never got around to. It also includes areas that intrigue you, even though you know nothing about them. You may want to learn how to change a tire. What about a new sport? Have you always wanted to learn a martial art? How to drive a stick shift? Want to learn how to mambo? Are there equipment and appliances you're not using because you're not comfortable with them?

"I'm half Latvian," said Shelly. "I want to learn the customs and the dances. And I want to learn how to relax."

"I want to know how to invest and to keep track of my money," said Mary Scott.

"I want to learn to mambo," said Jenny.

"I want to learn Italian and art history," said Alane. "And do more Bible study."

"How to be a force for change, and a force for good, within humanity," said Amy Jo.

Exercise: Identifying Incompletions

The following are categories that explore areas in which a lack of resolution is keeping you from moving forward.

Write down the titles of each category on its own page in your notebook.

1. Things I Want to Start and Am Not Starting
2. Things I Want to Change That I Am Not Changing
3. Things I Want to Stop and Am Not Stopping
4. Things I Started and Want to Finish
5. Things I Want to Have and Do Not Have
6. Things I Want to Do and Never Have Done

7. Things I Want to Be and Never Have Been
8. Things I Want to Say and Have Not Said
9. Anger I've Had and Have Not Expressed
10. Things I Want to Learn and Never Have Learned

Now, write down whatever you can think of. Don't agonize over this one; just jot down the things that come readily to mind.

INCOMPLETIONS IN PHYSICAL SPACE

Now that you've identified most of the incompletions that come immediately to mind, the next step is to allow your physical space to remind you of more pockets of incompletion. The way you'll do this is to throw out fifty things in one day.

That's right, fifty.

The idea of this task usually intimidates people. Fifty sounds like an awful lot of things! But people usually find, once they get going, that the exercise is far easier than they thought.

A look in your medicine cabinet may reveal all kinds of medicines you've been hoarding, in fear of the next time you get sick. Your makeup case may contain decade-old false eyelashes you once thought you needed to be attractive. Attics and garages are usually full of incompletions; rooting through the closet and tossing out those tiny suits that you never plan to fit into, your tacky polyester dress from college graduation, and the perfect blouse you got a spot on can be enormously satisfying. You may find incompletions in your broom closet, on your night table, in your computer files, in the glove compartment of your car, and in the kitchen drawer that has everything in it except your purse.

Throwing things away enables you to choose what you want in your life, and what you no longer need. When Amanda found the keys to the little studio she'd bought at twenty-three, she decided that, at thirty-seven, she had financial independence, and would have it even if she threw away the keys. But she also could have decided to frame the keys, to celebrate that precocious accomplishment. (On the other hand, Amanda also found that she was allowing a collection of plastic supermarket bags to accumulate in her kitchen; early on her mother had told her she was a slob, which had produced in her a resignation about the possibility of clearing up her clutter. In this case, Amanda decided to chuck the bags—and the outdated notion of herself as a slob.)

Many people find projects they're delighted to rediscover, and recommit to. Most women find that allowing themselves to complete the projects that have been nudging them for years—the letters, family videos, gardens, attics, and painting supplies—frees up an enormous amount of energy. One participant found that she'd bought the video equipment to make a home documentary on her genealogy and family history for her children—had bought the equipment, gathered all the photographs, paid a researcher to research the genealogy, and come up with a format for the film, only to leave it sitting, for the next six years, in her basement. It was an incompletion she was delighted to resolve, a project she got a burst of energy from completing.

Some people even find space and time! One woman, who thought she had to leave her apartment because it was too small, found that when she threw out all the clutter, her apartment felt quite roomy. Another participant, a writer who felt she never had enough time, had a stuffed file cabinet that was driving her crazy. Between the two days of our workshop, she stayed up until two A.M. cleaning it out. In the process of figuring out how to reorganize her files in the three drawers, Katherine realized she had three different professions: writer, editor, and teacher. Instead of seeing her jobs as competing, she realized that they were three aspects of one profession that complemented each other. Organizing her file drawers provoked a ripple effect of reorganizing her thinking—and it resolved her time management issue.

When you clean out your junk drawer, feel free to decide that you still believe that the sock fairy is going to return one day with the matches to all your single socks. The point is to choose actively. It doesn't matter what you do with the African safari brochure that's been on your desk for years: Whether you file it, throw it away, or call and sign up now, making the choice will release you from the energy drain that happens every time you look at it. You may realize that you *want* to keep the old sheets in the back of your linen cabinet because this summer you intend to take up painting. Discovering *why* you're keeping them—the commitment behind the hoarding—will enable you to stop chastising yourself for being a pack rat.

Similarly, as for that kit you bought four years ago to build a greenhouse: The important thing is not whether you decide to abandon the project and throw it out, or you decide that there's still a gardener inside you screaming to get out. The important thing is to make a decision. Though you will probably actually achieve some completion through this exercise, its point is simply to listen to yourself and make a decision based on what you hear. What you decide you need for completion depends completely and utterly on you. There is no "right" resolution to the pockets of incompletion you discover, no one answer to what you should do with the objects you find.

The bad news: a stack of magazines, a pile of old frozen food from your freezer, or the collection of twelve-year-old spices—each counts as *one* thing.

The good news: intangibles count.

Intangibles you might want to throw away include, first and foremost, resentments and regrets. Resentments are things you can forgive other people for; regrets are things you can forgive yourself for. You can simply declare that you're going to throw out the resentment you have toward your sister about comments she made when you were twenty-two. Or you can throw out a feeling you've been holding by making a phone call to someone and expressing it. We had an identical twin in one of our workshops who hadn't spoken to her twin in seventeen years. The workshop leader asked her what the fight had started over, but Gillian couldn't remember what she'd been holding on to for seventeen years! (That evening she called her twin, and on the second day she ended up designing a vacation that she could take with her twin.) In coming to terms with what's so, you also get to throw out the feeling of regret about actions you've been defining, in hindsight, as mistakes. Again, when you can really take in that your action was perfectly appropriate for how reality was occurring to you at the time, you get a lot more room to validate your past and leave it behind.

A note about phone calls: Before making the phone call, ask yourself: What's this for? What will this allow for? Is my commitment in the conversation to complete what's incomplete by communicating? Is it to build by asking questions and using my new listening? Or is it to convey how wrong the other person is or was? Where you are going to be standing in the conversation will, of course, have everything to do with its outcome. If you're trying to complete by making someone else wrong, and leaving them incomplete—by needing somebody else to do or say something—you're less likely to generate completion for yourself.

If you define the action required for coming to completion as coming from you and not someone else, then regardless of the response, your chances for completion jump way up. You may, for example, want to define the action required for incompletion as *stating that you wanted acknowledgment you didn't receive* rather than *asking for the acknowledgment itself.*

One last note: You can take actions to complete the past even if the person you need to communicate with is unavailable or dead. You can write them a letter and not mail it. Or you can mail it with the person's name on it but no address. In either case the simple action of writing down what was never verbalized begins to allow you to express what has been harbored as an old resentment or regret that has gone unexpressed and surfaces as incomplete, unfinished business from the past. A third option is to tell a close friend what you wanted to tell the person who died. A Greek tradition of dealing with bereavement is that you go to the person's grave every day for a year, and talk to him. What a great tactic for completion!

The basic process for reaching completion is first to acknowledge what's so by taking complete ownership of every aspect of the situation. Next, you'll decide whether there are actions to take to reach the point where you can declare the situation complete. If there are, you'll decide when you'll take them by; if there are no actions, you can move directly to what is always the last step, which is that you declare the situation complete.

....

IDENTIFYING MORE INCOMPLETIONS: THROWING OUT FIFTY THINGS

1. Look around your home, your office, your car, your gym locker. Look in closets and drawers, in the basement and attic. Notice the stuff that has been cluttering your life.
2. Ask yourself, "Why am I holding on to this? Is this serving a purpose?"
3. If you decide you want to recommit to whatever it is that feels incomplete, feel free to choose to keep it. If you decide it's no longer serving you, throw it away.

4. When you get to fifty, call a friend and tell her what you just did.

Congratulations!

··

WHEN ACCOMPLISHMENTS
BECOME INCOMPLETIONS

Recently, a luncheon was given honoring Wellesley professor Carolyn Shaw Bell, who is one of the best-known women economists in the country. Professor Bell was being honored by the many powerful women she had taught and mentored over the years; there were more corporate board members and CEOs than I have ever seen in a group of women before or since. At the question-and-answer portion of the event, Professor Bell was asked for the most important piece of advice she could give to young women. Her response wasn't "Earn your credentials," or "Network," or "Learn how to deal with numbers." Her answer was: "Boast!" Boasting, she remarked, is something that men seem to know how to do but that women have more trouble with. She advised: Share your delight in your accomplishments. And if you can't yet boast about yourself, boast about your colleagues, or your team.

Bell's advice underscores the idea that external recognition starts with internal recognition. Not that outward obstacles don't exist, or that we should deny them. But if there is one idea I want to communicate in this book, it's that the most powerful way of dismantling the "glass ceiling" is, first, to take off the glasses that frame and shape how you see the sky. How many of us have paintings we've never shown to anyone or accomplishments we've never mentioned because we're afraid or embarrassed about the way the world will receive them?

You've already begun to take some actions to begin to resolve some of the incompletions in your life. Acknowledging your accomplishments is simply another one of the actions you can take to get complete about those things you may feel unrecognized for, although you've finished them successfully.

Self-acknowledgment can be a difficult category for the many women who have heard, from some well-meaning person, that it's not good to brag. This belief sits in the cultural mores defined as the Protestant work ethic. Often communicated by a well-meaning teacher or relative who inherited an interpretation from her well-meaning teacher, it says that good breeding, or whatever, does not include the act of stating and acknowledging one's own accomplishments. As a result, women grow up feeling it's presumptuous, or arrogant, to tell people about their successes. For all these reasons, it's especially important for women to work on getting past this notion. I "grew up" in a company where "humility" was a core value. Being humble is okay, I guess, if that means not throwing your weight around, or having the ability to listen to other people's possibilities. But if it means not acknowledging your own accomplishments, not taking the ground you're entitled to, it's out of the question. In fact, it's unthinkable. Toss it out!

Most of the time, by acknowledging your own accomplishments, you help others. In one of our workshops, for example, there was a participant who had been a national amateur golf champion at nineteen. But Terri rarely told people about it, because she'd decided that other people would think she was bragging and they wouldn't care. But when we got to the point in the workshop where we ask people about talents they have that others may not know about, Terri publicly acknowledged her past achievement. When she did, another woman's mouth dropped open. "That's you?" she asked. "I've always wanted to meet you! I read about you years ago!" This other woman was a golfer, and had always wanted a mentor. Two other women in the group then jumped on the bandwagon, and the group made a plan to reconvene, after the workshop was over, on the golf course. Thus Terri created completely unexpected possibilities for the other women, simply by telling them what she'd done.

When we speak our of accomplishments, we allow others to access us as a resource.

The bigger point about acknowledging your accomplishments, though, is that it allows you to get grounded in an appreciation for what you contribute in the world.

The idea of getting grounded is an important one.

Say your life, in terms of its successes and failures, has been going along about like the jagged line on the following graph. Ever wonder why the overall slope of your growth is so flat, even though you're making extraordinary efforts?

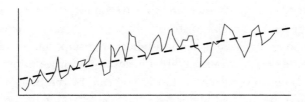

The way most climbers scale physical mountains, I think, can teach us something here. When climbers scale a mountain, they don't try to climb straight up to the top. Every so often, when they get to the top of their rope, they secure it on what's called an anchor. What this does is prevent them from falling too far back. The high-altitude climbers create a series of base camps for themselves, at increasingly higher levels: they stop, they rest, they look around, and maybe they eat something. They get used to the altitude, in other words, and they take in nourishment for the next challenge. Thus, while the overall slope (the dotted line) is much steeper, the actual graph of how climbers climb mountains looks a little more like this:

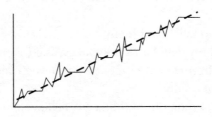

The flat places represent the plateaus climbers use to take their ground.

Emotional climbing functions very much the same way. To climb steadily, we need plateaus: places (or intervals of time) that establish a new, higher base level of functioning than you had before. This means resting. It means accepting, for example, that you now weigh ten pounds less rather than rushing in to try to lose another fifteen. And it means celebrating. In taking that ground, you distinguish what you've done that has allowed you to be successful, and you assimilate those techniques. What is now available to you that wasn't available to you ten pounds ago? What new arenas are open to you now?

Taking ground is crucial to steady progress, because it takes into account that sometimes we have to step back, regroup, stand still, or take another route—to go around a difficult slope—before continuing up. If all you do is climb vertically, as fast as you can, by the time you get up close to the top, you feel like, what's the point? You get tired and you backslide, or you look down and get vertigo, and suddenly you're terrified at how far you've climbed. But if you've taken your ground, you'll only slip back as far as your last plateau. Taking your ground is the difference between breaking out of your old habit on a single occasion and making a habit of change.

So, part of making yourself available and open to new futures is to acknowledge your accomplishments. Now that you've explored your incompletions, it's time to acknowledge some of the things you've done that have brought real satisfaction to your life.

"So, in the following areas of your life, what accomplishments have been the most extraordinary, fun, satisfying, and fulfilling? Let's start with Health and Well-Being."

"I lost twenty pounds," said Alane, "and I gave up sweets for Lent this year."

"We need to talk," said Jenny.

"I survived my daughter's pregnancy," said Debra.

"I go to chiropractic treatment twice a week and I have for two years," said Zully.

"You know, I didn't think I had any achievements in this area," said Jenny. "But I did change my diet to deal with my cholesterol problem."

"I didn't either," said Shelly. "But after a year of serious dental problems, I began flossing every day for the first time in my life. I think any real habit you pick up after forty is a triumph!"

"Great," said Hafeezah. "What about the category Family and Friends?"

"I gave my parents a European vacation," said Alane.

"My daughter sent me a lovely card," said Leslie, "that made me know she felt like I'm there for her."

"I've been a maid of honor four times," said Sara.

"When my relationship was thawing with my mother," said Jane, "she had a heart attack. I took a whole week off, unscheduled, and went down to take care of her. I'm glad I was able to do something concrete for her."

"I made friends with my brother when my son was born," said Julie.

"I had a birthday party for my mom's seventieth birthday that included a wonderful pictorial history of her life and a compilation of well wishes from family and friends," said Mary Scott. "And in general, I have three beautiful, self-assured kids."

"Terrific," said Hafeezah. "How about Profession and Career?"

"I was the founding executive director of the Chicago Sexual Assault Service Network," said Mary Scott.

"I survived the downsizing of my husband's company," said Debra.

"Not only did I have a best-selling CD-ROM," said Alane, "I created a new category of video games that take girls through travel and adventure challenges without having to get attacked or be violent."

"Excellent. What about in the area of Finances?"

"I have a great salary for a social services professional," said Mary Scott.

"I paid off all the bills in ninety-five," said Debra.

"I paid eight years in back taxes two years ago," said Josie.

"I allowed myself to get into debt to buy a house," said Elinor. "I've always been so financially responsible that that was a big step for me."

"I started my own business and took it to enormous success in under two years," said Leslie.

"What about the category of Growth and Personal Development," asked Hafeezah.

"I got a master's degree at twenty-eight, with two kids," said Mary Scott.

"I've learned three languages," said Alane. "And I've lived abroad successfully."

"I took this course," said Lynda. "And I learned more about

my own ADD this spring. And I stood up to my archdiocese in verbal and written form when they fired a priest we all really loved."

The last category of accomplishments we ask women about is Participation in the World. This consists of things we do to shape our environment in a larger sense—not our own personal world but the larger world and our sense of it.

"I organized community campaigns against drugs and crime," said Mary Scott. "And I am an antiracism activist in the city and community. I also participated in antiapartheid work and traveled to South Africa."

"I got my ex-boss a job at my current company, for a huge salary," said Elinor.

"I started an association for working parents that serves as a networking thing and a support network," said Leslie.

"I heard my son's teacher admit that he didn't know how to turn on a computer," said Jane. "So instead of railing and calling the Department of Education, I went to the public school and taught him and got my company to donate the hardware and then watched him teach kids."

"I was in the first M.B.A. class that allowed women at a top-ten business school," said Amy Jo. "I graduated a four-year advanced program in two years and four months. And I just graduated from law school, having been accepted to it in 1972, and passed the bar. I'm really proud of that."

"I'm having trouble," said Leslie. "Because, like, when I was going home from Harvard Business School for my last vacation, my parents were so proud that I was about to finish. I was one of the first black women to graduate. And I remember thinking, 'I don't want to do this.' But I couldn't not do it, because they were so proud. So all of the successes were not my successes. It was as if I was living someone else's life."

"That's very important," said Hafeezah. "If you aren't authoring and designing your own life, you can't own your accomplishments."

"I'm proud," said Page, "of something I created at my previous job, the financial services one? I was head of my division. Twenty years ago, I took a maternity leave to have my last son. About one week after the leave, my boss called me into his office and said, 'I don't like you leaving at five.' I went on to succeed him at his job and now, years later, they have a flex-time and job-sharing policy that I instituted. At first the company prohibited it, but I let my employees do it anyway, and then after two years I got up the nerve to show the management how well it was working. Anyway, last week I was visiting a close friend there, and I was in the hallway, and I overheard somebody asking, 'What kind of place is this to work for working moms?' And the answer was, 'A place where you get a memo that it's okay to leave early on Halloween.'"

"Fabulous," said Hafeezah.

....

EXERCISE: TAKING YOUR GROUND

1. Write down the following areas of accomplishment, giving each a separate page in your notebook.
   Health and Well-Being
   Family and Friends
   Profession and Career
   Finances
   Growth and Personal Development
   Participation in the World
2. Now, write down, in any category, any of the achievements you're proud of. Look down your list of accomplishments and see if there are any around which you need more acknowledgment or celebration.
3. This week, if you haven't before, tell someone important to you what you have accomplished. And find a way to celebrate the accomplishments you never celebrated.

Congratulations!

....

"I can't concentrate," interrupted Mary Scott. At the break, Ireen had announced that NBC, who had said they'd be filming our workshop in Chicago, wasn't coming because a bomb had gone off in Tel Aviv. "I feel so sad that there has been senseless violence. Last week another bomb went off, and there were some young girls, just like the ones I work with, who were killed senselessly."

Mary Scott couldn't concentrate in the workshop because she was incomplete about the information she'd received. The deed was done, the bomb was thrown halfway around the world, but Mary wasn't complete. As a result, she couldn't be present in the workshop. Incompletions keep us from the present, whether they happened three minutes or three decades ago.

"Is there something you'd like to add?" asked Hafeezah.
"I'd like us to intend world peace," she said, on the verge of tears. We all sat for a moment in the workshop, silently backing up Mary Scott's wish.
Once Mary Scott had identified her incompletion and shared it, Hafeezah helped her define what action she needed to take to get complete. After the group had given her the acknowledgment she requested, she was able to be present, and move forward with the workshop.

COMING TO COMPLETION

Now that you have some intuitive experience in coming to completion, I'd like to lay out a step-by-step process you can reuse whenever you need a burst of energy. The first aspect to coming to completion is to acknowledge what's so. In Mary's case, that meant acknowledging that she wasn't paying attention. It can also mean stating an accomplishment, or admitting that you no longer want to pursue a friendship with someone who lives in your apartment complex, or informing yourself about exactly which years you owe back taxes for, or acknowledging that you still care about someone you're trying to leave behind. Again, because completion is an interpretation and not a fact, it never depends on any specific outside reality. You can decide to take action to finish a goal in order to be complete about it, or you can decide you are complete with not finishing. You may feel comfortable abandoning your dream of becoming the world champion sand castle builder, or you may decide you don't want to go another summer without having entered Atlantic City's annual competition. In either case, you're going to take ownership for how things are for you. What completion is, then, is a responsible relationship with the way things are. Responsible not as in *I'm the cause*, but as in *Now that I admit how things are, and how I continue to feel about them, I can respond to this situation*. It's admitting what's so, without the judgment attached.

"But how do you declare yourself complete about something like the fact that though you have three grown daughters, you always wanted a son?" Page asked.

"I'll answer that indirectly by talking about the choices you have for how to deal with your incompletions," said Hafeezah. "But for right now, what you can say is that 'what's so' is that you have three daughters and you always wanted a son. Are you going to have more children?"

Page laughed. "I'm sixty-two," she said.

"And are you going to adopt a son at this point?" asked Hafeezah.

"No," said Page, after a minute.

"So, are you ever going to have a son?" asked Hafeezah.

"I guess not," said Page.

"Just out of curiosity," asked Amy Jo. "I wonder if I could ask that question Hafeezah keeps asking—because I have only a son, and not a daughter. What would having a son be for?"

"It was just—" Page began, "my father always wanted me to have sons. I love my daughters, but I wanted to make him happy. It just always made me feel as if I couldn't make up for being a girl."

"So the incompletion's about your father's approval, and not the sons you don't have?" asked Hafeezah.

"I guess so," said Page.

"Is there anything you can do to get complete now?"

"I'm going to write my father a letter," said Page. "Even if he is in a nursing home."

"Keep in mind," said Hafeezah, "completion is a place to come from. So that you're always generating what action you may need to take, in any one moment, to feel complete. It's not a feeling; the object of completion isn't to feel good. It's simply the place of clearing that enables you to move on. You don't have to feel great about something to be complete."

My next suggestion is to decide how you want to respond to your incompletions. Besides digging in your heels and doing nothing, there are three other possibilities for how to respond.

The first possibility is the most obvious: *take action*. In this case you probably already know what it is you want to do.

Some women have trouble with this option, because they feel that if they identify an action they want to take, then they'll *have* to feel complete afterward. But Mary Scott's experience points to the fact that completion is a moment-to-moment state. Sometimes you can take action and permanently achieve once-and-for-all closure. Sometimes you'll take some action, achieve completion, and then a week later find you're still incomplete and need to take more action. Mary Scott was "present" in the workshop—complete—for most of the morning. Then she realized something had happened that made her incomplete. Mary was able to ask for an action, a moment of acknowledgment from the group, in order to get complete around her feelings—about the bomb that had killed some young girls—so that she could get back to being present in the workshop. But that doesn't mean that Mary has to feel okay about the violence in the Middle East for the rest of her life, or that she won't decide, next week, to do something else about it.

If you know the action you want to take, and you want to set a concrete deadline by which you'll take that action, you'll be putting your incompletion in a category we'll call the "Now" category. By "Now" I don't mean "I have to act this second" but rather simply that you want to set a specific time frame for taking action.

The second option in dealing with an incompletion is to decide you'll *do it later*. With this option, you're remaining committed to doing something, but you're making a decision not to do it now. Declaring that you're taking no action for the moment means that you can stop harassing yourself because you're not learning French. You can decide that you'll learn French when your baby's born, or when you retire.

The third option is to decide that you're not going to take any action. Announcing "I'm not doing it!" is really satisfying when the incompletion is something you've been nagging yourself about, and apologizing for, but aren't really committed to. In this option, you simply *declare it complete.*

So if you had an old commitment to go back to school that's been nagging you for years, you have the choice of deciding on a date by which you'll enroll, or you could come to terms with the fact that you're not going back to school until you retire, or you could simply decide, once and for all, that you're content with the school of life. Recently, I declared complete my longing to be a pianist—or at least a bistro performer. "Not in this lifetime," I said, much to the relief of my family. And I drew a line through "piano lessons" for 1998, or 2000, or ever.

EXERCISE: COMING TO COMPLETION

1. Go back to your lists of your incompletions. In the left-hand margin, categorize them this way:
   - **N**, for now (interpreted loosely, this is something you want to assign a deadline to and complete within a specific time frame)
   - **L**, for later (meaning, you're committed to doing it sometime in the indefinite future, even if that means after you retire)
   - **C**, for complete

   There may be incompletions about which you can't decide what to do. That's okay. You'll have more than enough, right now, than you will know what to do with. Just try to investigate and notice why it is you're resisting completion in that area—what you think it would mean. The goal isn't completion in every single area of your life—there is no such thing as perfect completion—but simply to become familiar with a process you can reuse.

2. Now, to the incompletions that you have labeled "N, "write down what you're going to do and the date by which you're going to do it. Keep in mind, if you're squirming, that it doesn't matter what date you set. Pick a date that makes you feel a little edgy, but not so uncomfortable that it feels impossible.

3. Rewrite those actions on a To Do list. On the left, write

down "Actions" and on the right, write "By When?" Then, in two columns, list the actions you're going to take and the deadlines you've set to do them by.

4. Declare your list (excluding whatever is too private) to at least two other people in your life. Tell them exactly what you're going to do, and when you're going to have it done.

Chapter Four

Paradigms, Assumptions, and Rules

I n some sense, people are meaning machines. At the end of a decade or a century, or (good grief!) a millennium, we are spiritually compelled—driven—to search for meaning. Our religious practices, our art, our storytelling, the relationships we have—all reflect our drive to make our lives mean something. One of the reasons we're obsessed with the possibility of space aliens, I think, is that they'll come along and tell us what it all means!

It's almost impossible to have an experience without interpreting its meaning.

Since meaning exists in language, part of finding meaning is sharing it with anybody who'll listen. The meanings we find, the distilled truths we derive from our experiences, become paradigms for how life is.

A paradigm is simply a belief that defines how we think. It's an interpretation that someone else—our parents, the culture, our company—
says is the way things are.

There are paradigms floating around about everything anyone's ever
experienced (and most of what we haven't). Thus, as North Americans,
we have paradigms of January as cold and June as warm. As American
citizens, we may hold such paradigms as, "Our society is the most fair in
the world," or "Every society in the world should strive for democratic
ideals." Depending on where we sit in society, we may hold paradigms
like, "We live in a meritocracy," or we may believe that "Race plays into
every interaction," and "America is still a plantation society, owned and
controlled by whites." Our paradigms about males range from, "Men
must make more money," "Men are more competent at technical
things," and "Men won't do housework" to "Men are more aggressive"
to "Boys won't read books with female protagonists." We have paradigms about southerners—they're slow-paced, and polite, and wordy—
and we have paradigms about Californians being relaxed and healthy
and progressive. Our paradigms about artists and writers range from
"Artists are geniuses with unique vision" to "Artists are lazy and a threat
to society's moral fabric." Someone is either a night person or a morning person, creative or analytical. We have paradigms about whether
mothers should breast feed in public; about oldest, youngest, and middle children; about corporations and families; about blondes and Lati-
nos, Asians and athletes—and just about everything else.

The first step toward freeing yourself from the control that inherited
paradigms may be exercising over your life is simply to try to bring to
consciousness what's floating around in your head.

> "What are some of the things we hear on the street about
> women?" asks Hafeezah. "Women are . . . ?"
>
> "The weaker sex," said Page.
>
> "They're quiet, to be seen and not heard," Josie added.
>
> "They should be less successful than their husbands," said
> Debra.
>
> "Obviously," Hafeezah said.
>
> "Women are responsible for everybody," said Elinor.
>
> "They're too emotional!" said Lauren.
>
> "Women should be supportive," said Jenny.

"Women expect to be supported," said Lynda.

"Women are too aggressive," said Alane.

"Too passive," said Helene.

"Let's not forget passive aggressive!" cried Amy Jo.

"I'd say women are pretty talented," Hafeezah said, "to be all three at once! What other paradigms do we hear?"

"Women don't know what they want," said Sara.

"Women don't get what they want because they're indecisive; they change their minds," said Shelly.

"Women won't stick with it, because they're going to go have babies," said Elinor.

"Women are too competitive," said Jenny.

"Women are sexually fickle. *La donn'è mobile,*" said Amy Jo.

"Women are manipulative; they want to control men," said Amy.

"Men get distinguished, women get old," said Page.

"Women talk too much," said Jenny.

"Women can't drive," said Mary Scott.

"Women who sleep around are loose."

"Women shouldn't be priests or involved in the church," said Lynda.

"Women get PMS, so they can't make the big, clutch decisions," said Elinor.

"Mothers must sacrifice for their children," said Josie.

"I'm not exactly sure why we're doing this," said Julie uncomfortably. "It seems like we're just spouting stereotypes."

"Julie needs to know already!" said Amy Jo. The group, and Julie, roared at having been caught by one of their own.

Most of us, like Julie, don't like to get too close to these sexist paradigms, though we know they're out there—we know men who believe these things, and organizations that operate under these assumptions, we ourselves are supposed to be in a "postfeminist" era. We've done the consciousness raising. We're over it. These old-fashioned beliefs belong to the men, not us. They belong to our mother's generation, not ours. They're held by women who are less educated or enlightened or liberated than we are. Or they're held by women who've been more indoctrinated by the white male establishment—that is, rich white women who bought into the male patriarchal values. They're held by women in less industrialized countries. By southern women. By women on the stodgy, conservative East Coast. By rural women, not urban women. In other words, the women who believe these paradigms are anyone other than us!

Our staff, when they first began doing this exercise in groups, assumed that after their extensive training on paradigms, they'd would no longer find them operating in their own lives. Yet Hafeezah, who is African-American, found herself using highly intellectualized language, and trying to articulate overly clearly, because she was operating under the paradigm that white corporate women would dismiss a "black kid from the projects," thinking she wasn't smart enough to lead them. Amanda noticed that when the VCR needed to be programmed, she waited for her husband to come home. Jennifer noticed that if she saw a bug when she was alone, she calmly looked for a newspaper to swat it; whereas if her boyfriend was around, she screamed involuntarily!

At the same time, as we designed workshops for different groups, I think we all assumed there'd be some differences in the paradigms the participants came up with depending on their race or economics. What happened? The mostly African-American single mothers living in homeless shelters came up with "Women are heifers," "Women are chickenshit," "Women can't deal with money," and "Women are whores"; a workshop of mostly white corporate women came up with "Women should be thin," "Women don't have the guts to stick with anything," "Women can't crunch the numbers," and "Nice girls don't do that." The women in shelters were afraid to end up as bag ladies; the high-powered corporate types were afraid to end up as bag ladies. White corporate women felt they had to serve the company's needs first, and their own careers second; African-American community leaders from Brooklyn felt it was their responsibility to take care of everybody else in their personal lives first, and to put their husbands' and siblings' needs before their own. In other words, how the paradigms were operating on them changed slightly, yet they were virtually identical.

Still, we hoped, when we were preparing a workshop for college-age women, that at least *they* would be past this stuff. No man these days would dare say to them what Carolyn Stradley heard—"No one will lend you the money, because you're a woman"—or suggest what Supreme Court Justice Ruth Bader Ginsburg heard when looking for her first law job, which was that she didn't deserve to take the job from a man who needed the money. These young women, we thought, were the privileged daughters of liberation! But while these young women didn't list the antiquated paradigms that older women do, they worried about not having the facts to prove their ideas, or the qualifications to ask for a great job; they repeatedly apologized for their ideas and for disagreeing with one another. The white ones expressed an overwhelming preoccupation with being thin. The paradigm "Thin is beautiful" was fact; there didn't seem to be any point in even addressing whether it was an interpretation or not. It was so heartbreaking for the workshop leaders to see how much they'd absorbed, at such an early age, that one of them broke into tears at the break.

Though the language used to formulate the paradigms may differ, and though they operate differently in different age groups and cultures, our experience is that the gender paradigms women absorb are remarkably similar. And that it's nearly impossible to escape them.

....

EXERCISE: NOTICING GENDER PARADIGMS

1. On a fresh page in your notebook, before you read on, write the words *Women are . . .*
2. Now, for a few minutes, write whatever pops into your head, without stopping. Just keep your pen moving; do not evaluate what you're putting down.

....

THE PERVASIVENESS OF PARADIGMS

"So my next question is: How many of you buy into these paradigms?" asked Hafeezah, continuing the conversation.

The participants were all silent.

"This just feels like, you know, old stuff," said Alane.

"Let's do a little experiment," said Hafeezah. "Turn back to the page where you wrote down all your accomplishments. Just out of curiosity: How many of you wrote down nothing?"

As some women began to laugh nervously, a few hands hesitatingly went up.

"So, Zully," said Hafeezah, "all those articles about you in the

Chicago Tribune are about how you have no achievements?" joked Hafeezah.

"I guess, whatever I've done," said Zully, "I feel like, everybody should have done that. It's just part of the struggle I went through. It didn't matter that I did it; it was just, I saw an obstacle and overcame it."

"So your paradigm is that you should just struggle and accept all difficulties without complaining?" asked Hafeezah.

"More like, If I want to survive, I can't complain and I can't boast," said Zully.

"So are there any accomplishments you want to say?" asked Hafeezah.

The group sat for two or three whole minutes of silence, while Zully thought.

"I guess I have to say something, right?" said Zully. "Well, I was accepted to graduate school. And I spoke before the U.N. on disability. But that was a long time ago."

"So it has to be a recent accomplishment for it to count as one? How long does it take before accomplishments expire?"

"After two years it doesn't matter," said Zully.

"Good to know," said Hafeezah. "So who cares that Marie Curie discovered radioactivity. That was over two years ago."

Zully burst out laughing. "You know, I was also assistant to the mayor of Chicago," she said. "Even if it was ten years ago!"

"What about you, Julie?" Hafeezah asked. Julie had also raised her hand.

"My parents weren't around," said Julie. "I mean, emotionally. I guess they just weren't interested. So I think it's out of line, or unnecessary grandstanding."

"So in your world," says Hafeezah, "people shouldn't call attention to themselves. Is this women? Or everybody?"

"Just women," said Julie. "My brother had no problem showing off."

"So your paradigm is: 'Women shouldn't call attention to themselves.' Hmm. Not that I'm saying you buy into it or anything . . ."

Julie laughed.

"Amy Jo?"

Amy Jo was whispering a comment to Shelly.

"We haven't forgotten you, Amy Jo, even though you might like us to!" said Hafeezah.

"I can't think of any," Amy Jo pleaded.

"So, graduating from business school as one of four women, and graduating two years early, and getting your law degree after twenty-five years, is, like, just what everybody does all the time?"

"I'm forty-six, and I'm literally in a career place that a twenty-three-year-old should be in. It's like, out-of-step dilettantism."

"Ah!" said Hafeezah, her face lighting up. "So there is a specific age by which accomplishments should happen, and if they don't happen by then, they're not valid?"

"Well, yeah," said Amy Jo.

"So all the pictures Picasso painted in his seventies were dreck?"

"I get the point," Amy Jo said, sheepishly.

"You know, I also didn't think I bought into any of these," said Elinor. "But the other night I came home from work, and my daughter was singing, 'Some day, my prince will come.' And I was like, 'Where did that come from?'"

"Recently I was playing squash with another woman," said Jane. "And it was sick! Each of us was apologizing for winning a point!"

"Recently my husband and I were having dinner with another couple," said Julie. "They have one child, a two-year-old daughter. During dessert, the husband announced he was going to work with his father. And my husband said, 'Oh, now you'll have to have a son.' And the truth is, I didn't even think about it until weeks later."

"I was on a flight with another professor," said Helene. "After we took off, the pilot came on to speak and it was a woman's voice. I teach anthropology! And my first thought was 'We're going to crash.' I was so nervous I told this to the woman next to me. I had to laugh. She said she'd thought we'd be really well taken care of."

"That's what I was objecting to before!" Lynda blurted out.

"The paradigms we wrote are all so negative. What about the paradigm that 'Women take responsibility for caring for others,' that 'Women care about the big picture,' stuff like that?"

Regardless of who the women are who are sitting in our rooms, it usually takes a while before a participant brings up a "positive" paradigm about women. Not that there aren't empowering paradigms about women floating around—there are. But it seems as if the negative noise is more often in the forefront of our minds.

It is interesting to notice that while many of these paradigms are inherently negative and limiting, most fall somewhere in neutral space. "Women are responsible for taking care of others," for example, can operate positively or negatively in a woman's life. In the workshop of African-American community leaders from Brooklyn, for example, several participants came to the workshop feeling trapped because they were financially supporting siblings, grown children, and husbands; or they were supporting their husbands' dreams and working for them in their business. Some of the designs these women came up with included running a day care center in another state and operating a business in a Brooklyn brownstone that would include all the services—massage, nutrition counseling, and so on—women might need. The limitations these women felt were about having to take care of others; the dreams were about taking care of others. (The difference was that in the lives they designed, it was *their* dreams they were authoring and supporting, not somebody else's.)

Because we so often assume that those paradigms live "out there," and not in us, we assume that the versions we've absorbed are benign. For this reason, discovering that we're holding on to limiting beliefs can be really embarrassing. We especially don't want to think we're actually teaching them!

I myself was raised to be anything I wanted to be: I was an athlete and a scholar. The fact that Sleeping Beauty was in a coma, Snow White was dead, Cinderella and Rapunzel were imprisoned had nothing at all to do with me! Yet when I was looking for my first job in New York, people kept saying to me, "You're really attractive. You ought to go into public relations." What I took in was that I would get a job because I was cute. All sorts of things happened as a result of my assimilating these messages. Though I'd been raised to be empowered—I never once heard from my father or mother anything about what a woman "should" do—I began to focus on always looking cute. I started to believe that it didn't matter what I said, as long as I looked good. I remember toning down my vocabulary, and adopted an artificial, folksy way of speaking—using "gal" instead of "woman," and saying "workin'" instead of "working"—because I thought I might come across as intimidating. No one ever told me to do any of these things; I simply did them. And as much as I hate to admit it, I realize now that I dismissed other women who didn't bother to make themselves attractive, because I assumed they wouldn't be taken seriously. Now the niche was a narrow one: You ought to be cute, but not too sexual. Many years later, I actually said to a manager who reported to me, who had a particularly full figure: "More Eleanor Roosevelt, less Bette Midler"—and then watched her gradually cover up her beautiful body—and her physical confidence—with loose, disguising clothes. I was buying in to what my narrow paradigm allowed, which was: not unattractive, but not too female. It took me a long time to realize that I had bought in to limiting paradigms about women in my own life—that not only was I passively allowing them in my workplace, I was actively forwarding and enforcing them on my female staff.

Though we may not think it, we are living these paradigms.

Gender paradigms in the culture operate on us like a perpetual undertow—we can't see it or measure it; the only evidence of its existence is how it *affects* us. Though the force may not be obviously visible, its effects are very real. If you're part of the human race, the ocean in which you're swimming is language that contains these paradigms. No matter how conscious we're trying to be, these beliefs are swaying us all the time. Like the ocean, the culture is bigger than we are.

> "It's so true!" said Elinor. "My colleagues all love me and wish me well. But when I started interviewing inside the company, with friends—women—who said well-meaning things like, 'Elinor, you've already got one child; how are you going to do your job with two?' As if you couldn't both be a mother and have a brain. Or, when I'd go into meetings, people would say, 'Hi, Mom!' I wanted to scream."

"You can resist, though," said Sara. "I mean, you could have said something. My mother always said that, as a woman, a career was something you fall back on. You know, marriage was the thing. But I ended up single. My whole life is my career."

"Was there room in your mother's paradigm to have both?" asked Hafeezah.

"My mother never even had an idea of what she might want to do with herself, even when she finally retired and had the time!" Sara said after a minute. "I didn't want to be like that."

"So you swung way over in the other direction," said Hafeezah.

"I never realized I was buying into 'It's one or the other,'" said Sara. "I'm so sick of fighting this—I don't want to have to be single for the rest of my life."

"What strikes me, in what you're saying, is that when you're trying that hard to actively resist, you're still operating in it," said Shelly. "Because I was raised to be so deferential, I raised my daughter to be really independent. I raised her to take care of herself in every way. I always gave her a special present on the Fourth of July. But now my daughter's thirty-six, and she's so driven, she can't accept help from anyone. And her life is like yours, Sara: all work, no romance, and she's alone."

"I realize that a lot of the control I was talking about," Elinor said, "that other people see in me, is something I developed to avoid being a 'typical woman' in a work situation."

"It's exhausting," said Josie. "When I was born, my father wanted a boy. My whole life I've been trying to prove to him that I'm every bit as good as a man. I have always wanted to own my own business, because he owned his own business, and now I'm sitting here wondering if it's even a goal for me: always trying to prove that I was just as good as he was; and could do everything that a son could do."

Josie's comments brings us to family paradigms. If you think of cultural paradigms as a huge set of assumptions, then family paradigms are like a smaller subset of assumptions within that bigger set. They're the subset of paradigms that your family believes or adheres to. The rules we get taught in our family can be more specifically tailored to us than cultural paradigms. Because they're more specific, these hold a bit more sway for us.

"So what are some of the paradiigms your family taught you?"

"If I say what I want, people will think I'm a bitch," said Shelly.

"What if I do this and it still doesn't make me happy?" said Julie.

Hafeezah interjected, "So the paradigm is . . ."

"Don't try anything if you're not sure of being successful," said Julie.

"You can't manage money, how can you run a business?" said Zully.

"I'd have to totally renegotiate my marriage," said Page.

"I've never had a good support system; I was never encouraged," said Josie.

"Single women aren't supposed to do that," said Alane.

"I'm not as smart as I think I am," said Shelly.

"Ditto," said Mary Scott.

"My family will disapprove and will alienate me," said Amy Jo.

"Ditto," said Lauren.

"I'm a failure if I don't have a man," said Sara.

"Exactly," said Alane. "And: If I express any emotional needs, men will feel criticized and run."

"Dealing with the public might be unsafe," said Leslie.

"Men will never let you get away with job sharing," said Elinor.

"Great work," said Hafeezah. "Now, keep in mind, the goal here isn't bashing, but building. So for now we're not evaluating whether there are any facts in your noise."

"Always try to please. Never try to achieve too much. Stay where it's safe," said Shelly.

"People with money are bad and don't care about their families. If you want to be successful, you'll ruin your family," said Leslie.

"Get married and have children; a career is something you fall back on," said Sara. "You're nothing without a man."

"Hide your defects so you can look pretty," said Zully.

"Don't bother trying to lose weight if you come from a family that's big," said Jenny.

"I'm not sexy or attractive because I'm too tall and flat-chested," said Helene.

"Speak only when you're spoken to," said Josie.

"I'm the first African-American woman, so I should . . ." said Leslie.

"I'm the smart one," said Page. "I wanted to be an artist, but I had to do something smart."

"Making C's is unacceptable," said Julie. "And: Are you going to do it like that? My mother would always refold the laundry I folded. So I decided I should be perfect, and I'm not," said Julie.

"Don't waste money. My mom wouldn't give me a penny for the gumball machine. So I have this scarcity model and am obsessed with making enough money," said Elinor.

"I have to be like a son," said Jenny. "People are always saying, 'Oh, your poor father, with all those girls in the house.' So I thought I should be this big career person. It keeps me totally asexual."

Notice here that many of the rules we live under are personal interpretations of cultural paradigms. "I'm a failure if I don't have a man" is not the same thing as "I'm lonely, and I want a partner." It's a personal judgment that distills the larger cultural paradigms that a woman has less value in society than a man, and that success for women is measured by whether or not they have a male partner. "I'm just like my mother, and she's crazy," personalizes the gender paradigm that defines men as rational, logical—the standard—and women as emotional hysterics (the Greek root of the word, by the way, means "womb"). "Always try to please" is based on a paradigm that women have to *work* to be pleasing, that they aren't pleasing to men as they are. "I have to be like a son" can be based on the paradigm that men value sons more than daughters. And beneath these last two, of course, is the paradigm that women should take care of men's emotional needs first.

"The only thing I felt comfortable with was art," said Page. "It was my only strength, and the only thing I ever wanted. But I had no familial support because, God forbid, if I wanted to go off to art school, I might meet an artist, and that would mean I'd never have any money. I mean, I've succeeded in a lot of things I never thought I could, because I was stifled. Still, I just wonder if it had to be either/or."

"Well," said Leslie, "the expectation for me was always that I could do great things and set a real example of what's possible. The problem now is that if I don't want to go and get, who am I? My business is getting more and more successful, and more and more demanding. I have to go to London for two months. If I just sat down and gave that up, I don't know where I'd be. It wouldn't be unique or successful enough, especially as a black woman, just to own a restaurant where you could hang out with your kids."

DICHOTOMIES

One of the structures we often absorb, for rules that get transmitted through families, is the dichotomy. Dichotomies are sets of "opposites" that are supposedly mutually exclusive, like truth and falsehood, creativity and analytical skills, madonna and sex kitten, career and marriage. The assumption that two things are incompatible is a paradigm from an older culture with more rigid definitions of what people should, or could, do. Sometimes this assumption springs up at a point when somebody has to make a choice—usually a choice they didn't want to make—and gets extrapolated, and interpreted, as a rule. The cliché that "You can't have both" is embedded in our culture because we're so fond of simple schemes in which the world is either black or white. Yet as F. Scott Fitzgerald wrote, "The test of a first-rate intelligence is the ability to hold two opposed ideas in the mind at the same time, and still retain the ability to function." I think the test of a first-rate life is the ability to be both creative and analytical, sexual and nurturing, to have both a great marriage and a great career, if that's what you want. To live the "opposed" halves of a dichotomy at the same time and to flourish as a whole person!

The human tendency to divide things into opposites means that false dichotomies are often subtly embedded in our thinking. They crop up not just in negative female paradigms, but in male paradigms as well. We've all heard the stories of Eve; of Delilah, who stymied Samson; of Dido, who distracted Aeneas from founding Rome; of Circe, whose sexual wiles held Ulysses captive for five years. The prevalence of stories about women distracting men from their mission, I think, gives rise to a more diluted dichotomy which is so deeply held in our culture that it's almost invisible: that balance and greatness are incompatible. Thus, those who care for others can't make money; in this fixed reality (a world without corporate coaches and motivational speakers!), teaching and achievement are incompatible. We who get "entangled" with others emotionally are not the ones who have great breakthroughs or astonishing focus or dazzling success. Caretaking, even of ourselves, becomes mutually exclusive with genius. The model becomes the person who sits at her desk twelve hours a day rather than the person who meditates for an hour during her lunch break. We think we don't have time to exercise, because we've got to get back to work, instead of thinking that the quality of work we'll do will radically shift if our bodies are cooperating with our minds.

When I got my first corporate job, I was the first woman hired at that level. I wanted a typewriter in my office—I had always done my own writing—but I was told that it wouldn't look good. People would think I was a secretary. So though I'd had one the first few weeks, I gave it up and wrote longhand from then on. I can't imagine, now, that I traded in my independence for dependence on a support staff *in order to look good.* But at the time, in the corporate world, if you took care of yourself, you were a secretary. Without realizing it, I adopted the idea that caretaking, in the form of technical support skills, was incompatible with vision and genius. I didn't even realize how thoroughly I'd bought into this dichotomy, and kept myself technically incompetent, until I started Lifedesigns, where as an entrepreneur I now wear many more hats than I used to. Although I have learned to word process badly—a triumph for me—I still haven't convinced myself that I'm capable of mastering the intricacies of e-mail!

Leslie's experience, and my own, also point to another deep-seated dichotomy about women: that "extraordinary success" and traditional female skills are mutually exclusive. How many women have taken on the idea that in order to succeed they had to suppress what was best about them? Of course, it's a recipe for defeat if, in order to be successful, you can't be like all the other people, or those other women—that is, if you have to be unlike what you are.

While I have no statistics, I have a hunch that most great inventors succeeded not because they were working to be special—which, again, is all about defining yourself in contradistinction to the rest of the world—but rather because they were indulging their own passionate curiosity, pursuing their own vision of a world that included their invention. When "different" and "special" become values in and of themselves, we begin to value separation over community. And our focus becomes distinguishing ourselves in the eyes of others—seeking their approval—rather than following the idiosyncratic road of our passion.

This is the familiar crisis of many high achievers as they come to adulthood. Ireen, for example, grew up in a little town on Long Island where hers was the only black family in her school. She was also a gifted and beautiful multilingual girl whose talent and intelligence enabled her to break a lot of rules. Ireen had to petition to graduate, even though she had a very high grade point average, because she had missed many more days of school than was allowed. What Ireen absorbed from these experiences was that a large part of her identity came from being exceptional. When she got to Barnard, the paradigm "I am exceptional," which she'd absorbed in her past, played out again. Now, though she read all the books and did the work, Ireen frequently decided that going to class was a waste of her time. She had to work very hard to remain exceptional amid all the other high school valedictorians at Barnard who went to class! "I must be special" was so embedded in Ireen's thinking that it supplanted her dream of graduating from Barnard. Ireen's biggest incompletion, right now, is that she "specialed" herself out of Barnard.

Areas where we have trouble succeeding in spite of a strong commitment can nearly always be traced back to some paradigm or belief that is interfering with our honoring our own commitments to ourselves. Even when the past has been very positive, and has served you, it can limit and debilitate the present. The goal is to get to the point of *deciding* whether or not to reaffirm that past, or to choose something different.

EXERCISE: THE RULES BEHIND YOUR NOISE
1. Go back to the page on which you wrote what might get in

the way of you fulfilling your dreams, and look over what you wrote.

2. On a new page, try and translate some of your phrases about your fears into rules you would be breaking if you declared the things you want to do. Make as many translations as you can, from general fears to specific rules about how the world is and how you're supposed to operate within it.

3. Look at the paradigms you wrote down. Do any of them imply dichotomies? For example, do you feel something is impossible because you believe that if a women does X, she can't also be a good mother? If any of your rules have dichotomies inherent in them, write them down.

An Early Decision

Our strongest paradigms, I think, are not those the culture fed us, or that our parents taught us, but the rules—the meanings—we invented for ourselves as an ordinary part of figuring out life. Every one of us has had an experience and then made it mean something. We make a decision about somebody's actions, and then, for us, it *is* that.

"So, Sara, you said you wanted this guy to call, but he hasn't. So what do you make that mean?"

"I'm not interesting enough," said Sara.

"Maybe he's busy," said Elinor.

"Or gay," said Jenny.

"Or seeing someone else," said Leslie.

"He said, on our date, that this was a bad week for him," Sara admitted.

"Ah!" said Hafeezah. "So even with that information you still managed to make it mean you weren't interesting!"

When we make meaning out of stuff that's happening now, our interpretations are a little more flexible. Sara's friend could add new information to change her opinion, or she could talk about her interpretation with someone in a way that enables her to modify what she thinks.

What's more pervasive, of course, are the decisions we made way back when. Often we made them so long ago, we've forgotten we made them.

"I'll give you an example," said Hafeezah. "When I was four and a half, I was in the room next to my mother, and I heard her say to a friend, 'I'm so relieved: she was crawling backward until she was two and a half, and she didn't talk until she was four. I was afraid she was retarded.' So I thought, 'My mother's afraid I'm retarded. That means maybe I *am* retarded.' And that lived for me my entire life—either proving I wasn't or using it as an excuse. I was accepted to Yale in the first class in which they took women, in 1969. But a big reason I didn't go was that I thought, 'What if when I get there, I find out I'm retarded, and I just can't do the work?'"

"I have a big one," said Shelly. "When I was in third grade we moved from a rural farming community in Illinois to the center of New Orleans. My teacher asked, 'Who knows what the word *hosiery* means?' And I'd seen garden hoses all over the place. So I raised my hand and told her it meant a bunch of garden hoses. And she said, 'Why do I get all the dumb ones?' And that lived for me even after I made the dean's list in college. And I dropped out. Even now, I don't speak up with an idea unless I'm sure it's right. I'm afraid of being wrong again, afraid of rejection."

"So that's living for you all the time," said Hafeezah.

Shelly nodded.

"So, what is some of the more personal noise we have about why we can't do or have what we want?" asks Hafeezah.

"I also grew up in the South," said Josie. "One time we were in a department store. This was when they had separate colored and white water fountains. I didn't want to use the dirty water fountain, so I used the white one. When I got home my mother said, 'You don't do that! Always watch what you say around white men!' And I'm in meetings, and they're saying, 'Josie, say something, you know what he's saying is wrong!' I always check myself."

"In the eighth grade I was put in the cloakroom closet almost every day because I talked too much," said Jenny. "The men in my law school class said things like, 'You women are so bright, you should make fantastic legal secretaries.' And then, when I was named the chief managing director of my former investment firm, a guy said, 'I'd rather work for a black than for a woman.' And I thought, so where does that leave me? So all these developed my motto, which is, 'If it's a Mack truck, bring it on.'"

Jenny's motto, by the way, is an excellent example of a decision that helped her survive as a brilliant woman in a biased world, yet at the same time it is limiting to her present to have to stand in front of Mack trucks all the time!

"So what are some of the things you think might get in the way of living your dreams?" asked Hafeezah.

"I think my physical goal makes me shallow, that it's trivial, that people will make fun of it, that being fit and liking my body will make me seem greedy, as if I want too much. I have intellect, so I should be satisfied with that. I'm afraid to even say I want it, because if it doesn't happen, I'll be so exposed that I'll be too vulnerable," said Jenny.

"I'm afraid of the loneliness that might come from painting all the time," said Page.

"I don't have the energy," said Mary Scott.

"Me either," said Lynda. "I'm burned out."

"I'm too ambivalent," said Julie. "I have too much anxiety around making decisions."

"What if I have too much passion," said Jenny, "and I burn up like a star?"

"You have to start small," said Josie.

"I'm afraid of running out of money and becoming a bag lady," said Elinor. "And just, like, hyperpragmatism in general."

"That's a big one," added Lauren.

"I'm afraid of criticism," said Alane.

"If you do something different people will laugh you down," said Shelly.

"When you come from a family that keeps you in, you fear being disliked because you're doing something well—like, fear of others' envy and jealousy."

"Afraid of not being able to fulfill my family responsibilities," said Page.

"Fear of disappointing yourself, or letting yourself down," said Leslie. "What if you don't succeed at what you try?"

"I'm afraid my family's business would collapse," said Amy Jo.

"Waiting for permission," said Sara.

"I'm not analytical," said Zully. "And what if I don't invest my money well?"

"I have no credentials," said Lynda.

Say, for example, that you've written down: "I don't deserve it." This could be the tip of several different icebergs. It may be that you're believing that "You only deserve success if you slave away at it unhappily." Or you may feel, "I must be the most expert person in my field in order to deserve success, and not feel like a fraud." Or, the rule may be: "I must ensure everyone else's success before my own, to avoid envy and jealousy."

"I guess my shyness and passivity translates into, 'I must not stand out,'" said Shelly.

"'My family will sabotage me,'" said Amy Jo, "is really . . . I have to take care of everyone in my family, by not threatening them by becoming more successful."

"I guess mine is that if I don't slave twenty-four hours a day I'll end up like my parents," said Elinor. "That you must slave and work in order to have money."

"Making art is selfish," said Page. "I must serve others first."

"You can't change the world," said Julie.

"I must sacrifice to be a good person," said Lynda.

"I must not pursue a man," said Sara. "Because he might go out with me even though he's not interested. So I must always be passive to avoid being hurt later."

TRACING YOUR RULES TO AN EARLY DECISION

1. On a new sheet in your notebook, write *An Early Decision* at the top of the page.
2. Look back at the rules you've written down. Do any of

them correspond to an early decision you made based on something you saw or heard?

3. Write down the rule; then, underneath it, the story of how you came to the decision you did. Often women find, when they do this exercise, that whole sets of rules have been generated out of a single episode.

4. Rewrite a simplified list of rules so that it speaks to you in its clearest form.

5. For the next few days, keep this list of rules in a place where you can see it. Notice how it feels to be surrounded by rules and to have those rules outside yourself. Check in periodically. These rules are your handbook for the old you, so check them continually—especially if you find yourself upset, frustrated, or boxed in—and ask yourself if you're unconsciously obeying your handbook.

Some women decide that, for a while, the way they'll make decisions is to use their rules as the deciding factor. When in doubt, they do the opposite!

Fundamental Paradigms and the Anchors That Hold Them in Place

Notice, with all these paradigms, that it's not necessarily the paradigm itself that is the problem, but that we believe it can only be one way. Essentially, all these paradigms get held in place by the five fundamental filters to listening and thinking. Underneath the instinct to pick and choose in advance who we'll confide our dreams in, is the fundamental human habit to *judge and assess* every situation in advance. When we keep quiet about our accomplishments, out of fear of seeming to lack humility, it's springing out of the model that encourages us to *avoid risk*. Dichotomies remain anchored in our culture because the underlying assumption is that *reality is fixed:* "Women in the past were forced to choose between expressive sexuality and sanctified motherhood" becomes "Women will always have to choose, and it'll never be different."

When we assume that someone will find us unattractive because we're too large or too small, we're usually *taking personally* a cultural paradigm from out there, beaming it down to our own mind and interpreting it as an original thought. Whenever we assert the paradigm "The management will never allow you to job-share," the premise underneath is the assumption of *already knowing* how it is and how it is going to be.

These five anchors keep us glued to our past, and our parents' pasts, to the inherited "wisdom" we've learned throughout life. The culture spews so many paradigms at us that, in some ways, it doesn't matter which ones we've absorbed. No specific paradigm is as limiting as what I like to call THE paradigm inherent in these five filters, which is that reality consists only of what we've already seen, where we've already been, and what's already been proven. THE paradigm is not about the content of our thinking, which is that mothers must do X and not Y. It is the underlying structure that obliterates other possibilities.

When we are trapped within THE paradigm, because there's very little personal volition here, we start to think there's only one right answer. Many women spend their lives being wretched because they're trying to get it right, to get it perfect, to get their clothes and their homes and their behavior "right." The assumption behind this paradigm is that there's one right answer—and an ultimate authority who knows it. Many women's lives have been spent waiting for someone to come in and pronounce us right, and good, and perfect! For years I drove myself, and everyone in my family, nuts before my mother came to visit. I would be angry and snapping—and people would be snapping back—as I tried to get everything perfect so that she could come in and pronounce it perfect. She never did—not because she did or didn't think that, but because she didn't know she was supposed to!

After I realized that my mother was not the authority who would confer goodness upon me, I made up a lot of other people who were. Once, at a party at our house, my daughter heard a decorator say that while I'd done a great job decorating on my own, it was "a bit cluttered." My daughter recounted the comment, mimicking exactly the woman's clipped British accent. *"A bit cluttahed,"* Abigail repeated over and over. So, while each of my two million candles, pillows, and baskets is beloved, these three words shook me so much that by noon the next day, I had scourged the house of at least half my stuff! I was only lucky, that time, that Abigail, my own "earth mother," made me put them all back before I'd hurled them into the attic.

It's a story I laugh at now, but it's one I think a lot of women have their own version of. We spend half our lives being wretched, because we locate the authority to define what's good, attractive, or perfect outside of ourselves. We're waiting for that authority; in fact we *want* someone to come along and tell us we got it right. We're allowed to write a novel only if somebody outside tells us we're talented and declares what we have to say interesting. We decorate and redecorate incessantly, in pursuit of some elusive definition of perfection. We keep our living rooms so spotless that nobody can relax, so that when "company" or our mothers drop in, they'll exclaim how perfect it is. (Or we apologize to the people who come over that our house is a mess, asking *them* to reassure *us* that our house is okay as is!) Our relationships with men become fraught with anxiety because we hand over to them the power to pronounce our bodies or our faces attractive—not just attractive to them, but according to some larger, absolute, fascistically uniform notion of what "attractive" is.

The reason we resist locating the ultimate authority in ourselves, I think, is that we fear getting it wrong. There is no ultimate authority, but what if one suddenly appears and tells us we got it wrong? This is how we approach "rightness" and "authority"; though intuitively we know that the "right" answers live only in us, and we've had them all along, we go along with the seemingly authoritative paradigms and adopt somebody else's version of right and wrong, because that way we know that at least one other person thinks we're "not wrong." Locating the authority outside ourselves, then, is a form of hedging our bets: it's insurance against doing the wrong thing.

Longing for meaning and searching for answers is what defines us, spiritually, as humans. But choosing to believe in only one interpretation, in one fixed reality, in THE paradigm, is a bit like translating an infinite God into an icon of a goat. A fixed reality is safe because it's known and it's limited; at the same time, though, in a fixed reality, nobody ever flies an airplane, or runs a four-minute mile, or discovers radioactivity. Marie Curie, in this reality, sticks to what she can see. If we're listening in the world for the answer, and we buy into old paradigms, we're operating on autopilot.

Autopilot is the navigational system that came with your box. It's dead-on accurate for getting to safe, old destinations with the least possible uncertainty. On autopilot, in other words, you can't make a wrong turn.

The next chapter explores a different navigation, one based on steering toward the future—a future you get to define and make up. It's a method in which you get to choose, in every moment, a set of beliefs that, instead of limiting you, will open the unlimited in the everyday.

Chapter Five

Fact vs.
Interpretation

Ultimately, there are no facts.

—ALBERT EINSTEIN

So if you're swimming in the ocean of culture, and the undertow of paradigms is more powerful than you, how do you ever escape getting sucked into the past? And how do you avoid getting sucked in when you want to make a breakthrough?

As an indirect response to these questions, I'd like to propose two basic categories of things we experience.

The first is facts. The book you're holding in your hands is a fact. The food you ate yesterday is a fact. A thing is a fact, and an event is a fact. What someone said—if we could record it with a video camera—would be a fact. The decibel level of the volume of their speech is a fact. Facts have dimensions in time and space. They're physical, measurable, demonstrable. The test for a fact is that it can be demonstrated to be true. So, "The Mona Lisa is hanging in the Louvre" is a fact. It's true. "The Mona Lisa is a sculpture" is false.

What you feel about those facts, on the other hand, is a matter of interpretation.

While facts live in space and time, interpretations live in language. Beauty, for example, is an interpretation, because it exists in language. "The Mona Lisa is a famous painting" could be a fact, if we agreed what famous was. But "The Mona Lisa is a beautiful painting" is a subjective interpretation, because "beauty" sits in the realm of language, not fact.

The words someone uses, and the decibel level of how loudly they're speaking, are facts. Whether the person meant to be complimentary or insulting, and whether they were shouting or simply exuberant, are interpretations.

"So here's what happens," said Hafeezah. "Remember when Elinor passed you in the hall and she grumbled. Now what was it you decided about Elinor?"

"She just got some bad news about somebody's health," said Helene.

"Okay," said Hafeezah. "Valid interpretation. So the next day she does it again. And then the next day, you pass Elinor in the hall and the same thing happens. Now, you know she's just had oral surgery, but her chipmunk face is gone. Of course, today, even though she's recovered from her oral surgery, it so happens that because she was in so much pain yesterday, she forgot her appointment to get her car inspected, and she got a ticket on her way to work. Anyway, so even though you think she's totally over her surgery, she walks by you and she's gruff again, with her head down. What does it mean?"

"It means she's a self-absorbed grump who doesn't support or mentor others," Mary Scott said.

"Exactly," said Hafeezah. "Notice, now we're drawing conclusions about 'the way Elinor is.' We've started to interact with what happens based on the filter of what we experienced."

On a regular basis, we experience facts and then we interpret them, and then we collapse the fact and our interpretation into something called truth. The fact that Elinor grumbled gets collapsed with the interpretation that she's a self-absorbed grump to form a "reality," or "truth," in which Elinor just *is* a grump.

The fact/interpretation cocktail can have quite a potent influence over us, in the sense that our "reality" inevitably starts to predict something. You start treating Elinor like she's going to snap, interacting with her today through the filter of what you experienced yesterday. Because in your mind she's a grump.

The collapse of fact and interpretation is as human as making the interpretation in the first place! The problem, however is that how you have power with facts is vastly different from how you have power with interpretations. If you want to get to the door, for example, and a chair is in your way, you don't cause change by thinking about the chair differently. You either move it or you walk around it. Or you dismantle it. Or if you want to be dramatic, you set the chair on fire. The way you deal with things that are factual, in other words, is to use force.

As any of us who have tried to "force" our interpretations on others know—as men who have fought wars over interpretations know— changing an interpretation requires a slightly different approach.

"So what are some incontrovertible facts?" asked Hafeezah.

"Sun comes up every morning," said Alane.

"Okay," said Hafeezah.

"You're a woman, you have two children, you have to pay rent," said Leslie.

"Does everybody in the world always have to pay rent?" asked Hafeezah.

"I guess not," said Leslie.

"And is it a fact that you've always paid rent every single month, your whole life?"

"No," said Leslie.

"Other facts?" asked Hafeezah.

For a moment, it seemed, Hafeezah had stumped her workshop.

"I grew up in an Ecuadorian orphanage, and I have a disability," said Zully.

"The first one, okay," said Hafeezah. "The second one is an interpretation. It's a very valid one. But calling it a disability defines the playing field as physical movement alone, and not, for example, as an inspiration for creative production. This might be stretching it, but theoretically you could also define your weak leg as the innate physical gift that allowed you to see a previously nonexistent market for custom shoes, in Chicago. Let's look up on the flip charts," said Hafeezah, "at all your noise about what could get in your way. Any facts there?"

"Not really," said Shelly.

"And what about the paradigms about women? Women should be pleasing, women are nurturing. How many of these are facts?"

"Not many," said Sara.

"None of them, really," said Josie after a moment.

"What about your personal noise about what would get in your way. What were some of the things you wrote down again?"

"My husband isn't supportive," said Debra.

"Is that a fact?" asked Hafeezah.

Debra shook her head.

"But there are some facts," said Jenny. "That women don't get promoted in my bank is a fact. It's not an interpretation that there are only three women out of a hundred in senior management. And it's not an interpretation that though most of the women in middle management have been there ten years, they haven't been promoted, while ten men who've been there less than five have. It's not an interpretation to say the women's average salary is less than the men's, for the same job. And that I who have an Ivy League law degree get paid the same as men who don't have a law degree at all."

"I'm with you," said Hafeezah. "I can validate those as facts. Except for the statement that women don't get promoted."

"But that's what those facts are saying!" cried Jenny. "Or at least that women have to work enormously harder to get promoted."

"Women don't get promoted describes the future," said Hafeezah. "Given the past you described, it's certainly a valid interpretation. But it's not a fact. You could interpret the situation as being ripe for someone as qualified as you to come in and exonerate the guilty feelings of all those guys who aren't promoting women. You could interpret the situation as meaning that you need to redefine your job as setting up awareness workshops within your company."

"You could interpret it as meaning that you ought to sue," joked Helene.

"Or, instead of interpreting that women have to work harder, you could interpret that your company is a place you need to leave," Hafeezah said.

"I guess I could even interpret it as meaning I'm in the wrong field!" said Jenny, rolling her eyes at how her solid ground was shifting beneath her feet.

Distinguishing facts from interpretations can generate a profound re-thinking about what the possibilities are.

"But how do you know the difference?" asked Jenny. "The examples you gave are clear. But last night I was talking to my husband, who said he thought the world was turning into a matriarchy. And I nearly hit the roof! I practically screamed at him for forty-five minutes, because that's his white male frightened overreaction to tiny minuscule gains in female power. He said women have all the power in his life. But that's his life! My facts are that our Senate is 97 percent men, our Congress is 96 percent men, and fewer than 1 percent of CEOs are women. By every objective measure of power and money, women are still very disenfranchised."

"Okay," said Hafeezah. "I'll accept your facts as facts. And, of course, your interpretation as valid! But what I'm curious about is: Can I go in there?" Jenny nods, knowing that she's about to get zinged. "Okay. So your husband says that women are already powerful, and you bark. This is because . . . you hate female power? So you have to scream that women aren't empowered? 'Cause it's an awful thing to have a matriarchy?"

Jenny rolled her eyes at Hafeezah, for sliding her interpretations under the microscope. "Of course not! But when he says we're already there, it means no work needs to be done. It's complacent. We're fine just the way we are."

"And that would mean . . ." Hafeezah asked, continuing to dig to the core.

"He wants to keep women down," said Jenny. "Like every other man in the world, he finds a way to take himself off the hook."

"So what triggered you to scream wasn't what your husband said, but what you thought it implied? You know what we call that at Lifedesigns?"

"An interpretation," Jenny said sheepishly.

"Wow! What an interpretation!" erupted Alane. "Here I was thinking this guy was so enlightened because he measures power in his own life not like the men do—by money and the Senate and the corporation—but in a spiritual and emotional way."

"Also a valid interpretation," said Hafeezah.

"I'm sorry he's not single," asked Sara, as the group roared.

Based on Jenny's experience with men in her life, her interpretation was perfectly valid. The conviction that her husband wanted to keep women down was real for her. This is because our experience of any event consists of both facts and interpretations. What we know as "reality" is something that sits on both sides of the fact/interpretation line. What we tend to do, what Jenny did here, is collapse "fact and interpretation" into "fact." As a result, Jenny couldn't see that her reaction contained interpretations and not just facts. Jenny got stuck, as many of us often do, because she was dealing with her interpretation as if it were a fact—trying to use the force of her tirade to get her friend to accept it.

Now, this is not to say that you shouldn't affirm and validate your interpretation. But when dealing with people who have a different interpretation, if you can simply recognize that much of what *you're* affirming is probably interpretation rather than fact, it's a huge start toward being able to recognize, and deal with, *someone else's* interpretation. To put this another way: When someone holds an interpretation you don't agree with, the first step is simply to acknowledge that given the facts each of you has, both interpretations are valid.

Jane told a story about getting another job offer. The mode in which Jane subsequently negotiated a month off, and a raise, was reasonable and polite *in Jane's reality*. In her boss's reality, she was belligerent.

What's real in Sara's world is that no matter how many positive interpretations we may place on her life, she is sad about being single.

> "But what do you do with interpretations that really aren't
> valid?" Jenny asked. "What do you do when other people col-
> lapse fact and interpretation, and then try to pawn it off as fact?
> I mean, I see that I got upset because I put an interpretation
> on what he was saying. At the same time, there are outside
> facts in the world. And given those facts, I can't validate his in-
> terpretation no matter how hard I try. It's just inaccurate."

Often, what triggers our need to be right in a conversation is the belief that we all share the same facts. If this is true, it terrifies and angers
us that others seem to be willfully disregarding those facts.

Jenny's husband's interpretation is that the world is approaching a
matriarchy. Given his reality, which is that women hold most of the
power in his life, he would probably affirm this interpretation even if
Jenny locked him in a room and read Susan Faludi's *Backlash* to him,
word for word. *From where he stood,* given the facts *he* was seeing, his
interpretation was valid. Her husband hadn't majored in Women's
Studies; his government wasn't American. He'd grown up in a Cana-
dian town with a woman mayor; his boss, and his current mentor, and
the head of the dance company he danced with were women. Jenny's
opinion, in fact, was the most important in his life. Her husband's definition of power was not out in the structures of the world, it was within
him. It was spiritual power. Because Jenny was operating from within a
different set of facts and assumptions—including the assumptions embedded in the very definitions of each word in the sentence—she felt
he had a profound disregard for the facts, that he was confusing his
feeling of powerlessness with the "fact" of a society dominated or controlled by women. But these were her facts, not his! The problem Jenny
was having with her husband was that she assumed that they were interpreting the same facts, when they were really taking two different
sets of measurements. Jenny lives in a society controlled by men; her
husband lives in a society controlled by women. We know so little about
one another's occurring reality that maybe we need to ask the question
my husband sometimes asks when I'm acting odd: "What color is *your*
sky today?"

"So were you successful in getting him to adopt your point of view?" asked Hafeezah.

"He says he won't talk to me any more about gender," admitted Jenny. "What do you do in a situation like that?"

Hafeezah held up her palm like a traffic cop. "Another choice is to hold up your hand and say, 'That's YOUR interpretation.'"

James Carse talks about this gap of perception in his book *The Silence of God.* Carse suggests something quite radical about communication, which is that our listening is so filtered that often it's not even as if there is "an" event with two interpretations. That is to say, the fact of a conversation occurs when two people say certain words. But since most of us don't record every moment of our lives on videotape we can play back, all we have to go on are the self-selected set of notes our filters pick up. Because each of us is human, and therefore limited, we miss things! Thus, in a conversation, our two filters let in two entirely different sets of facts—creating the experience of *two entirely different events.* And even if we had a video camera and could agree on what had been said, we'd define them totally differently. So what we have is your interpretation of what you said and your listener's interpretation of what he heard. Because fact and interpretation are so easily collapsed into fact, these two realities are often seen as two different versions of "the facts." According to Carse, you don't even have to know what you said until the other person says what he heard. In effect, "the fact" of the conversation ceases to exist.

What Carse seems to be saying is that on a fundamental level, our experience mirrors the laws of quantum mechanics, which state that perception (or the act of measuring) so alters an event that the measurement influences what the event is. In plainer words, none of us is experiencing the same facts.

"Say we hang an apple on that fire alarm sprinkler up there," says Hafeezah, to illustrate this point. "Now, Elinor, who as we know has been having trouble with her contact lenses, looks up and sees something red oozing out of the ceiling. She thinks someone's been shot on the floor above. Lynda, who's been at home eighteen years without apples, is seeing a piece of fruit she wants to bite into. But Alane happens to have another view, she's able to see a worm that nobody else sees. And she's not going to bite into that apple no matter how delicious I say it is."

To adopt what Einstein stated as part of his theory of relativity—that "ultimately, there are no facts"—is terrifically scary and unsettling.

On the other hand, accepting the ultimate relativity of perception—realizing how quickly our hard ground of "fact" shifts into a quicksand of interpretation—gives you an enormous amount of freedom both in how you deal with others and, more important, how you deal with your life.

···

EXERCISE: FACT VS. INTERPRETATION

Part I

1. On a fresh page in your notebook, write down the basic outline of an episode with another person that you've been finding difficult or unresolvable.

2. Look at the language you used to describe it. Are the sentences you wrote facts? Do they have dimensions or weight? Are there any interpretations embedded in the way you described the other person's actions or intentions?

3. In two separate paragraphs labeled *Fact* and *Interpretations,* separate the various components of what you wrote into these two categories.

Part II

In the next few days, write down a story or episode that somebody else tells you, and repeat the exercise. Notice how much of what we all experience as fact, is "in fact" interpretation!

···

Recognizing the profoundly relative nature of facts—both yours and others'—grants you the freedom to truly and completely let others have their point of view. Because whether or not we give them permission to, others will have a different interpretation of the same set of facts—they've got a *different set of facts!* When we offer someone our luscious apple, and they respond by saying, "What? I don't want to eat that!," our acceptance of this relativity frees the same heap of emotional energy that Jenny spent yelling at her husband. Instead of launching into "You shouldn't feel that way" or "You got the wrong impression," we can simply say "I wonder what sets of facts you've been developing, that led you to that interpretation." To Deborah Tannen's now-famous phrase "You just don't understand," we can add the coda *but neither do I.*" Instead of feeling that we must bludgeon the other person's opinion to conform with "the facts," we get the emotional power to calmly reply: "Your interpretation of this beautiful red apple is that it has a worm. Hmm. You also have a point of view I've never seen before. I can't even imagine how you see that. Then again, I don't have all your facts."

"When I got promoted at the bank to a job that involved managing people," said Jenny, "my boss sent me to a people management workshop. In the workshop you had to rate yourself on how you relate to people. I thought, I'm warm, I'm friendly yet unintrusive. I gave myself a 9. But then they showed me the results of the questionnaire of my people. They gave me a 1.5. She doesn't know what's going on in our lives, the responses said. She doesn't know the names of our husbands or wives! I went to my boss and tried to dismiss it. I was like, 'That's not a worm, that's supposed to be there, and worms are good, and it's a design element!' You know? I said, 'I don't need to know their wives' names! Just because a few people complain . . . ' But my boss said, 'Jenny, the average is 1.5.' And I had to see that my interpretation did not relate to the facts in any way."

"But my question is," Lauren asked, "wouldn't it be great if in our lives we could have some management consultant come in and hand out a questionnaire that measures the difference between what we think and what's out there? I mean, what if it's not exactly a relationship thing you're struggling with? If you don't have another person to give you feedback, then how do you know what your interpretations are? I've been with a career counselor for a year, but I still don't know what I want to do. I mean, I should know by now. But I have no idea whether some interpretation I'm putting on is getting in the way of my knowing."

"Is it a fact or an interpretation that you should know?"

"I'm running out of money," said Lauren.

"Well," said Hafeezah, "your economics dictate that you make some money. Is that the same as 'You should know what to do'? What are the assumptions behind that interpretation?" Hafeezah asked the group.

"You should know by now," said Lauren.

"You should be working all the time, according to the Puritan work ethic," said Alane.

"You're doing something wrong in your job search, or being self-indulgent."

"But what if Lauren authentically believes that?"

"Yes, she may authentically believe that," said Hafeezah. "But sometimes if these are inherited thoughts—like getting a job should only take a certain amount of time—then even if we authentically believe it, it may not work for us."

"Then I would have to question every one of my values," observed Lauren. "How do you know if they're your values or somebody else's values?"

Authenticity vs. Authorship

The question of how to know what interpretation you believe can be answered in a way that contains one of the most freeing ideas I've ever encountered.

Focusing on *what we authentically believe* can be enormously helpful. The last chapter was dedicated to helping you discover beliefs you have but may not quite have realized you were authoring. At the same time, this search can create a paradigm in which there is one "true" interpretation and a bunch of false ones. Yet if all interpretations are made up by you or by other people, and if many of our "facts," upon close scrutiny, also reveal themselves to be interpretations, it means *your current interpretation is just one of many.* When you absorb that most everything everybody thinks was *made up by somebody,* it sets aside the question of which is the "right" interpretation. In this context, you're free to evaluate and choose an interpretation based on whether it empowers you. If somebody's going to make it up, in other words, it might as well be you.

"The thing is," said Page, in response to Lauren's job search, "it takes a long time to change jobs. It's a myth that it can happen overnight. I quit as president of the foundation I ran, and it took me twenty-two months to get a job in the corporate culture. By the time I got it, I was $10,000 in debt. I later became the top salesperson in the country, so the rewards were great because the risk is great, but it took time."

"Even the idea that it takes a long time," Hafeezah said, smiling slyly, "is an assumption. But for you, Page, it was an interpretation that empowered you to stick in there. For Lauren it might be one that makes her think she's got to chase down every possible option and find the perfect one before taking a risk and trying something out."

"I guess my question," said Elinor, "is that I can sort of see how, with one person, you're on equal footing, and you can say I have my interpretation and you have yours. But what do you do when you go up against a whole culture's interpretation? Like the corporate culture that makes you work all the time and yet says you're not producing? I guess I feel like, in that context, balance and greatness are incompatible."

"And that would be a . . ." Hafeezah trailed off.

"Paradigm," yelled the group.

"You have to bring that feminist consciousness inside the workplace," said Page. "Our generation made the room, in the sixties and seventies. Now you've got to carry that idea in, to articulate these concerns and change the culture. Band together and unite on these ideas!"

"I think it's a matter of taking responsibility for your own priorities," said Julie. "When I was pregnant with my son, I had a nurse teaching me nutrition and breathing. And I kept missing appointments. Finally, she said, 'You need to shift your priorities.'"

"I'm getting that I've got a responsibility to others," said Elinor. "And I make that time for my kids. But I feel like all of you are saying it's my fault. And it's not my fault that the culture creates stress! It's like you're saying there's always more I can do, but I want to do less!"

"Perhaps the first thing," said Hafeezah, "is to stand for what you're thinking. State, and keep stating, what your experience is. Who else has some ideas of what Elinor could do?"

"Well, collectively, you know," said Helene, "women are leaving corporate America in droves, because they don't find the structure supports them. You could gather some evidence, stats, and such. And you can enroll others who think the same way. Even those men who have daughters, who will have to neglect their grandchildren if they can't find balance. Enroll them any way you can. Even the boss who has no children and stays until one in the morning, and who has no life, and is working to avoid that, can be enrolled in the powerful idea that the people who do a great job are the ones who maintain their personal development."

"You know, at the first or second job of your career," said Leslie, "you do work hard. Then you need to say, where am I going to get new ideas? How am I going to come back refreshed? So take a stand."

"My boss does great and doesn't answer beeps and leaves it behind," said Mary Scott. "She's earned that."

"When you said your boss earned it," Jane said, "it may be that it's not that she got to a level where it was permitted as much as that she let people know what her boundaries are. No one treads past where you stand. My boss left a horrible message—abusive—because I'd made a mistake. I went in on Monday and said, 'I made a mistake, and I'm horrified, and I'll do whatever I need to do to rectify it. But that way of speaking doesn't work for me.' Now, my boss is still rude to everybody else, but not to me."

"You need to speak about a performance-based culture rather than a time-based culture. Write that language into your contract," said Leslie.

"What about asking human resources to set up a series of stress management workshops over the lunch hour?" said Mary Scott. "You know, little forty-five-minute presentations? What about getting your bosses to talk about the stress they feel?"

"What I find interesting," Hafeezah said, "is that you took what Page said not as 'I'm right and I'm going to celebrate that balance and enroll others in that balance,' but rather as 'I have a responsibility and I also need to manage the stress.' You took it as 'I'm still deficient and incomplete, and I need to change myself more.'"

"The fact is, the job is too big for one person," said Elinor, the relief visible on her face.

"How about redefining the job?" asked Hafeezah.

There are several things to notice about this conversation. The first is that Elinor realized her "reality" included an interpretation, which was that she was always deficient in some way. Thus she was holding on to the idea that there was only one way to respond to the situation, because she thought that allowing for the possibility of responding differently might mean accepting blame. Like "commitment," the word *responsibility* has a lot of baggage attached to it! So if "greater responsibility" makes you queasy because it lands on you as if you caused the situation you don't like, I'd invite you to allow yourself more "respond-ability." That is, simply consider that there may be a wider variety of possible responses than those you're currently considering. Saying that your current way of responding may not be the only way does not make the way you're currently responding "wrong." And it doesn't make you wrong, and them right, about what the problem is! It simply means that there may be another layer of resignation you can peel off about your situation to create a response for yourself that is more empowering to you.

Once Elinor accepted that the possibility of responding differently didn't make her "wrong," she noticed that five different people had offered five valid interpretations that she was authentically able to believe. There are as many interpretations out there as there are people to make them up. So though you can't authenticate all of them, there is usually some leeway to believe something different.

So, some questions to ask, when you're down, are: What interpretation have I put on myself that's getting me down? What interpretation can I invent that's genuine, and real, and authentic—and also empowering?

Creating — and Believing — Empowering Interpretations

I want to reiterate that if you're going to make up or create and speak a new interpretation, it has to be something you can stand in. A whimsical, superficial, or inauthentic version of the truth won't work very long. This is not about positive thinking. Positive thinking is sort of like pouring hot fudge sauce on cat food: You can speak all the affirmations you want, and say anything you want about the reality, but eventually you're going to taste the truth. It's one thing to say "I'm thin, I'm thin" when you're not, it's another to realize that "attractive" is an interpretation that for some people means thin and for other people means luscious and curvy. The choice then, becomes whose interpretation are you going to live in? Yours or your past's? In every moment, really, you want to ask yourself, "What do I want to author now? Can I invent an interpretation that's authentic to me, that is empowering, that I can actually live in?"

> "It's interesting," said Alane. "I never gave myself permission to have a positive interpretation. My mother wakes up every day with a smile on her face and is too cheery, and I've always wanted to approach it from wanting to understand the facts from all sides. It's actually empowering to think about which interpretations I might have are empowering. I've always thought people dupe themselves, people who didn't see the worm in the apple. But I think I didn't see the good side of the apple. Being willing to see how others see it might also give me some room to choose something authentic, that's also good."

Alane gets the record for inventing a new interpretation that was empowering: Before the end of the conversation, she had decided that it was okay to believe in an empowering interpretation!

There are many other ways to undo a disempowering interpretation. When you're operating under a paradigm like "Balance and greatness are incompatible," you may simply want to affirm another reality in which it's possible for these two elements to actually coexist. You may be able, after reading this book, to gain new tactics and pathways that will enable you to authentically believe that it really is possible for you to increase your earnings, have a great job, and spend more time with your family. Or you may want to dig up into the interpretations inherent in how you define notions of "greatness" and "balance." You may revise, for example, the idea that you need to be "balanced" in every moment. While nature contains outrageous floods, earthquakes, tornadoes, and avalanches, there's still a balance to the whole. So you may want to think about balance over the course of your life, not in the course of one day.

I call this "relanguaging." It's one of the best ways to invent a more empowering interpretation.

Relanguaging a job can mean something as simple as defining it in terms of specific performance goals, which then give you the freedom of how, and what time, to execute those goals. Say you have a situation in which, no matter how hard you work, your boss doesn't seem to be satisfied. Relanguaging could mean that you ask your boss to sit down and agree on a set of tasks that constitute the word *job* for you. In a broader sense, you could help your company define its "culture" differently by asking the powers that be to define, perhaps for the first time, what management thinks the corporate culture ought to be. You may need to interrupt the assumption that "productivity" is contingent on long hours, to state and restate that creative human beings are cyclical, that the nineteenth-century model of a machine who sits at her desk twelve hours a day creates drones, not inventors. The upshot here is that relanguaging a situation can be as simple as becoming aware, and making others aware, of the paradigms that operate beneath the words.

Controverting the paradigms inherent in others' speech, by the way, need not be done in direct confrontation. If your boss has a fixed reality in which no company ever pays for or sponsors day care, or assistance for women with children, you can do something as simple as speaking about an article you read about how, at the UNICEF headquarters, there's something called a Menstrual Room (as is the tradition, by the way, all over China), where there's a breast pump and a cot for women at work who want to attend to their physical needs. Or you can find a human resource person who has instituted a day care program and get her to give a presentation in your company.

Relanguaging internally gives us an enormous amount of freedom. Say your description of the problem is "My job leaves me feeling unappreciated." Sometimes a resolution can be as simple as changing your definition of "job" to include not just accomplishing tasks but also helping your boss reach completion on what's been accomplished. In this scenario, you would spend more time talking about your accomplishments, stating and restating—even boasting about—your, and your team's, performance. Or if, for example, you want to interview for a new job but can't deal with the fear. You might consider that the physical feeling you labeled "fear" is often the same sensation you've felt on a roller coaster when you were creeping up that huge hill, about to fly down the other side. Now, you paid for that feeling—even stood in line to get it! So what you're calling fear—especially the fear we feel when we're up to something really big—can often as easily be called exhilaration or anticipation.

Another option, in this case, would be to dig under the paradigm "Fear is bad." You may simply want to remember Eleanor Roosevelt's advice, "Always do what you fear most." Or you may want to decide, as a friend of mine did, that "fear" is an acronym for Face Everything And Recover. In any case, the next time you're feeling fear, you may want to language it differently, to try on a new and more empowering interpretation of your physical response.

> "I want to move," said Shelly. "But I know myself well enough to know I'm not so independent at going to a new place."
>
> "So here," said Hafeezah, "we want to ask ourselves: 'What are the things I say about myself that don't give me a whole lot of freedom?' What do you want to author and affirm? Your commitment to moving? Or your commitment to already knowing who, and how, you are?"
>
> "Given that plain a choice,why would I ever have to choose an interpretation that's not empowering?" asked Lauren.
>
> "My therapist was saying that people have a tendency to see negative patterns," said Sara, "and not positive ones. She told me about this couple she's working with who finally had this great sexual experience on vacation. But when they came back, she asked, 'How's the sex?' and they said, 'Terrible.' She said, 'But what about this great experience you had?' They said, 'But that was on vacation.'"

Sara's therapist was pointing out a basic human tendency. It's probably a survival skill we developed somewhere along the line to keep us from missing a potential threat. Even when we know that there are other interpretations, we often choose to hold on to, and indeed doggedly defend, interpretations that aren't empowering. Why?

The Benefits of the Box

Well, the benefits associated with remaining in the box that is your safety zone are not small.

One obvious benefit is that the rules are protective.

Nearly all the unexamined rules are lessons somebody else has learned—an attempt to protect us from a trauma that somebody else experienced. They are designed to serve as a sort of protective architecture against the dangers, threats, and disappointments somebody else experienced. You mother says, "Don't lose your reputation" to protect you from consequences she or one of her friends experienced after staying out all night. You say to your child, "Don't walk on the wall because you'll break your leg" in order to protect her. Who knew you'd be creating a box in which she doesn't have the balance to walk on a wall, or fulfill her dream of becoming a dancer?

So in this fixed reality, the box we take on protects us from known dangers.

It also protects us from the unknown—that is, from our fear of the end of the known. Another way of saying this is that the box is comfortable.

In the final months of the twenty-seven years he spent imprisoned for subversion, Nelson Mandela resided in a warden's bungalow at Victor Verster Prison outside Cape Town, recuperating from tuberculosis and meeting secretly with state visitors. After his release, he built, across the road from his ancestral village, a vacation home that was an exact brick replica of the warden's house. An interviewer asked him whether he'd done it out of nostalgia for the fraternity of the prison experience or as an exercise in humility. Mandela replied that the choice was pure pragmatism: He had grown accustomed to the floor plan and wanted a place where he could find the bathroom at night without stumbling in the dark.

Most of us hold on to our box because it's a place where we don't have to stumble in the dark. No matter how unsuited we are to our quarters, no matter how uncomfortable they are, they're familiar. Even if there are things we don't like about our house—its leaky faucet annoys us, the basement is being eaten by the termites that are our incompletions and forgotten dreams—the bad things we experience within our box are familiar. We know we can survive them. We don't know whether we can survive what might happen out in the world, because it's unknown.

Along with this safety, we also get to preserve our identity, which in some ways can be defined as what's fixed in us. And the older we get, the more fixed our reality tends to be. Staying in the box means staying connected. We may not want to succeed because we fear our siblings will feel threatened, and then they'll be distant. Or we may fear they'll attack us out of jealousy. In this case, continuing to "buy in" is a way of anticipating, and avoiding, the conflict that can occur when we challenge the status quo. Often, for women, the status quo is that we get to be the victim who takes the moral high ground. The world becomes shakier when there's no one outside ourselves to blame!

Or it may be as simple as that we don't want to leave our loved ones behind. We see them as static and unenrollable. Because we don't know what a new future might be, it can seem as if it's a choice between retaining connections to others or losing them, rather than a choice between connecting to our past and connecting to whom we want to be.

There are significant benefits, then, to staying in the box.

> "But I feel that, if I let go, there aren't any facts to how I've been living—so what do I base my life on?" asked Alane.

This question, I think, points to the very center of why we buy in to disempowering interpretations. The possibility of utter freedom of invention is terrifying.

"So what are the benefits of staying where you are?" asked Hafeezah.

"If you cancel your expectations, you can't get knocked over," Helene said.

"Yeah," said Lauren. "I hate confrontation, and my mother always said, 'Don't be too strong,' so I think I betray myself all the time, because I fear a fight."

"It's easier," said Elinor. "Takes less energy."

"Does it?" asked Hafeezah.

Elinor was silent for a moment. "I guess not," she said, "if you spend so much energy stressing about it."

"So what other benefits are there?" Hafeezah persisted.

"It's safe," said Leslie. "You're performing to other people's expectations and you don't have to deal with their skepticism and criticism."

"Exactly," said Alane. "You don't have to worry about making the wrong move."

"You get to be right," said Jenny, "which I guess is just another way of protecting yourself from disappointment."

For women, I think, getting to be "right" is one of the biggest benefits that keeps us where we are. If we maintain the role of being the most responsible, considerate, and sensitive—martyrs, in other words—while it's true that we're often able to prove that we're "right" and they're "wrong," this interpretation allows us to continue suffering, to continue not to have to take the risk of changing anything, while feeling good about ourselves! Martyrdom is the interpretation that allows you to feel self-esteem from getting through a bad situation: It transforms a situation you could do something about but are passively allowing into one you have no control over, which makes you a heroine for bearing it. I slip into this all the time!

In any case, all of these benefits are, as we say, "valid." This isn't an exercise in chucking out everything from the past, but simply in making committed choices that you can stand in and own. Simply looking at your world differently will put a crack in the box. Some rules you may want to keep. But you'll be keeping them because you want them.

"That's true," said Ireen, the young woman who sits in the back of our workshop as one of our room managers. "My father worked at the U.N. his whole life, and his whole life was about third-world empowerment. So in my family saving the world was just what you did. But then I got to college and joined all kinds of committees, so many that I didn't have time for my courses. I wasn't enjoying it at all, and it was one reason I was asked to take a leave of absence. It took a long time to examine that commitment, and once I did, I reinterpreted it. What I came up with was: I must make a difference. But in this case I defined the rule, so it works for me and in fact motivates everything I do."

The next thing to consider, once you know the benefits and comfort associated with not moving forward, is to consider what the cost is.

"My traveling so much and striving so much is costing me closeness with my kids," said Leslie. "That I might never get back."

"Giving upon life cost me my marriage," said Helene.

"Living to my full potential," said Alane.

"My health," said Mary Scott.

"I think it's cost me a lot of money," said Jane.

"A sense of being authentic," said Shelly.

"Peace of mind," said Debra.

"Hate to be a broken record here, but it's costing me great sex," said Alane.

"Fulfillment in using my potential to do good in the world," said Amy Jo.

EXERCISE: COSTS VS. BENEFITS

1. On two facing pages in your notebook, write the words *Benefits* and *Costs*.
2. Now ask yourself: "What are the benefits of staying the way I am?"
3. List all the benefits you're getting from staying in your own unique box—the reasons you feel you need to stay in it.
4. On the opposite page, ask yourself: "What is it costing me

to continue to empower this paradigm?" And write down all the things you're losing out on.

5. Compare the balance sheet. The obvious question is: Is it worth it?

So the basic answer to the question posed at the beginning of the chapter, which was how to keep your sense of direction amid all the paradigms in the undertow, is: first to be aware that you are interpreting, and then to get in the habit of actively choosing what interpretation you want to author in every moment. Choose the interpretation that enables you to keep moving toward your destination. It's sort of like driving past billboards you don't like on your way to an important appointment: You may notice them, and you may acknowledge to yourself that you don't like them. But you don't pull off the highway and rail against the billboards, or write down the phone numbers of the advertisers so that you can call the designers and try to change their ideas. You simply notice them and keep going.

Of course, this implies that you know your destination. That's what we'll explore in the second half of this book: tactics for defining and designing your own independent direction, neither fighting, nor trying to conform to, the undertow's sway—in other words, techniques for swimming sideways.

PART TWO

DESIGNING THE LIFE OF YOUR DREAMS

"So what happened last night?" asked Hafeezah on the morning of the second day of the workshop. "Anything shift for you?"

"In the middle of the night I got a phone call from the burglar alarm company for my family's business," said Amy Jo. "Normally I would have jumped in my car and driven down there. But instead I pulled back and said, 'Call me back if you start seeing movement in the store.' For me, not being the hyperresponsible one is just unheard of."

"I don't have family here in this country," said Zully. "My girlfriend Phyllis and I are very close, but I never had a feeling that I was, you know, needed in someone's life. I always do stuff for people but never think it matters. Her boyfriend called and said there had been an explosion in her apartment, and she was in the hospital. She had him call me back to make sure I knew. It was great to feel like what I did was recognized. And it mattered to her."

"You know, Zully, I felt it when you said, 'Nobody needs me,'" said Sara. "If I didn't come home, no one would know and it wouldn't really matter. At least, when I was a therapist, I knew that I mattered, a lot, in the lives of my patients. I want someone to matter to."

"My best friend died when I was nineteen," said Leslie. "Her mother called from the hospital and said Selma had been shot by her boyfriend, and wasn't going to make it. The week before she had come and stayed with me because she was afraid. When her mother called me first, that was special. I felt like she knew how much I cared. Losing her has just, you know, stayed with me. And it's really behind this feeling I got last night—I woke up in the middle of the night terrified that I'm missing my kids' childhood. I travel all the time—I'm going to London for six weeks next week—but I just can't keep living just to set an example for others of what a black woman with a Harvard M.B.A. can do."

"How many people are in our lives that we kind of take for granted?" asked Hafeezah. "Often an incompletion can be as simple as giving appreciation to people in our lives, or even people who have fallen out of our lives."

"My daughter isn't out of my life, but I figured out one reason we're not connected," said Lynda. "I started cleaning out my medicine chest, and I'm realizing I have all these medicines in there that I've saved, from the time I was on public assistance with three kids. It's like eight years later I'm saving up and hoarding them in case I have to go back on Medicaid! There's no room for anything new in there, and there's no room for my daughter's stuff. I keep complaining that she's so distant, and that she has to keep everything that's hers in her room. Last night, I understood one reason why she does that—my past wasn't leaving her any room!"

"Something really odd happened to me," said Debra. "My husband must have got wind of something happening, because he said to me—completely out of the blue, he's never said this before—'I think we need to spend some quality time as a family.' And even though he's the one who's usually impossible to pin down, he wanted to set a time."

"Is that new?" asked Hafeezah.

"Hasn't happened in over a year," said Debra. "I mean, I don't even know if I want to start patching. He must have gotten wind that something was up."

"It isn't magical thinking," said Hafeezah, "to say that when we identify what we're committed to, the world pricks up its ears. I don't know if you're committed to ending the marriage, Debra, or just to ending the discord in your family. But it's interesting to notice how shifting our resolve also shifts those around us!"

"It's true!" cried Jenny. "But mine wasn't quite so positive. Driving home, I got this crazy idea that I would train for the marathon. I smoke and, obviously, I'm overweight, so it's totally nuts to think I could do it this year, but anyway, I got all excited to exercise last night. But when I got home, with that huge thunderstorm, the basement was flooding. I picked everything up off the floor and we turned on the sump pump. More than that, there wasn't much I could do. So I went upstairs. Just as I'm getting on the treadmill, my husband says, 'The basement is really flooding!' So I go back down. There's nothing I can do. So I say, 'I'm going upstairs to run.' Again, just as I'm getting on the treadmill, he says, 'It's really coming in down here! You better come down!' So I come down. The pump is working. I ask: 'So what do you want me to do?' He doesn't answer. I tell him I'm going upstairs to run. He grumbles under his breath. I say, 'So what do you want me to do?' Then he says, 'NOTHING,' meaning, you know, 'DO SOMETHING!' It made me wonder if maybe the best way for me to grow would be in the office of a divorce lawyer."

Jenny's describing a situation we've all experienced: We're arguing yet we don't quite know why, or even what we're arguing about. Very often, when this happens, it's because the obvious is not being made evident. Like the other participants' stories, Jenny's story depicts a shift that occurred because she had identified a strongly held commitment—in this case, the commitment to care for her body. But Jenny hadn't declared it to her husband.

So her husband keeps summoning her; he wants something, but he's not stating what. Perhaps he's operating within a paradigm of "As the man, I must fight the natural disaster," and he is balking at the impossible responsibility that paradigm lays on his shoulders. Or perhaps he is operating within the "My wife is responsible for the house" paradigm. At the same time, Jenny repeatedly asks, "What do you want me to do?" as if her husband has ultimate responsibility and she is only responsible for executing his commands. Or maybe Jenny thinks she must push forward with her first day of training even if a Mack truck—in this case a flood—is coming at her!

Without knowing the history behind Jenny's story, I can't speak with authority about which paradigms are operating beneath the surface of this conversation. I want to point out, though, that simply the fact that Jenny had identified a strong commitment to herself shifted her external reality. What it did was to challenge the underlying assumptions structuring the automatic conversations she was having with her husband.

Now that you've come to a clearing, Part II details how to design and create a new future, using a step-by-step process to take you from the assumptions that have created the reality you're living in now, to some strategies to create the life of your dreams. First, we'll examine the two cornerstones of interrupting these sorts of circular, automatic conversations: committed listening and committed speaking, which I call declaration. When you listen committedly, focusing constantly on what you want to create and build, you will begin to hear possibilities in a way you never have before. And when you declare your new reality, you create an opening in which that new reality can occur. It sounds obvious to say, but a huge piece missing from Jenny's conversation is that she neglected to tell her husband about her newly discovered commitment to exercise. Identifying the commitments operating beneath what's getting said and done enables you and your partner in conversation to decide whether you're committed to continue being the way you're being. In sum, Chapter 6 looks at what happens when we declare a new reality, without evidence, permission, know-how, or proof that it will happen.

Chapter 7 invites you to explore what lights you up. It's based on a series of questions designed to expand your sense of who you are: your past accomplishments, present loves, and future passions. It addresses the issues that hold women back from identifying and exploring their passions—the fears of selfishness and isolation. I plan to convince you that living passionately and fully is the most generous gift you can give anyone. Especially your kids.

Once you've explored the breadth and variety of your interests, and have chosen a few fields of passion where you might like to roam, I'll detail a method for constructing a reality. Chapters 8, 9, and 10 lead you through a step-by-step process for creating and mapping out a concrete, workable plan toward your dream. It's a process that can be used again and again to create any breakthrough, in any field of passion, as you gradually sculpt a reality you can live in, and love.

The first steps will be to get specific about what you want, which enables others to connect to your dream and offer you new possibilities for exploring it. Once you've identified a domain or two that interest you, you'll assemble a group whose purpose is to brainstorm for possibilities you may not see—to create what I call a Conversation for Possibility.

The next step will be to declare that you're going to create a breakthrough. From the slew of possibilities your brainstorming group offered, you'll develop—either right away, with that same group, or later, with a smaller "design group"—a project that lights you up. A series of questions coaches you, and your group, through this process. When it's done, you will declare a clear and measurable result to your group—one that now sits somewhere between highly improbable and nearly impossible—as well as a date by which you'll accomplish that result.

The next step will be to map out pathways to your dream. Using the technique I call "thinking from the top of the mountain," your group will help you map out more than one pathway, or set of steps, to the result you've declared. In the way that Chapter 8 expanded your possibilities for *what* you could achieve, Chapter 10 will broaden your sense of possibilities as to *how* to achieve your dream. And Chapter 11 describes how to use the skills you've acquired to create a support network that will hold you to your dreams.

Then comes the scary part: declaring your breakthrough out in the world, before you accomplish it. Because your loved ones are people whose support is crucial to your success, we'll discuss how to use your committed listening to convert the skeptics around you into willing, and even enthusiastic, supporters. When you're prepared to enroll the people whose support you'll want on a daily basis, the final exercise will be to declare your radical new plan to the most important people in your life.

By the time you finish Part II, I hope you will feel like one workshop participant who said, "You took my dream out of my head, and put it in my face." You will have a concrete project, many possibilities for how to get there, and new resources, including a support group. More important, you will have acquired a set of skills—a process—that you can use again and again. I hope the project you come up with is a giant step toward your wildest dreams, but even if, six months from now, you decide you want to go in a different direction, what you will have is a step-by-step method to translate any dream into a passion you live.

Chapter Six

The Source of Action

I was going to die sooner or later, whether or not I had ever spoken myself. My silences had not protected me. Your silences will not protect you. What are the words you do not yet have? What are the tyrannies you swallow day by day and attempt to make your own, until you sicken and die of them, still in silence? We have been socialized to respect fear more than our own need for language.

—AUDRE LORDE, AFTER SHE WAS DIAGNOSED WITH BREAST CANCER

When our leaders ask women how they'd go about achieving breakthrough results on a big project, they usually agree on one thing: You have to take actions.

"So if you wanted to get some really outrageous results in your organization," said Hafeezah, "what would you do?"

"Take actions," said Elinor.

"So we all agree that actions produce results?" asked Hafeezah. Most of the women in the workshop nodded, as Hafeezah made a chart that looked like this:

"So what actions do you take?" asked Hafeezah.

"There are two ways," said Sara. "You offer rewards for the desired behavior, and suffering and penalties for the undesirable behavior."

"Okay," said Hafeezah, writing down "Rewards/pain" under "Actions." "What else do you use?"

"Motivate people, and inspire them with your vision," proposed Leslie.

"Enroll everybody and make them feel that their participation is crucial to the success of the project," said Elinor. "And then assign them very clear tasks."

"You have to make an example of yourself," Julie interjected, "as a productive member of the team. You can't just assign and assign. You have to roll up your sleeves and let people know you're as willing to do the drudge work as you want them to be."

"And give them the training to make sure they know how to do what they're doing," added Zully.

"You have to analyze the possibilities and communicate why this project is needed at this time, I mean, why it's necessary," said Debra.

"When they get stuck you have to coach them," said Mary Scott.

"Great," said Hafeezah. Her chart now looked like this:

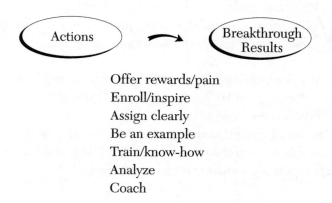

Actions → Breakthrough Results

Offer rewards/pain
Enroll/inspire
Assign clearly
Be an example
Train/know-how
Analyze
Coach

"Any other actions? That about covers it? Okay. Now, are any of these foolproof?" Hafeezah asked.

The women of the workshop sat silent, considering the question.

"My question is," continued Hafeezah, "have you ever offered obvious rewards for the behavior you wanted, that people didn't take, even though they knew about them?"

"Sure," said Elinor.

"Leslie, you ever inspired people with your vision, only to watch the whole thing go up in smoke?"

A roll of laughter rippled over the participants. They seemed unanimous in having shared this experience at one point or another.

"Julie? Have you ever rolled up your sleeves, assigned other people clear tasks, and jumped in, and then looked around and everybody else was way back there?" Hafeezah asked, pointing back over her shoulder.

"That's, like, the M.O. at the foundation where I work," said Julie.

"Okay," said Mary Scott, becoming playfully argumentative. "But you know when things break down you have to coach people to get them back on track. You can't just make an initial effort and then sit back and watch it go to waste!"

"Great," said Hafeezah. "So there's never been anybody that you've trained or coached who didn't give you the results you wanted? Coaching is foolproof?"

"Well, no," said Mary Scott. "I always take on these causes, but last week I had to fire someone I'd invested two years in."

"What about knowing?" asked Hafeezah. "Does knowing how mean you always achieve results? How many of us know how to lose weight, but don't?" Hafeezah's warm eyes drifted down over her own body, which is ample. When she looked back up at the group, over half the hands in the room had drifted up.

COMMITTED LISTENING

If all that was required to achieve a breakthrough was the knowledge we needed, I'd have my driver's license by now, and Hafeezah would be exercising, and Ireen would have graduated from Barnard. Unfortunately, our actions are not produced by know-how, or even will or desire. And no matter how much enrolling and exampling and training and analyzing and communicating and coaching we give others, they don't always act the way we want them to.

A few years ago, just as I was starting Lifedesigns, I was struggling with exactly this problem. I had taken a management workshop to deal with the fact that my staff wasn't executing my requests. I had clearly stated my need for Jennifer and Ireen to get to work on time; I'd held a special, follow-up meeting to tell them how it had to be; I had pleaded, cajoled, and even threatened, and still, they regularly straggled in after ten. In the management workshop, as I was expressing my frustration that the phones at my new business were not getting answered in the morning, the workshop leader tossed a Magic Marker at my face without warning me. I caught it; she held out her hands and I threw it back. Then she threw it at me again, and again reflex prevailed. Then she asked me if I knew what the marker was.

"Sure," I said. "It's a Magic Marker."

She asked me if I knew what you do with a marker. I replied, "Of course I do!" wondering if she thought I was retarded.

"So what do you do with it?"

"You take off the cap and write with it," I said. The simplicity of her questions was getting tedious.

"So the action you take with a marker is to take off the cap and write with it?" she asked again.

I nodded again, ready to throw the thing back at her.

"So why didn't you take the actions appropriate to the marker?" she asked.

"Because you threw it at me!" I replied, at my wits' end.

The leader then proposed that what was coming at me wasn't a marker. It was a flying object, a projectile coming at me the way the world comes at us, day by day by day. A light went on in my head. I had not taken the actions appropriate to "marker" because the marker was occurring to me as a thing flying toward my head. And the action appropriate to "thing flying toward your head" is to catch it or to duck.

In that moment, she taught me something crucial: that we all respond—and *act*—not according to what is "appropriate" to whatever's coming at us in life, but according to how that thing is occurring for us in that moment. I got it—again—that our actions are always a function of how reality is occurring.

When people take actions we judge as "wrong" or "not valid," it's worth considering that as their reality was occurring, those actions were perfectly appropriate. In the moment, every action anybody ever takes is the perfect response for them. Hard as it was for me, I had to consider—to imagine the existence of—a reality in which lateness was an appropriate response to my requests for simple punctuality. I realized that Jennifer and Ireen had been working nights and weekends without the incentive of extra money; I was expecting them to do this uncompensated, as part of their regular job. And my confidence in them made me expect it to be easy! So I wasn't giving them the appreciation they felt they deserved for the contributions they were making. Their occurring reality regularly included twelve-hour days in workshops, evening meetings with Lifedesign alumnae, and nights when they stayed until after ten to finish something I'd assigned on the spur of the moment. From their point of view, Jennifer later said, I was taking for granted the huge after-hours responsibilities they'd taken on, and then demanding an even further commitment of punctuality, which was not where they judged their effort needed to be spent. My reasonable request to arrive at nine, then, was coming at them as a failure to acknowledge the enormous investment they were making to my business on a daily basis. In their reality, my simple request was not so simple; it was a request to mindlessly obey my every demand, regardless of priority. And the appropriate action was to duck.

Possibly, then, when we ask ourselves what new actions we need to take to get breakthrough results, our attention is focused in the wrong place. Rather than trying to impact people in the realm of actions, perhaps we ought to be focusing on shifting the occurring reality that dictates which actions seem possible.

Now, shifting how reality occurs may sound like an even more daunting task than taking different actions. But the fact is, it's a lot easier than you might think.

"Let's do an exercise," said Hafeezah. "Who's willing to talk for two minutes about a big inspiring project they're all excited about?"

Jane raised her hand, and Hafeezah motioned her to come

up and stand in the middle of the U-shaped tables. "Hold on a minute," Hafeezah said. She began to go around the outside of the circle, whispering one by one in the women's ears

Standing in front of the group, Jane was beginning to blush.

"Jane, what's going on in your mind about the fact that I'm whispering?" asked Hafeezah.

"That there will be flaws in my speech," said Jane.

"My ESP senses a paradigm about having to be perfect!" teased Hafeezah.

"Who, me?" said Jane, laughing.

Here's what Jane said.

"Education ought to be engaged throughout our lives," Jane began. "It's womb to tomb. We need to position our society to have education be a constant aspect of our entire lifetime, not just a segment that has closure. The learning needs to be focused and specific as we move through our life cycle: When we look at "lifelong learning" or "welfare to work"—there are lots of buzzwords like these going around—the key is that we benefit from a group of people who are learning with a variety of ages and experiences. So the wisdom of the elders gets tempered by the enthusiasm and questioning of the youth. And the idea of mentorship needs to be expanded so that we bridge the traditional gaps between K through 12 learning, higher education, and corporate America. Learners will have greater access to finding mentors who understand and can work with them. The political environment needs to support this by facilitating the technology and networks. This isn't about p.c.s, it's about providing the infrastructure and enabling technologies so that people can easily learn anything, anywhere, anytime.

"The cultural environment needs to address the idea that it's a normal thing to get disintermediated. An example of being disintermediated is that in ten years we will no longer need travel agents, because airlines will make it easy for us to go on-line and compare fares and buy over the Internet. We need to start looking at how people learn globally and to utilize those resources: If we need an expert, we should have access to an expert. If we want to learn more about Einstein, we should be able to access a video of him talking. Not everybody's an expert, but everybody can be a learner who has access to an expert, even if the education isn't formal. Education does not mean schools."

"Thanks, Jane," said Hafeezah. "That was terrific! So what did all of you hear in what Jane said?"

"I was seeing this great movie with Sally Field—you sort of look like her—in which a woman connects all the people in her life—" began Debra, "her children, her corporate world, some academic experts—to solve some environmental crisis. That she becomes a hero because of how she connects them and everybody cries at the first preview."

"I noticed that Jane was wearing very modest clothes that didn't distract from what she was saying," said Zully. "But I thought she might wear some colors, to translate the fun in what she's saying into a visual message."

"I wondered how much this was going to cost," said Josie, folding her arms across her chest skeptically. Her authoritative tone and posture made her look like an entirely different person from the meek woman who had entered the workshop on the first day. "There's a lot of great ideas here, but who's going to pay for them? Where will the tangible results be to motivate somebody to give that kind of money? It's like the dream of eradicating hunger or total world peace: It's great, but who provides for it?"

"I was really impressed," said Lynda. "She was so articulate, and confident in front of the group. I was counting the 'ands' and 'ums'—she said 'and' once and didn't say 'um' at all. I got all wrapped into the fact that I could never speak that well."

"What did you think about what she said?" asked Hafeezah.

"I didn't really catch it," said Lynda. "I was thinking about my own attention deficit disorder and how I could never have given such a coherent speech. Then I was too busy trying to get them counted the right way. But I wanted to!" she cried, turning to Jane, and laughing. "I heard something about a wider learning, that I was interested in—I did think that Jane's ideas would be great for special learners, like gifted children, or kids with ADD, so that they didn't have to get trapped in the local structures that are designed by small-minded people and districts that won't allocate resources."

"So your listening shifted from one filter to another," observed Hafeezah. "What about you, Shelly?"

"I wondered what happens when the expert you get access to tells you something inaccurate," Shelly said. "I mean, who's going to be liable for when you say that person X is the expert in gallbladder cancer, and they give information that's only partial because of their particular bent, or because your satellite time runs out, and then somebody gets the wrong stuff? I mean, there's a lot of possibility here, but there's also a lot of responsibility, and liability."

"I wondered who would design the games for people to navigate where their information could come from," said Alane. "And I loved the idea that education would move more toward play, due to the expansion of possibility. I also," she added, smiling, "want the patent on the connective technology."

"I wondered what Jane meant by the political environment facilitating the technology," Julie said. "I wondered what laws in what area might do that. Whether you'd want tax incentives for corporations to donate the technology. Or breaks for nonprofits that organize volunteers to implement the technology? Or a government project like the superfund, to be used in a flexible way by applicants for grants that are chosen by a foundation?"

"I wondered about what protections you were planning to put in place for the people who are acting as resources," said Amy Jo. "Are they going to be called upon at any hour of the day or night just because some psycho in Bora Bora wants to build an explosive device? Will the experts be exploited or harmed?"

"Great," said Hafeezah, her eyes twinkling with amusement. "Anybody else thinking about psychos in Bora Bora?"

Laughter rippled over the group at the absurdity of this question.

"Just checking," said Hafeezah. "Helene?"

"I wondered how you'd protect the learners from frauds who pawn themselves off as experts," said Helene. "I mean, one reason a university exists is that the experts there have credentials that are bona fide and checked out. What checks are there on the Internet where it's a free-for-all?"

Then Sara jumped in. "I just thought, what a wonderful, spiritual, connective vision she has, and how confident she is in that! It makes her an incredibly attractive woman and I would think she would have men swarming all over her."

"I thought it'd be a fabulous resource for mothers who wanted to do home schooling of their kids," said Leslie.

"I wondered how the experts would go to the bathroom during the teleconferencing," said Jenny.

"Anybody else concerned with bathroom facilities?" asked Hafeezah. "Just checking. Okay. So, Jane, what did you notice?"

"Each person had a different point of view," said Jane. "Some people were coming out of left field. Just like they do at my job," she added.

"And why was that? Because they wanted to come out of left field?"

"It was like, because of who they were being," said Jane.

"Wonderful," said Hafeezah, nodding. Jane had intuitively perceived the fundamental point of the exercise. "So who were they being?" asked Hafeezah. "Who was Debra being?"

"Hafeezah asked me to listen as a movie producer," said Debra.

"Whose card I would like to get before the end of the workshop!" added Zully.

"You got it," said Hafeezah. "And who was Josie?"

"Josie was a money person," said Elinor.

"I was a CFO," said Josie. "And Zully was a costume designer. That was obvious. But who were you?" she asked Shelly.

"I was a lawyer," said Shelly. "I had to listen for liability. After what Alane said about possibility and play in Jane's project, I can't believe that I didn't get excited about what she was saying!"

"Were you listening for play?" asked Hafeezah.

"No," said Shelly. "Just for risk."

"So 'play' got tuned out," said Hafeezah. "Interesting. So who was Julie?"

"Some sort of politician," said Leslie.

"A senator," said Julie, grinning widely. "How about you?"

"I was a stay-at-home mom," said Leslie.

"And who was Amy Jo?" asked Hafeezah.

"I was a police detective," Amy Jo said. "So I thought about psychos in Bora Bora, and union protections. What about Alane? I couldn't figure out who she was being."

"I was just myself!" Alane said, laughing. "I didn't realize that I was listening through any filter until I heard what everybody else heard. I never even thought about the liability Shelly heard, which, even as me, I should be thinking about."

"Good," said Hafeezah. "Lynda, I guess you were also yourself, thinking about your daughter?"

Lynda nodded. "Doing this made me realize how obsessed I am with my daughter and her problem," she said. "And my problem, because I have ADD, too. So it's really that I'm focused not on her but on her problem. I couldn't even do what I was supposed to do, counting the 'ums' and 'ands,' even for two minutes! It makes me realize I probably don't hear most of what my daughter says, I mean her feelings as a person, because I'm so obsessed with her problem."

"Great catch," said Hafeezah. "So who else? Helene, who were you?"

"I was a university president," Helene announced proudly.

"Sara?"

"I was a yenta!" said Sara.

"Who was Jenny?"

"I was a plumber," said Jenny, laughing.

"Anybody we didn't hear from? Jane, what did you think of the exercise?"

"Well," said Jane, "I'm sitting here thinking that because my background is in education and language, I'm always predisposed to someone who speaks articulately, but now I realize that I'm probably missing a lot of good ideas because I'm not open to people who don't express themselves as well, or have the skill. And also, I realized that I wanted to persuade everybody. So because Mary Scott is a mentoring professional, I especially wanted to hear from her. I figured that she didn't say anything because I'd gotten past the amateurs but not the expert."

"Fascinating," said Hafeezah.

"I didn't say anything," said Mary Scott, "because I'm completely stunned—what a great idea! I'm a techno-idiot. I want you to pilot the technology in the community mentoring program I run!"

After a moment, Elinor spoke up. "Hafeezah, I figured you didn't whisper anything in my ear because, when we were talking about my job and stress, I'd done something wrong in the conversation. So I spent the whole time Jane was talking wondering what I'd done wrong, and how I had to be more agreeable!" said Elinor.

"Wow," said Shelly.

"Elinor's doing some serious catching on herself," said Hafeezah. "Now I have one more question. Debra, how long have you been a movie producer?"

"Not long," said Debra.

"Josie? How long have you been a CFO?" asked Hafeezah.

"Five minutes," said Josie.

"Jenny, how long have you been a plumber?"

"Since last night," said Jenny ironically.

Hafeezah's listening exercise demonstrates how quickly we are able to completely alter the reality that is occurring for us when we listen in a committed way. Though most of the women had barely two minutes of experience in the new "box" Hafeezah had assigned to them, they were able to project themselves into a new reality and hear new possibilities. Their commitment to listen in a certain way, then, actually altered what they heard. It wasn't just that they had seventeen different new interpretations of Jane's speech; they heard seventeen different speeches. And the actions they took—the questions they asked, and the concerns they were prepared to respond to—were based on what they were listening for.

So when we replace our automatic listening with committed listening, we perceive a different reality. We have observations we've never had before; we hear things we've never heard; and we respond differently, simply because we're committed to listening for a different set of possibilities

This sequence:

becomes

Committed listening, while it takes practice, isn't rocket science. It simply means that, first and foremost—like the participants were doing in the above exercise—you commit yourself to being who you're being. The simple willingness to recognize the filters you're already listening under produces choice. If it's working, you can recommit to being who you're already being; if it isn't, you may want to commit to generating a new reality by listening for what you want to build. As the head of a software games company, for example, Alane remained committed to listening through the filter of play and possibility; yet realizing she was listening through that filter also opened up the possibility that she could also listen for liability. Lynda, on the other hand, realized that her filter of hearing everything in terms of ADD was getting in the way of her fully perceiving her daughter. Whatever you decide to commit to listening for, the act of committing automatically enables you to see new possibilities, which in turn create results consistent with your commitments rather than with your past.

This is not to say that you're going to reject your old filters in every moment. We bring our filters along with us the same way we bring along our hands, without even thinking about it. And sometimes they serve us. I grew up in an all-white Ohio town with parents who loved and supported me; my father constantly drilled in the message that I could be whatever I wanted to be, and accomplish whatever I wanted to. I hope that my commitment to empowerment and self-fulfillment, which is for me almost like a religion, has enabled me to empower Jennifer and Ireen and everyone else who's worked at Lifedesigns. And that the Lifedesigns workshop, which was created out of that commitment, has empowered thousands of participants. At the same time, in my rush toward my vision of empowerment, I tend to rush others toward my vision. Sometimes this means that I steamroll over other people's difficulty, causing them more difficulty, in an effort to bring them to the joy I envision for them. And because I'm in love with my own vision, I sometimes have a hard time accepting that others have a different vision, which may be better for them.

So, for example, as I sat in the back of our first workshop for black single mothers living in homeless shelters, and listened to their experiences of family, I found myself dismayed by their past suffering. I was actually finding it difficult to listen to their pain, because I wanted them not to have been treated that way. I wanted not to have been so much more privileged than they. And I even felt a little impatient, wanting them to get over the past and start designing their glorious new futures. Because I have the filter of wanting a better world *now*—on a certain level I don't "get" how hard it still is for them, how pervasive racism continues to be, or how valuable it was for them simply to have Hafeezah acknowledge their suffering.

Both the strengths and weaknesses of my upbringing—my facts, my conviction in my own and others' empowerment, my impatient desire for an equal world, my joyous visions for others, my assumptions as a white person about what's easy or difficult, my paradigms about how things should go, my automatic listening, my "box"—means that I continue on occasion not to "get" how it is for others. In my charge toward a wonderful, empowered universe, I prejudice my own vision over that of others. Because I so anticipate others' strength, and their ability to handle, to manage, to overcome, I don't always listen to their struggle. And I'm so invested in my kids' and my employees' success that I sometimes find myself cutting them off, with stock reassurances, when they bring up the difficulties of their process. When I inadvertently dismiss their concerns, I can sometimes even disempower them. It's another example of how we can undo the very thing we seek to do—spread joy and strength—by not listening!

So how to respond? I can either pretend that I have no biases and shout, "I'm a good person!" and "I'm this way because I want a better world for you!" Or I can look inside myself and say, "Wow! My confidence and vision sometimes make me insensitive and prejudiced." Now, I didn't *create* that prejudice, and recognizing it doesn't make me responsible for it. Prejudice got on me, the way it got on everybody else in the United States: it was raining; I went outside in the culture; and I got wet. But if I can actually *own* that prejudice was one of the things I got, I may have a choice in how I respond in the present. Instead of committing myself to being an already perfect, unprejudiced white person, I can commit to being a person who is continuously willing to recognize the prejudice in herself. When I realize I'm listening to others from that first commitment—in which everything is already great, just because I want it to be—I have the choice to shift my listening toward empowering others starting from where they are rather than where I want them to be. In this way I own it rather than letting it own me.

> "It's interesting," said Jenny. "When I took that workshop where I got evaluated as a 1.5—I began to feel as if all this background I had was just like huge, enormous baggage. I was preventing myself from being happy, and looked at myself as all negative. But I guess I'm hearing that it doesn't all have to be so negative. I'm starting to turn all those negative thoughts into positive thoughts. It's okay, they're filters. They also made me stronger. In fact, they've made me who I am, and got me here."

In her comments, Jenny hit on something crucial. This is the good news about the huge box of filters we've been lugging around: Our past got us to today. Though whole industries are based on the premise that we have to get rid of the past, simply owning what interpretations we actually carry, by continually subjecting our thoughts to the fact/interpretation test, enables us to choose what we're generating. You don't necessarily need to decide that everything you thought in the past was "junk" that you now have to get rid of. You can embrace, cherish, and even love your past. Yet moment by moment by moment, your willingness to recognize your filters and interpretations gives you the choice of whether that past reality is the one you want to continue to build and affirm in the future.

With respect to my staff, for example, as the boss who's ultimately responsible for generating the income to pay them, I can *decide* to have a moment of judging and evaluating, in which I say that I think Jennifer and Ireen spend so much time at work not because of my excessive demands but because, as best friends, they waste a lot of time gabbing. Or I can decide that what I'm indirectly getting, in the form of their defiant lateness, is a rating of 1.5 on the issue of acknowledging others' reality. As the head of the company, I can decide to prioritize the basic functioning of my business over the special projects and onetime events. In this case, I can decide that Jennifer and Ireen's first priority ought to be showing up at nine.

Or I may decide that there are some steps—some missing acknowledgment and appreciation—between how enrolled they feel now and how enrolled I want them to be. In that case I could begin to listen for what they need from me to feel empowered, rather than telling them what they need to do to be empowered.

However I decide to deal with the situation, I'm making a choice, because I'm aware that my commitment to empowerment, great as it is, also creates blind spots in my vision. I need to ask myself, continually, whether I'm committed to empowering—that is, to continually taking cues from others about what they need to become empowered—or whether I'm committed to asserting that a state of perfect empowerment already exists, in which everything, including my management style, is already perfect.

I'm trying, even as I write this, to play with catching myself locking myself in my box. At least, as I sit here writing at 5:30 A.M., this is what I'm hoping to do once I get into the office later this morning, even if my phone doesn't get answered until ten. That's basically what I'm suggesting you should do: play with catching yourself. Once you get in the habit of catching yourself listening through your old filters, you get to choose, in any one moment, who you're committed to being. Owning the choice of who you're being, in every moment, radically shifts how the world occurs for you.

And yet . . .

And yet, there's something that happens even before we commit to listening in a new way. In the listening exercise Hafeezah did, the first thing that happened was not that the participants decided to listen differently. It was that Hafeezah declared to them who they were going to be.

DECLARING A NEW FUTURE

A declaration is when we suddenly say, "It's not going that way anymore, it's going like this." Often other people around us have no idea what we're out for, and what future we're committed to, until we say so! It may be that the failsafe method of creating breakthroughs—outcomes between highly unlikely and nearly impossible—is simply that we say it will be so.

Declaring a new future isn't based on evidence. It's not like, "If I was sure I could get a job as a chef, I'd invest the money in cooking school." On the contrary, it is the people who declare a new future *without evidence* whom we call heroes and visionaries; people who say, like Martin Luther King said, "I have a dream"; who say, as Gandhi did, "India will be a free country without violence"; who say, as John F. Kennedy did, "We will put a man on the moon in ten years." What declaring means, in fact, is saying how the future will be—*not* based on evidence in the past. Breaking through to a new reality that's a wild rupture from the past means that no proof exists that this new reality can occur. It's hard to prove that what doesn't yet exist, can!

The beauty of declaring is that you don't need proof—or much of anything else—to do it. You don't need know-how: Kennedy did not know how a man would be put on the moon, and Gandhi, surely, did not know how India could nonviolently wrench itself free of British colonial rule. Each declared what he declared in the absence of know-how or a plan.

And you don't need permission. Who gave the signers of the Declaration of Independence permission to decide that the United States was no longer ruled by the king of England? Who gave Gandhi permission to say that India would become free by nonviolence? Of course the answer is no one, and especially not the British who created the old system. Nobody is *ever* really given permission to declare an outrageous vision; they simply do it. And if you think back to the times in your life when you made a radical break with the past—when you decided you were having the baby or leaving the relationship or buying the house or asking for a raise—you first made a declaration that *that* was how it was going to be. If you think back to a time when you broke with your past even in a modest, almost trivial way, you probably said something like, "It's not going to be like that anymore!" "I want a light, breezy house!" "I hate this maroon chair my aunt gave me, and I'm throwing it out now!" Women who have been abused, for example, usually remark that it ends when they stand up and declare "I will not allow you to hit me anymore." The point is, the Wizard of Oz did not come in and pronounce, in a thundering voice, "YOU MAY NOW DO WHAT YOU WANT." More likely, the person who gave you permission to create this new future was you.

The more we look for them, the more opportunities we see to disrupt "how it always is." We don't often recognize that just before we got a breakthrough result, we usually declared that we were going to disrupt the usual. Even if we didn't declare a specific, outrageous result, like a free India or a man on the moon, we declared the existence of a hypothetical new future *without evidence of it* by saying something like, "There has to be a better way." Declaring that a better way exists is what enables us to start listening for it. Declaring, simply, that a different way could exist enables us to choose.

So it is a declaration—nothing more, nothing less—that produces a breakthrough. In the absence of evidence, know-how, permission, or even courage, what a declaration does is push out a space of clearing for the possibility of a new reality.

What you need to declare is simply a voice to say it and an ear to hear it.

The reason you need an ear, and why you can't just say it to yourself or write it down, is that you don't get any richer transferring your money from your cookie jar to an envelope under your mattress. It's only when you make a transaction with the outside world—an investment in something—that you have the possibility of gain. Similarly, you can collect dreams and schemes and plans for years, but transferring them from one hiding place to another doesn't break open your current set of possibilities. You don't send a ripple into the universe until you say what future you want, in front of somebody else. In speaking it aloud, you are investing in the possibility that the world might just provide you with the future you want. So while it may be more prudent to first try your declaration on someone you know will be encouraging, it's not necessary.

It doesn't even matter if your listener says "No way," or "You're nuts!" The fact that you've dared to put yourself out there shifts your internal reality.

It's enough, believe it or not, for you simply to say you're going to bring this new future into being *because you say so*. As a little kid, when your parents gave you a reason you couldn't do something, you probably knew you could argue them out of it. If they said, "You have to stay home because I can't drive you," you could come up with ways around that by telling them that Joey's dad would drive, or that you could walk, or that you could ride your bike. But the one reason kids can't argue with is "Because I say so." When a parent declares "because I say so," he or she is asserting a kind of ultimate authority to define reality. Which is why it's so frustrating for kids—it's nonnegotiable! The great news is that, as an adult, you're the one who gets to say how things are going to go, just because *you* say so! When you declare a new reality for yourself based on your passionate commitments, your declaration—which in some ways is a declaration of who you really are—becomes virtually unarguable. It's almost like saying, "It's going this way because I *am* so." In announcing a reality consistent with what you love, and what you're passionate about, you claim an authority to create a new future that's immense. What you are declaring, in other words, is a nonnegotiable part of your identity.

So, declaration is what enables us to make the transition between our old, automatic results and the new futures we want to create.

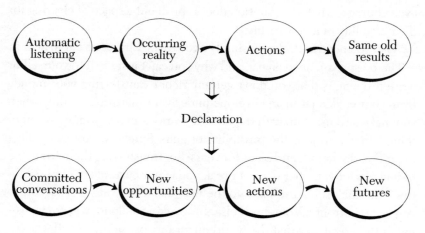

It's worth saying again that what you need, in order to make a decla-ration, is simply a voice and a listener. The source of your power is not thinking your commitment, or believing in it, or knowing the pathway to get there; it's not encouragement, or support from others, but simply your voice. Results happen simply because people say they will.

"But it's not that simple," objected Julie, when Hafeezah made that point in the workshop. "I'm committed to restructuring the corporate tax system and engaging more corporate people in their community. Now, I can say it, and when I say it, I'm committed. But I can't pass a law alone; I need other people. And even though I say it, they don't necessarily get enrolled. And then other stuff happens and I get pulled away from my commitment."

"Spoken like a senator," cracked Amy Jo.

"So, Senator Julie, when the other stuff happens, do you stop saying it?" asked Hafeezah, once the laughter had subsided.

"Yeah, I guess I do," Julie said thoughtfully. "And then it sort of dissolves. Or I think of how I'm going to do it and then I groan and think, Oh, I can't think about that now."

It is true that declaring, and standing for your commitment, means that you may be alone for a little longer than you like.

One of my favorite movies is *Rudy,* the true story of a little guy from an Illinois steel town who said at age eight that he wanted to play football for Notre Dame. He was told in high school that he wasn't smart enough to be accepted there, and was dissuaded from even applying. Rudy was profoundly alone in his declaration; his father and brother, who worked in the steel mill, told him he was crazy. He got a job in the mill, where he worked for three years, until one day he watched his best friend—the only one who had supported his dreams—die in an accident. It was the catalyst for Rudy: He committed to his dream and declared it. He told his father and brother he was going to play football at Notre Dame, quit his job, and took a bus to South Bend, Indiana. When he wasn't accepted at Notre Dame, he got a job as a groundskeeper on the Notre Dame football field and went to a junior college next door. He found a tutor to help him academically, and every semester, he applied for a transfer to Notre Dame. Every semester, he was rejected. Still, his grades were improving, and he continued to enroll everybody else—his tutor, other students, his family, his boss at the football field—in his dream. Finally, at the end of his sophomore year, he was accepted. He joined the boosters—the students who paint the helmets—and eventually got on the squad of sparring partners, who the football team charges into and knocks down during practice. After a year in which his tenacity earned the coach's respect, Rudy asked if, one game next season, he could be placed on the active roster and actually suit up for a game. The coach agreed, but he quit that summer, and the new coach didn't know Rudy. Finally, though, before the last game of his senior year, all the players went to the coach and said they wanted him to play. Each turned in his jersey and asked if Rudy could play in his place. With his family watching, and with a minute to go, Rudy got put into the game. And he is the only player in Notre Dame history who has been carried off the field in victory.

Rudy knew he was a Notre Dame football player before he ever was one. And he *was* that player, with all his being, until the people who had the power to send him out on the field saw the same being. So the choice, in every moment, is not really what actions you're taking but *what commitment you are being*. When you declare it and when you start to *be* it, this commitment, whatever it is, will open up a radically different world. You may need to stand alone for a little while, in your new identity, until you are able to enroll those around you. But by my own way of thinking, that temporary aloneness is a lot better than the aloneness that comes from *not* standing for yourself, or with yourself, with what you're committed to.

Thus, a more accurate version of Hafeezah's chart might read like this:

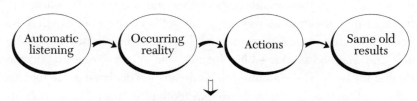

Declaration + continuing to stand for your new reality

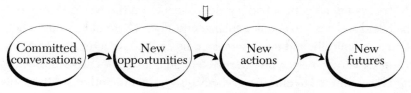

If you can keep standing for your commitment regardless of current evidence, if you can just keep saying "This is the way it will be," the authenticity of your declaration will eventually shine through. Most of us spend our lives desperately looking for something to authentically believe in; because we care so much about it, we tend to attack inauthenticity. On the other hand, a genuine commitment is something people nearly always love to get behind. It enrolls others more quickly than confidence; it yields more respect; it's the act of defiantly flying a flag *without* knowing you've got an army behind you to thrash your opponents. There was no way to tell, in that first moment, whether Kennedy had announced we'd put a man on the moon because he wanted to sound good or because he was committed to a dream. But when he continued to stand behind his words, and kept declaring that they would happen, the excitement accelerated overwhelmingly. And there is nothing more seductive or appealing than someone who takes that kind of risk!

So, the question that remains is, What—or who!—will you declare?

Chapter Seven

What Lights
You Up?

*Our worst fear is not that we are inadequate. Our deepest fear is
that we are powerful beyond measure. It is our light, not our
darkness, that most frightens us. We ask ourselves, "Who am I to
be brilliant, gorgeous, talented and fabulous?" Actually, who are
you not to be? You are a child of God; your playing small doesn't
serve the world. There is nothing enlightened about shrinking so
that other people won't feel insecure around you. We were born to
make manifest the glory of God within us. It is not just in some of
us, it is in everyone. As we let our own light shine, we unconsciously
give other people permission to do the same. As we are liberated
from our own fear, our presence automatically liberates others.*

— MARIANNE WILLIAMSON IN A RETURN TO LOVE:
REFLECTIONS ON THE PRINCIPLES OF A COURSE IN MIRACLES

In our culture, we like to ask kids "What do you want to be when you
grow up?"

It's a question that implies a fixed, finished destination you're supposed to reach and stay at. So it teaches us to think in terms of arrival. This is probably why, when kids get to be about eighteen, we stop asking it!

But the idea that we become something and stay it, that we "finish" establishing an identity, is a myth. It's a myth that reflects our belief that we know all there is to know about the world. Think back to the circle in Chapter 2 that represented all the knowledge there was to know in the world. If you just narrowed that circle to represent all that there is to know about your husband or child, I would ask again how much do you really know about this person? An even scarier question is: How much do I really know about myself, my talents, and my possibilities?

The myth that we ever finish establishing an identity is one a lot of the culture buys into. Why? Because it serves efficiency. Most structures that are designed to be efficient—hospital work schedules, military hierarchies, corporate ladders, factory floors—encourage us to come from a place of knowing where we fit in the puzzle. Rather than being designed to enable us to explore who we are, they're designed to keep us performing in our designated role.

In companies, especially, we often take someone who has many identities, or areas of interest, and we shut them down with the instruction that they, and they alone, will keep the books. Again, this comes from a mechanical model of organization in which each person is a cog in a machine that performs a single function. We take someone who has a second career in opera singing, and we say to them, speaking very slowly so we're sure they understand, "Your job is to keep the books." It may be that we're trying to market our company's product to an upscale, classical-music-loving population, which this singer probably knows something about. Or, she might suggest the perfect music for the commercial we're producing. Or, she might think up a terrific public relations campaign in which we do pro bono work with artists. Yet inside the Newtonian cog-in-wheel model of how people function in companies, we like it when the jobs are rigidly defined and people do only the job they're assigned to do. It makes us feel safe; this way, we know how to keep the structure working. If something breaks down, we know how to fix it—we get another bookkeeper or another receptionist. So if a circle represents the whole of anyone—not what they do or accomplish but simply who they are in terms of what they're committed to and what they love—what organizations often do is collapse all of that person's skills, passions, and commitment into a dot. That dot is the tiny cog the organization needs a person to be to perform the needed function. Ironically, organizations do this—and confine you to only being the last cog you were—even though what they now need, as they enter the twenty-first century, is flexibility!

And the worst thing is, again, that, as adults, we "cog" ourselves. As adults, we spend an enormous amount of energy maintaining a fixed, recognizable identity. Our boss tells us she'd like us to present an idea at a conference, and we reply that we're not good at public speaking. Someone calls and invites us onto the board of a children's foundation, and though we love children, we say, "Oh, but I'm not good with numbers." Someone suggests we might consider interviewing in an entirely different field than the one we've been pursuing, and we dismiss our chances of being qualified. Having long ago decided I was a "creative type," I still tend to limit my own possibilities by constantly saying that my left brain doesn't work, that I'm not good at technology or math, or a whole slew of other things I'd love to master.

The notion of "efficiency" demands that we keep the machine running, rather than taking it apart, every so often, to see how it works. It demands that we be one fixed thing. Like focused, efficient listening, focused and efficient notions of identity keep us sitting in what we know about who we've already been. In other words, it keeps us in our box.

So the question I love to ask is, What lights you up?

It's a question, I think, that reflects our constant process of becoming. My hope is that it will give you permission to think about issues you haven't thought about since you became a "grown up." In some ways, What lights you up? is the opposite of a "grown up" question, because it asks you to think not about the ways in which you're done but about the areas in which you're *not* all grown, the areas in which you're green and eager to explore how to continue growing. So when you ask it of yourself, give yourself some room to explore your passions outside the framework of what's appropriate or feasible or reasonable given your current niche.

The question is a fluid one, implying that passions—and people—change.

HOMING IN ON YOUR PASSIONS

Like everything else, What lights you up? can land on people in a variety of ways. It can seem wonderfully freeing, or it can seem terrifying.

Some women are delighted and respond with a 128-page full-color catalogue of all their many passions, fulfilled and unfulfilled.

Other women have an idea of what they love—or at least, a secret itch to try underwater welding—but immediately get caught up in judging and assessing, sometimes even before they can allow themselves to say it aloud. What comes to mind is how underwater welding is selfish or unrealistic, that pursuing it would disrupt the family; and then the imagined consequences of pursuing the passion overwhelm the ability to declare the dream.

Other people are neutral: They can't think of an immediate answer, but they like the idea of exploring.

Still others find the question upsetting, because they worry that they can't come up with *the* answer to what their ultimate passion is.

All of these responses put you just where you need to be.

• *If you have many passions,* and are eagerly looking for a way to integrate them into your life, this chapter may be one of the easiest for you to complete.

• *If you have a vague idea of your passion,* but feel that exploring it would make you a selfish person, read on.

Keep in mind, when I ask What lights you up?, I'm not asking, What are you allowed to be lit up by? As women, we sometimes think we have to be lit up by something hypergood, that what lights us up has to be a version of being Mother Teresa. Certainly, all of us want to make a difference and affect the lives of others. For some of us, what lights us up *is* some wildly ambitious form of contributing to society—like connecting learners and experts all over the world, or restructuring the laws of capitalism to encourage more community participation from corporations. For others, making a difference can also be as simple as cooking dinner. One of the most moving answers I've ever heard to this question came in a workshop we offered that included men. One guy, after trivializing his answer by saying that we'd find it sappy, confided that what really lit him up was going home every Friday, turning on an oldies station that played solid Frank Sinatra, and cooking dinner for his family. Imagine the joy that Friday dinner brought his children! Imagine what the example of just one dinner like that might create for his children's friends, some of whom may have been living in families that were less loving! Those Friday dinners, I knew, would have a huge unspoken effect on how his kids raised their kids. I had the kind of revelation for him, in other words, that Jimmy Stewart is given in *It's a Wonderful Life,* when an angel allows him to see how awful the lives of his family, and indeed the lives hundreds of people in his tiny town, would have been without him.

Because our own joy always serves others in ways we can't see, I'm not asking what your favorite way of making a difference is. I'm not asking about your responsibilities, or about the good you want to do in society, your company, or your family. Rather, I'm asking: What do you think might bring you great joy? What is it that makes you uniquely you?

Even things we think of as "selfish"—nice lingerie, a manicure, quiet time to think, a vacation alone—make us richer, more joyful, more able to give. If what lights you up is nice lingerie and a manicure, you will be doing the world a service by giving them to yourself. I have never known why women are so often taught that their pleasure, and the pleasure of their loved ones, are two different things! When you get these messages from the world, which women get all the time, you might consider asking yourself this basic question: If you were picking a mentor, would you pick the martyr who did your laundry and dutifully cooked for you, or would you pick the joyful, fun, fully alive human being who taught you belly dancing but let you wear dirty socks? Would you eagerly await a visit with the person who was a perfectionist, who had to do everything, and keep the machine running efficiently, or the person who'd just come back from Italian cooking school?

I love the quote at the beginning of the chapter because, more than any other single statement I've ever read, it speaks to the enormously strong paradigms in Judeo-Christian culture that tell women they need to sacrifice their own pleasure for the good of others. Williamson makes loving ourselves and expressing ourselves the first and foremost way that we can love others. My interpretation of what she's saying is that pursuing your most joyful self, rather than being selfish, is a profoundly spiritual act. Allowing ourselves the joy of shining in our own unique way is our best shot at contributing to the good of the world. The greatest gift you can give anyone—your parents, your professors, your kids, your friends—is to be living the life of your dreams. That's what gives them the freedom, and the permission, to live theirs.

• *If pursuing what lights you up scares you* because you think it will mean separating from your family or husband—I'll address this more in the next chapter—I ask you to consider Hafeezah's take on the question What lights you up? In her workshops, Hafeezah likes to ask the question as follows: Say you're in an airport; you're on the verge of being late for your plane. In the middle of this, you see some people engaged in a conversation—people you'd ordinarily avoid because your filters, whatever they are, would tell you not to talk to them. These people, in other words, belong smack in the middle of a group you're biased against. What topic could they be talking about that could be so compelling, so interesting, and so valuable to you that you would stop then and there and jump over all the obstacles of time pressure, shyness, and even prejudice? What would make connecting more important than staying in your box? What subject would compel you to interrupt and say, "Excuse me, I couldn't help hearing your conversation . . . and I just *had* to know more about it!"?

What I like about Hafeezah's formulation of What lights you up? is that it reflects her belief, and mine, that the ultimate result of exploring and pursuing your passion is that you create a whole new community for yourself.

This is another idea that's especially important for women, because so many of us are taught that indulging in a life we love will disconnect us from the people we care about. The way Hafeezah asks the question takes for granted that the end result of declaring your passions is that it *connects* you: connects you to new people, connects you even more profoundly to people you already know and love. The act of declaring your passions and commitments creates an almost instant community, enabling you to quickly connect to people you're wildly different from, via those shared commitments. These quick yet surprisingly profound connections are the kind people experience in churches, in A.A. meetings, at an exciting professional conference, in a group of disaster relief volunteers, or with the other parents at their kids' softball games: all groups in which people of wildly different backgrounds and cultures are often able to jump over their differences because they can align themselves on a shared commitment.

• *If the question* What lights you up? *strikes you as too broad,* too wide open to answer, it may simply be because you've never been asked a question that's not about achievement or performance but about ontology, or being. If this is the case, trying to answer What lights you up? can be disconcerting. If the fact that you don't have an immediate answer makes you queasy, congratulations. Even the ability to approach the question indicates that you've completed a bit of your past and challenged some long-held interpretations and assumptions. The wide-open feeling the question is evoking is proof that you're actually in a new place; it is the space of clearing you have created for yourself by cracking open your "box." The more uncomfortable it makes you feel, the farther you've probably come, in the course of the book, toward creating a new space of freedom for yourself.

The good news is that the message behind the discomfort is not: Turn back now! but rather: Welcome to a wider playing field!

"I'd like you to answer a series of questions," said Hafeezah. "First of all, what would others say are your talents, your distinctive competencies, your gifts?" asked Hafeezah.

"I'm known for being fearless in the face of a technological problem," said Alane.

"An eye for beauty and a love of beauty," said Page, "that always shines through, even in twenty years of corporate life."

"An ability to laugh at myself and my mistakes," Amy Jo said. "Which hardly ever gets used, you know, because I make so few mistakes . . ."

"Even though I keep talking about solitude solitude solitude, I think others would say I have an ability to bring people together," said Debra.

"My boss always tells me I'm a great facilitator and trainer," said Mary Scott.

"My friends say I'm an excellent mentor and manager, and a good listener," said Julie.

"Even though all I want to do, after working in cosmetics, is wear jeans and a sweatshirt for the rest of my life, other people say I'm an elegant dresser," said Lauren.

"Okay, good. The next thing I'd like to ask is: What *you* think your talents, distinctive competencies, passions, and gifts are?"

"I think I'm great at understanding all elements of a complex problem," said Jane.

"Good thinker, and very good mother," said Julie.

"I won't break a confidence; I'm a true friend," said Lynda.

"I'm good at overcoming almost impossible obstacles by the force of my persistence," said Jenny.

"Terrific," said Hafeezah. "Now the third thing I'd like to ask is: What are the things you like doing the most?"

"I have a passion for family pictures," said Mary Scott, "a passion for justice."

"I like helping people come up with new ideas for generating income, while fulfilling my creativity," said Zully.

"Changing how the system views ADD," said Lynda.

"Entertaining at home," said Debra. "And decorating my home."

"Great," said Hafeezah. "Now, this is a version of the previous question, but it may allow you to bring up some other things: What things do you feel most strongly about?"

"I feel strongly about education, and about helping people solve problems through change," said Jane.

"I love spirituality, and cross-cultural experiences," said Alane.

"I never do it, but I love singing and dancing and movement," said Mary Scott. "And I love creating stories and spaces where multicultural living and understanding is possible."

"The spirituality in working with my hands, learning, inventing, and creating programs to help people do what they want to do," said Zully.

"My social and political concerns, and participating in reinventing society," said Julie.

"What lights me up," said Leslie, "is just spending time with my kids."

"Great," said Hafeezah. "My next question is: What are some of your favorite ways of expressing yourself?"

"I love writing multimedia presentations," said Jane. "And panel discussions."

"Cooking Italian food for my friends," said Alane. "And e-mail. I've become a letter writer again."

"Dressing," said Debra, who had shown up at the second day of the workshop in a dazzling crimson suede pants suit.

"Writing and hugging!" said Zully.

"Biking with my son," said Julie.

"Painting," said Page.

"I never do it, but . . . dancing of all sorts," said Jenny.

"Taking a special trip to New York to go dancing with my husband at the Rainbow Room," said Helene.

Now it's your turn to explore what lights you up. Having dealt with all the hesitations I can think of, I invite you to momentarily set aside your ideas and judgments about what your answers imply. The goal here is not to plan the whole thing out, or to set up a deadline for you to find and speak out about the ultimate one thing you want to do for the rest of your life. It's simply to explore what happens in the field of a passion, once you begin to speak your passion to yourself and to others. Just allow yourself to begin to define what great looks like without getting bogged down in how to make your dream life happen. The exercise is designed to help you check in with yourself, to rediscover what your passions are at this moment in time, to explore who it is you want to be next month or next year.

EXERCISE: WHAT LIGHTS YOU UP?

Give each question a page in your notebook; write them down and then give yourself some time to come up with the answers.

Answer the questions in the order of what excites you the most.

- *What would others say are your talents, your distinctive competencies, your gifts?*
- *What would you say are your talents, distinctive competencies, passions, and gifts?*
- *What are the things you like doing the most?*
- *What things do you feel most strongly about?*
- *What are your favorite ways of expressing yourself?*
- *What would you like to experience during this lifetime?*
- *What is it you love?*
- *What are you passionate about, even if you have no experience of it?*

DOMAINS OF INTEREST

Because we're so practiced at focusing our identity, it's incredibly important to take the time to acknowledge our own multifacetedness. The routines that provide structure and security in our lives also force us to cut off sides of ourselves that we might just as easily have developed as the paths we've taken. Pausing to acknowledge all of what we love is sort of like traveling: even if you don't decide, each time you visit a foreign country, that you want to live there, the simple act of putting yourself in a different cultural structure and way of thinking opens up possibilities for how you view home.

That said, the next thing you will be doing is exploring and documenting all your fields of interest, which I call domains. A domain is not necessarily something you have a real relationship with, something you've ever done anything about, or have any experience with. It's an area of fascination. This includes anything from gardening to spirituality: sex, artistic fulfillment, piano playing, scuba diving, nature, dogs, sports and fitness, financial security, a six-figure income, folk dancing, yachts, Latvian singing, jewelry design, African art—anything in the world that excites you.

You will be doing a simple exercise in which you draw a circle and then list within it the domains that excite you.

Here are some examples of the circles of the workshop participants.

Lynda's circle: children, reading books, knowledge, family, and losing weight.

Julie's: changing the world, "Seinfeld," social justice, hiking and back-packing, church, kids, mentoring, cooking, restructuring the corporate tax laws, yoga, travel, laughter, rafting, teaching, and friends.

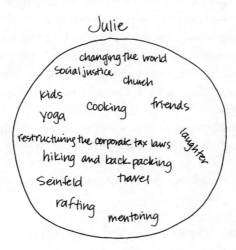

Mary Scott's: stained glass, learning, creating community, life stories and storytelling, spirituality, dancing, her mom's life, her granddaughter, swimming, and double Dutch rope jumping.

Debra's: decorating the house, health and well-being, financial freedom, quality time with kids, highly organized surroundings, having and being a fabulous mate, and an Afrocentric art collection. As an afterthought, she revised decorating the house to "making a home refuge."

Zully's: fashion—texture, colors, and creativity—and money, traveling, activist, international leader and activist, giving advice in creating business opportunities, dance, dance related to other cultures, and designing costumes for that dance. Up in the corner, outside her circle, she wrote "Coty Award," which is an award for dance costume design she wanted to win.

Alane's: spirituality, art, intimacy and sex, cross-cultural experiences, eating great food (Italian!), cooking, traveling, sports, languages, and fashion.

Notice the incredible range of answers each woman came up with!

....

EXERCISE: EXPLORING YOUR DOMAIN OF INTERESTS

1. Draw a big circle on a piece of paper. This is the circle that encompasses all of who you are: your past glories, present passions, and your interests and dreams for the future.
2. Within it, begin to write down some of the major areas of interest in the life of your dreams. What fascinates you? Jot down whatever comes to mind, quickly, as a way of picking up all the threads of love that connect you to the world. The ideas you ought to be paying attention to here are not the developed, dutiful responses of the person you've worked to become, but the almost dreamlike associations and the flash connections they induce.

....

Chapter Eight

Creating New Possibilities

Now that you have expanded your sense of yourself, and have set down all your domains of interest, you may be feeling as if you finally have some air to breathe in terms of possibilities. On the other hand, once women set down their fields of passion and get a fuller, richer sense of all they are, they sometimes begin to feel as if they have too many interests! Those domains of interest can feel like a lovely sky of stars—nice to contemplate and dream about, but unreachable.

So how to get there? How does anybody ever get anywhere? We've all experienced that twinge of regret of watching someone take advantage of a possibility we think we should have seen but didn't. "How did they get that idea?" you may have asked yourself. "Why didn't I think of that?" Or, "If only I'd had her connections!"

Well, this chapter is about making connections—with yourself, with others. It is these relationships, often founded on commitments, that will help you get from where you are now to the realization of your wildest dreams.

Often when we think about how to cross a field of passion and make a dream real, we instinctively feel hopeless; we think we have to reinvent the wheels on which other people are already speeding down the highway. In fact, possibilities are all around you if you know how, and where, to gather them. This chapter contains a strategy for harvesting possibilities, especially those right around the corner, or next door, or in your gym, your church, or your doctor's office. I hope to persuade you that most new possibilities come from unexpected, and even unpredictable, sources.

DARING TO GET SPECIFIC

As the participants' experiences suggest in the Overview to Part Two, identifying a commitment you hold, even before you say it to someone, begins to shift the world around you. Your possibilities will expand even farther once you formulate a clear declaration of what you're committed to within your field of passion. This section will help you hone what you want as precisely as possible.

Even before you receive input from others, simply the act of getting specific with yourself can open up possibilities. In the workshop that you've been observing in these pages, for example, Lauren's field started out as healing. But she hadn't acted on it, even in the months after she quit her cosmetics job, because she thought it would mean going to medical school, and she didn't feel she had the money or the years to do that. When her group pressed her to be specific, though, she said, to her own surprise, that what she was interested in was healing with plants. And she lit herself up before anybody could say anything, because pursuing "healing" had suddenly become possible for her!

Specificity is also what enables others to understand what it is you want. When you begin to declare what you want to pursue, and what you think the life of your dreams might consist of, the words you use will be crucial to their ability to support your dream. For example, say you ask for help with the domain "job." The person you're asking might not know what you mean. One woman might say "job" and mean "career," another might even cross out "career" and write "vocation," and finally end up with the phrase "creative and passionate work." Someone else who wrote down "career" might mean "six-figure income with travel." Still another might interpret "career" as "fulfillment"—that is, as a sort of spiritual satisfaction in everyday tasks. For one person the generic "solitude" may mean having the time to read the great Russian novels; for another it may mean giving herself the time to explore her creative potential by taking piano lessons; for a third, solitude could mean spending time in a Buddhist monastery. Because you will be reaching out to a group of people to help you explore possibilities, the more specific you are in stating your field of passion, the easier you make it for them to know what help you might need.

Your specific declaration connects you not just to what you see of any one person—which is often, simply, their "cog" function in your life— but also to their cousins, friends, past experience and education, and the article they read last week in the doctor's office. What you do, when you declare, is that you enable them to connect you with all the elements in their lives that you may not have noticed in your usual encounters with them. You may discover, for example, that your friend's next-door neighbor works in your field of interest, or that your colleague's niece is dating someone whose family business does something similar to your career goal, or that your neighbor's college roommate teaches a course in just what you want to study. When you declare to others, you're creating the opportunity to connect to the whole of what their life is, rather than just the part you know about.

When you speak about a specific commitment, the resources you can access are almost infinite.

EXERCISE: DARING TO GET SPECIFIC

1. Look at the circle with all the areas of interest in your life. Now draw another circle on a different page and begin to transfer your fields of passion.

2. One by one, restate your areas of interest in this new circle. As you do, reword as many of them as possible into more

precise language. Are there any specific things you're interested in pursuing that light you up? For example, instead of sailing, is sailing across the Atlantic what you really want to do?

....

The next step will be to pick a domain you'd like to work on, and then to narrow your declaration to a clear statement both of what you want to explore and what it's for. Believe it or not, this actually widens the space for possibilities to rush in. In one workshop, a participant, Nancy, said that what really lit her up was entertainment. After she had identified her domain, though, the group sat in silence. Nancy seemed to be a socialite who already threw and attended tons of parties, so no one could quite understand what she meant by this or why it mattered to her. Then Hafeezah asked Nancy what "entertainment" would allow for? Nancy clarified. A few months earlier, Nancy had spent time in a pediatric cancer ward where her niece was dying, and while she was there she'd thought, again and again, about what a difference it would make in some of these children's lives to have some entertainment to cheer them up. So "entertainment," a generic term the group couldn't quite connect with, got narrowed to the very specific and inspiring "entertainment that would give joy to children with cancer." In that moment, the women in the room went from being detached and disaffected to feeling moved, amazed, and ready to help, because they understood Nancy's commitment to bring joy to sick children. They threw out possibilities for foundations, for Nancy starting a volunteer network, for her learning to sing and dance, for her teaching a class at a community center—and they got so excited that they continued to yell out ideas even after Nancy had enough to last a year. By making her language more specific, Nancy enrolled the group, who then began to help her generate possibilities.

"Let's explore what might be possible by fulfilling one of your domains," said Hafeezah. "How about you, Zully?"

"I'd like to explore the domain of dance with culture," said Zully.

"What would that allow for?" asked Hafeezah.

"It would enable me to combine my craft and my art," said Zully. "And to fulfill my dream of winning the Coty Award for dance costume design," said Zully. "Also, I want to get involved in designing costumes for films."

"What about you, Page?" asked Hafeezah.

"I know this sounds odd, but my domain is de-stressing," said Page. "Within that my commitment is to find a way to use art or nature to allow for me to feel more integrated and self-expressed, the way animals are."

EXERCISE: HOMING IN ON YOUR DOMAIN OF PASSION

1. For the purpose of example, pick a few domains—two or three—that are the most exciting to you. These are not the only areas that you will develop, but simply the ones you might like to practice on for now.
2. Within the domains you have selected, ask yourself a few questions.
   - What am I committed to within this domain?
   - What would fulfilling this domain make possible?
   - What would that allow for?
3. Based on the answers to these questions, decide which domain most lights you up. Some people like to dig in and start with their biggest problem area; others like to start with an area that's a little less emotionally charged. Either way is fine, though I sometimes recommend to people that they momentarily set aside huge areas like "marriage" and "financial security," which I think often come as a consequences of living a life you love. In any case, because you're practicing a process you'll use over and over, it doesn't really matter what domain you choose. My only requirement is that just thinking about pursuing it makes you feel joyful and excited.

A CONVERSATION FOR POSSIBILITY

Now that you've identified a field of passion that most excites you, the next step will be to create what I call a conversation for possibility. This conversation can generate many possibilities where none previously seemed to exist.

My first example of this is one that occurred around Zully's declaration that she wanted to combine culture and dance.

> "Okay," said Hafeezah. "We ready? Everybody's going to throw out possibilities for how Zully could combine culture and dance. And Zully, all you're going to say is, 'Great idea.' Who's willing to write down the possibilities for Zully?"
>
> "I will," said Lauren, who was sitting next to her.
>
> "Thanks," said Hafeezah. "Who'd like to start?"
>
> "You could get involved in the next Olympics," said Jenny.
>
> "You could design costumes for a music video," said Debra.
>
> "You could do theme parties for children, with cultural costumes for them to wear," said Josie.
>
> "You could start designing a new line of dance shoes," said Mary Scott.
>
> "You could open a store," said Leslie.
>
> "You could visit a museum for inspiration," said Page.
>
> "Get on the board of the Costume Institute of Metropolitan Museum of Art," said Jenny.
>
> "I couldn't do that," said Zully. "I'm not that rich."

The first thing you need in order to begin to harvest some possibilities you don't now have is a *stance*. The stance I'm asking you to take is that you suspend your disbelief for the duration of the conversation. If the conversation goes as it's designed to go, your contributors will begin to offer possibilities that threaten, or even crack open, your box. When you feel your resistance mounting, and all you want to do is raise your box like a shield against the new, my advice is: *don't*. Later on you will have time to actively engage the fact/interpretation test on your own resistance. In the conversation, though you may be dying to interrupt with "I can't do that because . . . ," or shoot down with "I already tried that . . . ," I strongly suggest for the purpose of this exercise, that you keep the list of generative questions in front of you. In your own mind, practice your new generative listening. Try not to "already know" about the suggestions your contributors offer.

In Amanda's workshops, she likes to ask participants to avoid getting the Charles S. Dual Award: In 1899, Charles S. Dual was the head of the patent office of the United States. One day, so the legend goes, he went to President McKinley to discuss closing the patent office; everything that could have been invented, he said, had already been invented. So if and when participants feel that way, Amanda asks that they bracket their sureness about what's possible or impossible, at least for a little while.

When you're listening to the possibilities that others are offering, rather than considering whether the idea is "valid" or not, possible or not, feasible or not, interesting or not, try to think like an inventor: keep in mind that invalid, impossible, unworkable ideas are, with a little modification, what lead to great ones. Suspend the judging and assessing, and keep asking yourself what each suggestion would allow for, and what you could build from that. Is there anything about the idea that might lead you someplace else? If you want to become a chef, someone may suggest you become a restaurant reviewer. You may not want to do that; at the same time, you might become a cookbook reviewer for a local paper to start getting free cookbooks. Or you could volunteer in a soup kitchen to get practice cooking meals for a lot of people. Or you could . . . well, you get the idea.

> "Okay," interrupted Hafeezah. "Looks like we're starting to crack Zully's box, because we tapped into some of her noise about why things can't happen. Remember, Zully, your job, for now, is to respond only by saying, 'Great idea.' Even if contributors frame their suggestions as questions—like 'Could you try doing such and such?,' avoid getting into a lengthy answer, or indeed any answer at all. Simply say 'Great idea,' or 'Great suggestion.'
>
> "Jenny, getting on the board of the Costume Institute at the Metropolitan Museum was a wonderful idea," said Zully playfully.

When you're trying to get others to generate ideas, it's not enough just to be neutral. Creating the most wide open channel for receiving input means actively encouraging people's initial, less-than-perfect attempts. We don't look at a child's first steps and call her a failure because she didn't make it across the living room; similarly, people's first attempts to generate ideas are not necessarily their best. Even if you don't critique, but remain silent . . . well, how does it feel when you say something you think is a great idea, and you're all excited, and you blurt it out, and somebody responds with silence? Do you want to continue to try to think up more fabulous ideas for that person?

So, when you're asking for possibilities, the best way to keep the ideas flowing until someone tosses out a gold nugget is to confine yourself to one response, and one response only: "Great idea!"

"Any other ideas for Zully?" asked Hafeezah.

"You could volunteer to design for dance," said Julie.

"Get involved in community theater," said Mary Scott.

"Work with dance schools," said Jane.

"You could research five people who are doing small independent films and volunteer to design costumes for them," said Debra.

"You could get on the board of some Ecuadoran dance troupe and design their shoes," said Lynda.

"You could contact the Chicago Film Commission," said Debra.

"Do a contest for children," said Josie.

After a moment, a silence settled over the room.

There's always a point, in a conversation for possibility, when there's a lull in the exchange of ideas. This doesn't mean that people don't have any more ideas, but simply that the group has collectively tossed out all the things that come to mind as imminently possible. Sometimes this first casting of your net is enough to generate great possibilities you hadn't thought of. Other times you will need the members of your brainstorming group to dig deeper, and more wildly, into their imaginations.

So our leaders ask participants whether something's opened up for them in the conversation. If it hasn't, they initiate a second round of brainstorming in which they ask people to get really outrageous, and go *way* outside the "box" of what they imagine might be possible.

"So, Zully," said Hafeezah. "Has something opened up for you?"

"Sort of," said Zully.

"Only sort of?" asked Hafeezah. "Okay, folks; let's go way, way out there for Zully. Anything you can think of."

"You could found a dance troupe here, get funding, and take it to Ecuador," said Shelly.

"You could travel around the world with a group of designers or young artists, and get corporate sponsorship from my company," said Elinor. "We did this once with a singing group. And you could study design in say ten different cultures and mentor your design students on your trip."

"You could fly to the Latin American director you love the most, and find him or her," said Amy Jo. "And just show up with your portfolio and stand outside where he or she is staying until he or she lets you in. No one's impolite enough to leave someone with a cane standing. Work that cane, Zully."

"You could found a world-famous shoe museum with an architect, and get funding for it from Nike and other shoe companies. Get some great architect to design it," said Page.

"Wow," said Zully. "Wow."

For many women, the conversation for possibility is the most empowering section of the workshop. So when I was writing this section of the book I wanted to make sure you had some terrific ways of creating this group experience for yourself. I had one or two ideas for how you might do it; ultimately, what I did was gather the Lifedesigns staff to have a conversation for possibility, over lunch, on the subject of how readers could create their own conversation for possibility. After a half-hour conversation, we had gathered five wonderful options.

Ireen, our workshop manager, who comes from a large family and loves large gatherings, suggested that the easiest way to construct a group would be to throw a brainstorming party. Using this option, you would call as many people as you can, invite them and whomever they'd like to bring, to a brainstorming party. Though this option probably takes the most effort, it's probably the most fun. Besides, it puts people together face-to-face. Suggestions spark other suggestions; ideas generate ideas. A sort of momentum develops where your contributors bounce off each other and come up with more and more ideas. You may even find, after your contributors have finished generating possibilities for you, that they'll want their own turn at gathering possibilities for their own lives!

As Ireen offered her idea, it occurred to me that there might be reasons you might not feel comfortable throwing a party. If economics or shyness or home decor is in the way of assembling a group—perhaps your house is "a bit cluttahed"—or, if you're like me, you and everybody in your life have more time commitments than you can possibly fulfill, you could also set up a conference call. This limits the number of people who can give input, but you could easily set up a series of conference calls with different participants.

Like throwing a party, a conference call enables people to generate more ideas by bouncing off what they hear. In addition, it removes geography and social skills as obstacles. You can create this conversation anywhere there's a phone, and you can put together the ten absolutely most creative and optimistic individuals you know without having to worry whether they're in town, or whether they'll mix well in a social gathering. It may require a little more organization to track down your contributors and pin them down to a time, but your phone company can execute this call quite easily. You may like it so much that you choose to set up a regular phone date with your group!

Hafeezah said her house wasn't big enough to have a party. What she wanted, she joked, was to go to Ireen's party. Out of that joke came her idea. If you're not a big social initiator and the idea of announcing your passions and commitments in a structured way makes you uncomfortable, a third possibility would simply be to go to a gathering place of any sort where you'll know people—a church party, a local hangout, an aerobics class, your hairdresser—and have a series of conversations. As with the first two options, you would declare what you wanted to explore within your domain of interest. You might want to offer a short explanation of your Lifedesigns work and the process by which you came to harvest possibilities, or you could simply mention what it is you're interested in pursuing and ask if the person you're speaking to has any ideas. But because people have not been assembled for your purpose, they might feel compelled to contribute the limitations on your vision. Because you're getting a somewhat more random response, you'll need a commitment to keep standing in what you want, even in the face of negativity.

After Hafeezah spoke, there was a lull in the conversation. The only person who hadn't offered a possibility was Jennifer. As usual, she had waited until she had taken in everybody else's ideas before she spoke. (Jennifer is a big advocate of allowing people to respond at their own pace.) When she finally did speak, she came up with a wonderful idea—an option for people like her who don't like having to respond on the spot but rather like having more time to consider the question.

In some ways, Jennifer's suggestion was the simplest. It required nothing more than that you send out fifty blank white postcards, which you would stamp and address to yourself, in envelopes that include a short note. The note briefly explains what you're doing, sets out the field of interest you want to explore, and then encourages your addressee to contribute any ideas or possibilities. There are several advantages to this method: First, as I said, it allows people to think at their own pace. Next, it's extremely low effort: All your contributors have to do, in this case, is think, write, and mail. It's also valuable if you're living in a part of the world that's radically apart from the life of your dreams—for example, you're living in France and you want to move to a ranch in Idaho. A final benefit of this method is that although it doesn't allow people to hear each other's ideas, giving your contributors this privacy allows them to propose wackier and more outrageous ideas.

Using Lauren's domain in the workshop, which was earning a living with plants, Jennifer then gave an example. Lauren's commitment was to help people heal with plants. If Lauren had used this method instead of coming to the workshop, Jennifer suggested, her note might have read like this:

> As part of a course I'm doing in designing my life, I'm exploring ways to incorporate gardening into my marketing work. I'm committed to connecting people with the healing plants can offer, to learning about plants, and to earning money with it. I thought of you as someone who might have some great ideas for me for possibilities around how to pursue this. If you have time, would you jot down any thoughts you have—no matter how specific or vague, serious or silly—on the back of the enclosed postcard? Thanks!

After Jennifer finished describing the postcard option, Ireen came up with a variation on it, which was sending a sort of chain letter that each contributor writes a possibility on, then sends to somebody else, until the fiftieth person sends the list of ideas back to you. Ireen's idea was that this method of using the mail would enable people to be sparked by other contributors' suggestions. I mentioned that this one seemed a bit high-risk to me, because one contributor could easily interrupt the whole process by allowing the letter to sit there. But because we were in the middle of a conversation for possibility, everyone reminded me to say "Great idea," and save my reservations for later.

After a lull in the conversation, I bounced off Jennifer's idea of requesting input through the mail and came up with what is perhaps the easiest of all options: Sending a letter out on the Internet to a whole bunch of recipients. In this case you'd state your declared commitment, and ask for input, via an e-mail to multiple people. You would also ask them, when they reply, to reply to all recipients. In this way, everybody gets to "hear" all the other ideas and you can generate some of the same group momentum you'd have in person. If you're already on the Internet, this option is terrific in terms of ease and convenience. And like Jennifer's "snail mail" option, it allows contributors to respond at their own pace. You can also send out queries to people you don't know, through chat rooms or newsgroups organized around your area of interest.

After a lull in the conversation, Hafeezah wondered aloud: What if, for whatever reasons, the reader can't throw a party, can't set up a conference call, and isn't on the Internet? Then Amanda showed up.

Amanda, who spends half her life in airports, contributed a simple, easy solution that is also a low-effort variation on Hafeezah's suggestion. Amanda's idea was that for one day, you could tell everyone with whom you came in contact what your field of interest is. This includes grocery baggers, taxi drivers, dry-cleaning people, your pharmacist, your hairdresser, your colleagues, the janitor in your office, and, of course, the person who sits next to you on the plane. Amanda had recently done this because she wanted to house-swap with someone in the United Kingdom; after three days, she'd found somebody.

Incidentally, since Amanda proposed this one, I've adopted it as a habit. Whenever I travel, I take my declarations along with me and I make a point of telling the person in the seat next to me on the plane, or at my table at a conference, what I'm committed to exploring in that moment. I'm always surprised, when I use this technique, at what great stuff I come up with!

What the conversation for possibility demonstrated, at least to me, is that there are always many more possibilities out there, and many of them terrific, than any one of us can currently imagine! One thing that came out of ours, completely unexpectedly, is that we sat around designing what the Lifedesigns website would look like—an idea we'd had for a while, in the abstract, but which became concrete and exciting as we brainstormed around it. The Lifedesigns website is for anyone who's looking for, or wants to offer, resources and information for other women! Check it out, at www.lifedesigns.com.

In this and the following chapters, you will be doing a few group exercises: brainstorming in a conversation for possibilities, designing a breakthrough project, mapping pathways to it, and declaring it. Because each method of assembling a group has its own unique advantages, I decided to offer all of them and let you pick how you'd like to create your own conversation for possibility. My instinct is to encourage you, if at all possible, to assemble a physical group, There's something about group chemistry that makes the outcome a little more unpredictable than dealing with one person at a time. Plus, doing it this way means that once you've harvested possibilities from your brainstorming group, you can proceed right away to the next steps, which are to define a breakthrough project, declare it to the group, and design pathways to get there. If you assemble a group in person, you can use the momentum to accomplish all these steps in one sitting.

On the other hand, using more than one method of gathering up a group allows you to be more flexible with your contributors. Not designing right after you brainstorm enables you to create a more focused design group from the most enthusiastic contributors in your brainstorming group. Breaking up the sessions also has the advantage of allowing you to do some research to explore the various possibilities before you define your breakthrough challenge.

So my most expert advice, for this first group exercise, is to create a conversation for possibility in the way that seems easiest and most fun to you.

Guidelines for Your Conversation for Possibility

The basic guidelines for how to create your conversation for possibility are as follows.

How to Pick Your Contributors. After nearly every workshop, women ask, How did you know to put this group together so perfectly? The answer is that we use a very scientific method called first-come, first-served. And the mix always turns out perfect.

Assembling the group depends on your approaching the task from a premise of not knowing. While it's probably preferable to choose the enthusiasts rather than the cynics, it's a good idea to suspend your idea of how much you think you know about the resources any one person might have to offer. Do not think of the people you gather around you as your "bookkeeper" or your "doctor"—a person who knows only about bookkeeping or medicine—but as people with a wide range of interests, experience, education, friends, cousins, and neighbors you probably don't know about. All of these, of course, may become resources for you. So choose your contributors from a stance of not knowing.

What to Say, in Your Approach. Tell your contributors that you're setting up a "conversation to brainstorm for possibilities." Tell them you know they'll come up with ideas you haven't thought of. Tell them you're interested in all of their ideas, no matter how wacky. And offer to allow the group to be used for anything they'd like to brainstorm about.

Though this is not a requirement, at the same time you invite each guest to contribute to your future, you may want to invite them, if they've expressed any interest or enthusiasm, to design their own breakthrough project at the same time. If they seem interested, invite them to prepare themselves by reading this book. The advantage of this, for you, is threefold. First, it may make it easier for you to ask for an afternoon of your contributors' time if you're also, at the same time, offering yourself in the service of their dreams. Second, the more contributors you have who have read this book, the more likely it is that the conversation will stay on track and successfully broaden your possibilities. Third, the last chapter discusses ways to create a continuing support network for yourself, women who know your breakthrough project and are committed to helping you make it happen. Engaging the members of your group in designing their own breakthrough projects means that your contributors will need your next meeting as much as you will! If they feel something's at stake for them as well as for you, they'll continue to show up for you, if and when you falter. Consider the possibility that the entire group section—the brainstorming group, and the design group that hones your project, and the pathway mapping session—can work for every member of your group who wants to design a life they love.

How to Neutralize Skeptics. Even if somebody's initial response is to tell you you're crazy, stand behind your idea of what you want to explore. At the same time, don't pressure anybody to participate. You may find that even the skeptics will start calling you back, both before the event and after it happens, with ideas.

How to Set Up the Conversation. In whatever version you choose to do the exercise, speak about your area of passion and what you're committed to. Tell your contributors as specifically as possible what it's for. Ask them to throw out whatever ideas come to mind, no matter how outrageous. At the same time, ask them not to get bogged down in offering detailed how-tos, and not to ask questions that require a response (e.g., "Do you think you could . . . ?"). Tell them you want them to fire off as many possibilities as they can think of, especially those outside your normal framework.

How to Harvest the Possibilities. Record the conversation! If you're having a party, ask somebody to write down everything that's said, so you can concentrate. You may want, at the party or during a conference call, to tape the conversation. If you're using e-mail, save the responses and print them out for later. If you're simply gathering possibilities by telling a series of conversations in public, you'll need a small notebook—the kind journalists use—to write down every idea you gather. If anyone asks you what you're doing furtively scribbling notes, tell them it's an old habit from your spying days and leave it at that.

One last note: The activities of the next chapter are also group activities. For the sake of convenience, you may want to read through Chapters 9 and 10 before you assemble people. That way, you can do the brainstorming, the design of the project, and the mapping of pathways all in one afternoon.

EXERCISE: CREATING A CONVERSATION FOR POSSIBILITY

1. Choose the way you'd like to assemble your group. Once you've made a decision, write down what you plan to do in your notebook.
2. Set yourself a deadline by which you will create this conversation, no more than three weeks from today.
3. Read through to Chapters 9 and 10 to prepare yourself for all the group activities.
4. During the conversation, keep the generative questions where you can see them. If you find yourself judging and assessing, bring yourself back to listening for what you could create. For the duration of the conversation, suspend your judgments.
5. Create a comfortable, nonjudgmental space for ideas by confining yourself to one response, and one response only: "Great idea!"
6. If your group finishes one round and nothing's opened up for you, speak up. If you're getting ideas that don't quite fit your vision, without shooting down what's been said, state it more precisely for your group. If they're simply not going far enough outside your box, tell them—hound them—into thinking more outrageously. Tell them I said to go "way out there."
7. Watch your world expand!

Chapter Nine

An Inspiring Challenge

"Be bold, be bold . . . be not too bold."

—ADVICE TO BRITOMART,
IN SPENSER'S *THE FAERIE QUEENE*

Once you've had a successful conversation for possibility, your "box" should look pretty cracked. In fact, it ought to be just about demolished.

Hopefully, you've got a list of possibilities that sets your mind spinning. Now that you're prepared for it, this chapter contains what you've been waiting for: a step-by-step process for creating a breakthrough in your life.

> "So what's a breakthrough?" asked Sara. "Last year I got all excited, and took a course in flower arranging. I passed the test, and never did anything about it again."

Our usual understanding of a "breakthrough" is something that happens that's unlike your reality up to that point. It doesn't mean finishing a project or activity spectacularly; what a breakthrough does is begin a spectacular new chapter in your life. When Roger Bannister ran a four-minute mile, it was a breakthrough not just because he did something no one had done before, but because he was then able to run other four-minute miles, again and again and again.

What we will be designing, from all the possibilities you've gathered from your brainstorming group, is a result you make happen (rather than something that happens to you), something you'll design and commit to simply because it excites you. And to make sure you expand your sense of possibilities permanently, it will be a result that right now seems somewhere between highly improbable and nearly impossible.

> "Seems a little daunting, trying to do something nearly impossible, that you have to do again and again," said Josie.

First, it's not that you *will* repeat your breakthrough over and over, but that you *could* if you wanted to. The idea is to bring you to a new place, not to force you to perform. Still, if this feels intimidating, keep in mind that everything you do in this book is practice. This is not the one and only breakthrough you will ever design. Because nothing works forever, the fact is that we are called upon, throughout our lives, to redesign and to create new breakthroughs. So while I want you to feel enough pressure that you can't go back to hiding your dreams in your cookie jar, the way to regard this exercise is as a test drive.

If the prospect of creating one seems daunting or exhausting, keep in mind that a breakthrough doesn't necessarily mean expending more energy or effort. Let's go back to the graph of your successes and failures.

Within this pattern, you have your range of predictable outcomes—the outcomes that basically nobody will be much surprised by. You get promoted, then laid off in a merger; then you get another job in your field. You lose some weight, gain it back, lose it again. In this scenario, your life might go up or down a little, but will basically continue along the same path.

Then there are stretch goals, which are the especially good outcomes you get if you work harder and strain a bit. These would include the best possible outcomes to your current set of conditions. For example, though you're not sure you're committed to remaining in the industry you're in, you get the best job in your company. Stretch goals are extensions of the predictable and are included by the dotted line.

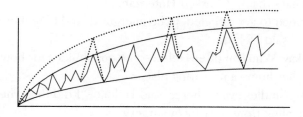

A breakthrough project is different from any of these. It is a complete break with the past that leaves you in a life that may even be unrelated to your current life.

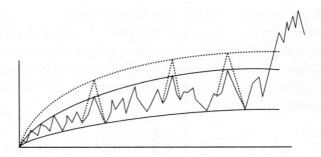

Breaking into a new future doesn't mean working enormously harder. It means knowing, perhaps for the first time ever, what you're working *for*. It means choosing what you'll do based on your deepest passions rather than trying to motivate yourself to work harder at something you're only half committed to.

Look back to your domain and commitment, and look over the many possibilities you gathered. If it's not yet clear to you exactly which outrageous result you ought to commit to, the way to pick is to keep asking yourself, "What's this *for*? Is it a result that would really let me know that I'd done what I now think is impossible?"

Watch how Debra is able to home in on a goal when Hafeezah focuses the discussion on what her commitment is for.

> "The domain I picked is my home," said Debra. "And my commitment within that is to make my home a refuge for myself."
>
> "What's that for?" asked Hafeezah.
>
> "I need to get refueled, to be energized, and to feel nurtured," said Debra.
>
> "Okay. Who can offer Debra some possibilities for how to make her home a nurturing place?"
>
> "Put candles everywhere," said Helene. "I did that when I was healing from my cancer surgery."
>
> "Set aside an area of your home that focuses on comfort," said Lynda.
>
> "Get a water garden in your house," said Jane.
>
> "Get rid of clutter by studying Feng Shui," said Amy Jo.
>
> "Have a music system throughout your house," said Mary Scott.

"Start meditating in your house and include your family," said Elinor.

"Make your bathroom a pampering zone," said Jenny. "I'll do the plumbing," she joked.

"Ask other members of the family what sorts of areas they would like," said Jennifer, from the back of the room.

"Have each member of your family design their own sacred space," Ireen called out.

"Hire Shelly," said Alane.

"Make it a family project," said Leslie.

"Grow some plants or vegetables together," said Lauren.

"Write notes to each other and leave them in unexpected places to let the people in your family know you love them," said Zully.

"Keep your house stocked with great health food and set as a goal that you'll cook one meal a week together," said Alane.

"You could get special things," said Jenny, "like a piano, or a flower garden, or equipment for the kids."

"You could offer to hold community events in your house," said Mary Scott. "Make it a home for more than just your family."

"Okay," said Hafeezah. "Debra, anything you can use there?"

"Almost too much," said Debra, her face a combination of delight and shock.

"Are you overwhelmed by the number of ideas?" asked Hafeezah.

"Wow," said Debra, a bit stunned.

"So, Debra," Hafeezah began, "this may be an obvious question, but what is having a home as a refuge for?"

"It's feeling safe, like things weren't about to crumble," said Debra.

"And what result would let you know that you had a refuge?"

"If everybody else in it felt safe, too. I can't believe I didn't realize all this time that I was planning a house for me but not for my whole family. I love the idea of making it comfortable for everybody rather than trying to make it perfectly the way I think it should be. That would feel like a real refuge."

Say your passion is travel, and your commitment within that field of passion is to go West. Would that mean a half-hour drive to a state park to watch the sunset? Would it mean driving cross-country to California? Would it mean moving to Montana for a year? What result would show, beyond a shadow of a doubt, that you had fulfilled your commitment? What would prove to you, in other words, that you'd done what you set out to do?

EXERCISE: CREATING AN INSPIRING CHALLENGE

1. Look over the slew of new possibilities you've gathered and ask yourself which, of all your possibilities, lights you up the most. On a page in your notebook, write down the ones that delight you.
2. Now rewrite your commitment within your domain.
3. Given your commitment within that domain, what specific result would let you know you had fulfilled your commitment? What would prove to you that you'd broken out and achieved something radically different? Pick something between highly improbable and nearly impossible, and write that result in your notebook.

By the way, it may be that you have two possibilities you want to pursue. Zully, for example, firmly held on to the idea that within the domain of design she had two commitments: to help others do what they want, and then to further develop her creativity while making money at it. So she had people brainstorm for her in two different fronts and came up with two separate declarations.

On the other hand, if two seems one too many but you don't know how to choose, it may be that you can combine two possibilities into one project. If you remember, Page's commitment was "de-stressing"; within that, she had two different domains in which she thought she might operate—animals and painting. Her first idea was to create an animal shelter that would take in pets for people who were traveling, and also get contracts from hospitals and hospices and elderly homes to bring pets to people to cheer them up. Her next idea was to go off and paint by herself. What she eventually came up with was a project of having an exhibit of her paintings of animals from her farm, as well as homeless pets, that would somehow make an event out of getting the people who attended, and perhaps even those who bought the paintings, to adopt animals as well. So she combined her two favorite de-stressing activities into one breakthrough project.

SHAPING A BREAKTHROUGH PROJECT

In designing a breakthrough project, the first and more important message is that it's crucial to think big. The result you will be describing ought to feel as if it's somewhere between highly improbable and nearly impossible—something that, when you say you're going to do it, makes you feel something close to vertigo. If you're not a little uneasy, the result you've picked is too predictable, probably one you'd accomplish anyway. The idea is to think bigger and scarier than you normally would.

> "Okay, so say I say I'm going to run my $300 million corporation," said Jane. "But I know I can't do it for years. Where does that get me?"

The second characteristic of your breakthrough project should be that it's possible. While it's crucial to think outrageous, your breakthrough ought not to be so bold and all-encompassing that you'll be overwhelmed, lose your momentum, and get derailed. So when you're deciding how much to take on, aim for something you think might be possible in about a year. In other words, it needs to be a big hurdle—a result that sits outside the predictable curve of what you'd expect of yourself—but not so big that it's unwieldy. Certainly, your breakthrough project may be part of a larger picture, in the way that enrolling in pastry school may be a step toward your dream of becoming the dessert chef at the Plaza. But for our purposes, you may want to set the goal of completing one semester of pastry school. Framing the project this way enables you to stretch yourself while still keeping a sense of possibility about getting it done.

So, "I will take over my corporation" becomes "I will become the head of a division that does what I want to do." And "I will travel around the world" becomes something like "I will visit one continent I have never been to."

All you have to stand for, here, is that it's not impossible. You don't have to see how it's doable, or even be firmly convinced that it's possible (because our view of what's "possible," of course, is based on what we already know—or think we do!).

The next step is to state your inspiring challenge in language that makes you want to do it. If your breakthough is stated as something you'll avoid, or not do, it's harder to keep motivated. The breakthrough projects that are easiest to stick to are those stated in a positive and empowering way—as something you're motivated to walk toward rather than something you want to leave behind. For example, "I want to stop being afraid to walk on the street," could be reworded as "I will overcome my fear of walking on the street." And "I want to stop fighting with my daughter," could be rephrased as "I will make friends with my daughter."

> "I guess rather than saying all the time how much I want balance in my current life, what I want is to unbalance it and jump off the seesaw. I want my freedom!" said Elinor.
> "Great," said Hafeezah.
> "I was saying I wanted an overhaul, but what I really want is to create a family," said Sara.

Now, the final criteria for your breakthrough declaration is that it's very specific. So the final questions are: Exactly what? And by when?

We all have ways of undermining our breakthroughs and denying our successes to ourselves, minimizing our accomplishments. Defining a breakthrough that consists of a specific set of conditions you want to achieve—again, a result you now consider to be between highly improbable and nearly impossible—means that when you achieve it, you will have no way of discounting your accomplishment, or rewriting it into your narrative of how things never change.

So, for example, "I will overcome my fear of walking on the street" can be further refined to "I will become a brown belt (or a mauve belt, if you prefer!) in Tai Kwon Do." And "I will run a division of my company" becomes "I will found a division called Brainsmarts and become president of it; this division will connect experts with learners all over the world."

For our purposes, I'm suggesting you shape a challenge that can be accomplished in three to eighteen months. Then I'll ask you to pick the date by which you'll do what you say you're going to.

In Shelly's breakthrough project, watch how the group helped her home in specifically on what she should do.

"I'd like to explore my creativity by decorating other people's houses. Even, you know, without getting paid," said Shelly.

"That's not okay," said Amy Jo. "You need to get paid."

"Shelly's going to do that, and keep her real job!" said Jane.

"Does that mean that it's not a real job if I don't get paid?" asked Shelly.

"We tell our clients at the Women's Self-Employment Project that when you finish a job," said Josie, "you have to be happy with what you get. If you do it for free, it's a hobby. Once you start, it's always harder to get those clients to pay more. Go for what you're going to feel good about."

"Although it's not always true that you can't raise your prices," said Zully. "When I started making shoes, I started by charging one twenty-five and ended up charging eight hundred as I learned to look at my real costs."

"Another rule interrupted," said Hafeezah, clearly delighted.

"Go for the value you're providing," suggested Leslie. "I don't charge for my time because of the value I'm adding to their business with my consulting work. I charge for more than just my time."

"It's interesting from an education standpoint," Jane said, "to notice how all the noise really comes up once we start trying to declare. Suddenly it's Do I need security? And, If I start this way, will it have to be this way forever? And, How much am I worth?"

"Great catch, Jane," said Hafeezah. "If you've got a lot of noise going, then you know you're up to something really big. Outside the box, it's a little scary! But keep in mind, about your declaration: This isn't a practice life you're designing. So does this really challenge and excite you?"

Shelly shook her head as if to say "So-so."

"Who else has a breakthrough declaration they're excited about?" asked Hafeezah.

"I'm really excited," said Page. "I'm going to do an art exhibit, which will be shown either in a small museum or a gallery, of my nature paintings of animals, in sixteen months."

"By June of next year, my daughter and I will create a fun self-development video magazine for girls," said Mary Scott. "And I will have done the research for a PBS documentary on the art of double Dutch rope-jumping, and the cultural tradition it passes on, for black women and girls."

"By December of this year," said Amy Jo, "I will have a minimum of seven clients per week, at $125 per session, for my divorce coaching business."

"Okay," said Shelly. "I've got it. By the end of the year I will have redone ten homes for $500 each, using materials that people already have."

"*Fabulous,*" said Hafeezah.

EXERCISE: CREATING A BREAKTHROUGH PROJECT

This exercise will sculpt your inspiring challenge into a specific breakthrough project. Rewrite your challenge—which contains your dream within your domain of interest—and submit it to the following five tests.

1. Is it compellingly calling you forward? Do you feel exuberant at the very thought of it? If not, is there a way to frame it so you'd be more passionate about it?

2. Is it somewhere between highly improbable and nearly impossible? If not, think bigger—to something that you think would just be absolutely, dazzlingly, terrifyingly wonderful.

3. Can you stand that it's at least possible? If not, scale back—but just enough so that you can admit it's a not impossible.

4. Is your breakthrough project stated positively and empoweringly? If not, reword your inspiring challenge so that it is.

5. Is it specific? Have you stated a precise result that you will achieve? And have you stated a specific date by which you'll achieve that result? Pick a date between three and eighteen months away that makes you uneasy and excited but not horribly uncomfortable.

"One year from today," declared Zully, "I will have created a nonprofit called Causes for Change International. In addition, I will have had five interviews to do costume design and will have one contract six months from now. And I will have enrolled in a Ph.D. program."

"I will own 51 percent of a fast-food soul food restaurant, by November first of this year," said Leslie.

"I'm going to make my home a refuge for the whole family by the end of the summer," said Debra.

"I can't believe I'm saying this—I'm glad you don't quite have to feel perfect about it to commit to it—but: I'm going to run the New York City Marathon this year."

"I'm going to write an ADD book for children who have ADD, with my daughter," said Lynda.

"By September of next year," said Jane, "I will have a radio call-in show on education issues, sponsored by other people. And I will begin writing a book on education."

"I will have spoken to a hundred women about my cancer survival by the end of the summer," said Helene. "And by the end of October I will go on and pay for a vacation with my estranged husband. And we will get back together by December first."

"I'm going to start an herbal practice to promote healing with herbs," said Lauren. "By next summer I will have at least ten regular clients."

"I'm going to get to Italy by next fall," said Alane, "if it kills me. By September I will be working in either the food or the fashion industry in Italy, and will be dating at least one wonderful Italian man."

"I'm going to adopt a baby from Russia," said Sara.

"By one year from today, I'm going to get my company to institute a flex-time policy that gives parents—not just mothers—options for how to work with kids," said Elinor. "And the day after we announce that it's in place, I'm going to take a year off!"

Exercise: Declaring Your Breakthrough Project

The conclusion of this process is that you actually commit to it out loud. Use your design group as an audience: Tell them *what* you're going to do and *by when* you're going to do it.

Chapter Ten

The Mountaintop

My hope is that you have now hit on something you want so bad you can taste it, so bad that not pursuing it seems absolutely unbearable.

But your asking yourself, with not a little terror, "How am I going to get there? What if I spent all this time identifying what I want, and there's no way to get there?"

To answer these questions indirectly, I'd like to first propose how you plan for a trip. When you go on a physical journey, you make plans for it by starting where you are. If I'm in New York, for example, and I want to go to Cleveland, I first pack a suitcase in my apartment, then I get in the elevator, then I walk to the street and get a cab to take me to the airport;

I check in, walk through the scanner, get on the plane; I get off the plane and get my luggage and go down an escalator and out of the airport and I take another cab, unless my mom and dad are there to pick me up.

And when someone gives me directions somewhere, my assumption is that the directions start from where I am and proceed toward where I want to go, in a logical order: Turn left at the light and go five miles; then, after you pass the gas station, go right at the fork, and you're there.

This way of planning your physical path contains two assumptions that make the trip possible. First, it assumes that there's a "there" there—that is, the destination you want to go to exists. It also assumes that somebody else has already gone where you need to go. Even if the directions are fuzzy, and you get lost, you still assume that a pathway exists to your destination.

The problem with breakthrough projects—and why I'd be surprised if you *weren't* feeling a bit uneasy right now—is that it feels as if no one can give you directions. The defining characteristic of a project that's radically different from what you now know of your life, in fact, is that you *don't* have any idea how to get there. If it's truly new, its foreignness precludes a whole lot of knowing in advance. This means that you don't know how many ways there are to get there; you don't know if anyone has ever done exactly and specifically the thing you want to do; and you may not even know whether it's possible.

On the other hand, if you think back to a challenge on which you did achieve an unpredictable result: When you got to the finish line, and looked back at your journey, you may have said or thought something like, "If only I'd known that when I started!" If you did, you intuitively realized that pathways to your achievement, perhaps easier ones than the one you took, existed. It was simply that you didn't know about them until you got there. What you were expressing was the wish to have begun your journey with the benefit of top-of-the-mountain vision.

Taking for granted both that the destination exists and that there are several ways to get there is the difference between standing at the bottom of a mountain and looking up, and standing at the summit and looking down. When you stand at the bottom—as we often feel we do when we're beginning a big challenge—you can see, at most, one or two pathways. Yet if someone were to helicopter you to the top of that mountain, and drop you there, you could see many, many trails that would enable you to reach the top. This is why humans find mountaintops so inspiring: They allow us to see more possibilities than our narrow, limited, day-to-day vision usually allows for.

The way we will be mapping our pathways to get you to your breakthrough will be to mentally helicopter you from the bottom of the mountain, and set you at the top. Using the committed listening exercise the group did when they committed to listening from a new identity, the next exercise asks you (and your group) to think and listen from the top of the mountain, having all the knowledge you need in order to get up there. Starting from a vantage point where your breakthrough project has already been successfully completed sets aside the whole question of whether it's possible, and shifts your attention to how it will happen.

So the way I want you to design the pathway to your breakthrough is to use hindsight vision at the *beginning* of the process. You'll do this by thinking backwards. You'll imagine what it's like to be there, and then you will think backwards, step by step, until you reach where you sit right now. This technique is an incredibly empowering way to make plans, and one you can use whenever you're having trouble imagining how you'd get to some place in the future from where you are today. And hopefully, your group will also map at least two possible pathways down the mountain.

The first step will be to close your eyes and fully imagine yourself standing in the future. Imagine that it's the date you set as your deadline, and you've accomplished exactly what you committed to in your breakthrough project.

Design what the celebration will look like. Will it be a party? A quiet dinner at your favorite restaurant? A vacation? A night on the town? Who will you be celebrating with, and exactly how will you be celebrating?

Now, to begin to navigate your pathway down the mountain and back to where you were, the question is simply, What would have happened just before to allow for that? So, if your goal was to sail across the Atlantic, for example, what would have happened just before was that you would have checked your boat and supplies one last time before taking off from the launch party.

The question you'll want to keep asking is: And what would have happened just before that, to make that possible?

With each step backwards into the present, your breakthrough project shifts from being almost impossible, to more possible, to doable, until finally the bridge from the future to the present seems one that you can easily walk.

"Okay," said Hafeezah. "So it's November 1, 1997, and Leslie owns 51 percent of a fast-food soul food restaurant. What happened just before that allowed for that?"

"She had a grand opening," said Debra.

"Debra designed and sent out the promotional materials for the grand opening," said Shelly.

"Okay," said Hafeezah. "And what would have happened just before that to make that possible?"

"She found a great location and rented it," said Josie.

"She hired me to design the uniforms," said Zully.

"Great," said Hafeezah. "And before that?"

"She met the other 49 percent, and gave him a business plan," said Jenny.

"Or, she put an ad in the *Chicago Tribune* inviting restaurateurs with business plans to apply to her," said Julie.

"Everybody got together and got a mailing list of potential investors," said Lynda.

"She determined who she's catering to," said Josie.

"She got her finances together and decided how much she was willing to invest," said Mary Scott.

"She learned the rules of the restaurant business," said Page.

"But you missed a step: Just after she learned the rules, she broke them," said Alane.

"She got the chefs and created a menu," said Alane.

"And what allowed for that?" asked Hafeezah.

"She had a tent at Taste of Chicago to see how her food would go over," said Sara.

"Amy Jo called her and said 'Run toward your fear,'" said Shelly.

"Wonderful," said Hafeezah. "Now, so you don't get stuck thinking there's only one way, let's create another way down the mountain. It's November one of this year, Leslie, and you just had your grand opening. What else could have happened just before to allow for that?"

"The p.r. firm Leslie just sold for millions of dollars handled the publicity," said Jane.

"Bert Wolf on PBS came to her to talk about soul food," said Debra.

The graph of Leslie's first pathway down the mountain looked like this:

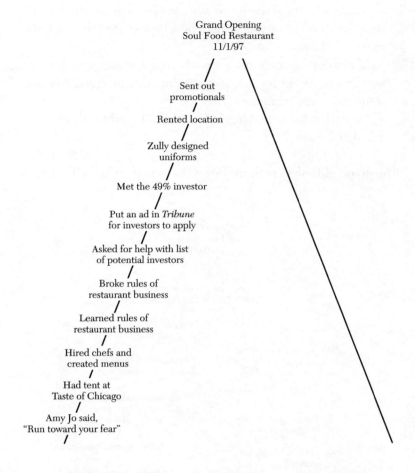

Grand Opening
Soul Food Restaurant
11/1/97

Sent out
promotionals

Rented location

Zully designed
uniforms

Met the 49% investor

Put an ad in *Tribune*
for investors to apply

Asked for help with list
of potential investors

Broke rules of
restaurant business

Learned rules of
restaurant business

Hired chefs and
created menus

Had tent at
Taste of Chicago

Amy Jo said,
"Run toward your fear"

"I saw her on the cover of *Today's Chicago Women*. She was one of the one hundred most influential entrepreneurial women," said Shelly.

"I convinced the committee I'm on to pick her as Woman Entrepreneur of the Year," said Zully.

"During the planning, Leslie is on the phone from home, hugging her children a lot," said Lynda.

"Leslie signed a contract with Sylvia Wood's in New York to be the silent partner and open a second Sylvia's Soul Food, like the one in Harlem, in Chicago."

"And before that?" asked Hafeezah.

"She hired a restaurant consultant," said Shelly.

"Leslie identified the restaurants she loves most and talked with the owners and asked them how they started their restaurants," said Alane.

"She went out to dinner everywhere in Chicago with her design group, except for me, because I'm in training and can't eat soul food," said Jenny.

"And what happened just before that allowed for that?" asked Hafeezah.

The graph of Leslie's pathway down the mountain looks like this now:

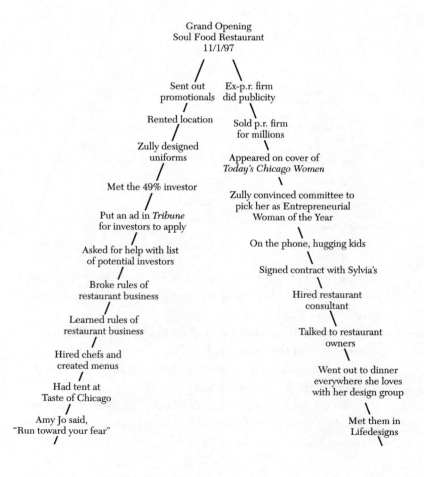

"She declared that she wanted to own a soul food restaurant, and asked her Lifedesigns friends to go out to dinner with her once a week," said Page.

"And before that?"

"She came to this workshop," said Lauren, creating the final link between Leslie's future and her present.

"The last step, Leslie," said Hafeezah, "is that after you decide which actions you want to take, you will assign a date by which you'll do each one of them.

"Uh-oh," said Leslie, laughing.

In the next example, the group charted a pathway for Shelly's breakthrough project of becoming a decorator.

"Okay, it's New Year's Eve and I have four thousand from the ten houses I redid," said Shelly.

"What happened just before that allowed for that?" asked Hafeezah.

"I deposited the checks," said Shelly.

"And before that?"

"She called the one person who hadn't paid and very sweetly asked her to pay before the end of the year," said Mary Scott.

"And before that?"

"She spent the weeks before Christmas picking up last-minute things for her clients in flea markets."

"Shelly found a whole set of furniture for Mrs. Jones's house at an auction, and because she'd been coming regularly, the auctioneer told her about it," said Julie.

"Mrs. Smith visited Mrs. Jones's house in the middle of the decoration, and loved what she was doing, and hired her," said Ireen from the back of the room.

"I did Mrs. Smith's house, she had a party, and invited three other clients," said Shelly.

"Somebody got her brochure in the mail," said Josie.

"I got the brochure in the mail," said Debra, "and called to hire her to help make my home a refuge for my entire family."

"She created the brochure and got a mailing list," said Zully.

"And before that Debra designed the brochure."

"A photographer came to shoot one of her first houses, and left her some pictures, and she used those pictures in her brochure," said Jennifer from the back of the room.

"She did a demo house and took a lot of pictures and got an article in the paper. These were the pictures she used for that brochure," said Sara.

"She found someone willing to have her design her first house," said Hafeezah, raising her hand to volunteer.

"She joined the Interior Decorators' Professional Club," said Zully, "and started going to meetings so she could get all the talk sounding very professional."

"And what happened just before that?"

"She designed the pathway with her design group," said Helene.

"Okay, here we go again," said Hafeezah. "Out to the future again," she said, walking toward the front of the U-shaped table where the participants were sitting. "It's New Year's Eve and we're celebrating. She's got four thousand and ten houses. What happened just before that?"

"Shelly realized she had eight thousand 'cause she's charging eight hundred for the residences," said Zully.

"She had a photo spread in *The New York Times*'s 'Living Section,'" said Amy Jo.

"The editor of the 'Living Section' went to a party at a house she designed," said Page.

"Shelly networked everyone she knew until she found someone who knew someone who knew someone who knew the 'Living Section' editor, and then invited that person to the party and got her to invite the editor," said Julie.

"And before that?" asked Hafeezah.

"She got an article in a local magazine," said Josie.

"She did a cable-access TV show about decorating your house with what you already have," said Jennifer from her table at the back of the room.

"And before that?"

"She did a volunteer speech at the YMCA about making your house a home," said Debra, "and the cable person was in the audience."

"She looked for assistance," said Josie, "and called me at the Women's Self-Employment Project for some help."

"And before that she declared what she wanted at the Lifedesigns workshop!" said Hafeezah. "Shelly, are you ready to assign some dates to your steps?"

"Now I know how Amy Jo feels, because now I'm really scared!" said Shelly.

Exercise: Mapping Pathways

This exercise can either be done just after the exercise in Chapter 9, with your brainstorming group. Or you can assemble a design group just to design your pathways. Often it's more convenient to do it all at once.

1. Ask someone to record your pathways for you, so that you can be fully present.
2. On a big piece of paper, draw a simple dotted-line diagram of a mountain. Put it up on the wall.
3. Now, state your breakthrough project to your group: what you'll do, and by when you'll do it. Write your goal, and your deadline, at the top of the mountain.
4. As part of registering your accomplishment, describe the celebration you're going to have. Then ask your group to answer the question *What would have happened just before that to allow for that?* Keep asking the question until the group brings you back to the present.
5. Design at least two pathways to your breakthrough result so you can't get stuck in the "there's only one way of getting there" mentality.
6. Give yourself a day to create an action plan from all the possibilities you gathered. Then: Assign your deadlines!

Chapter Eleven

Completing Your Breakthrough

The final step in making sure you achieve your breakthrough will be to ensure the support of those people whose support you need. The first step to getting it, of course, will be to declare your breakthrough project to them, just like you did to the people in your design group.

The bad news is that a bold and specific declaration—the kind that you created in Chapter 9—often generates resistance in the people who know you best. Most of us have had the experience of declaring to a loved one a great new idea for the future, only to have it shot down. And when we get shot down, we often decide that what our loved one really wants is to sabotage us. Either we begin to argue with the "skeptics," or we tune them out, resolving not to tell them about our dreams and plans again. Neither of these responses helps you get the support you need to achieve your breakthrough.

The good news is that there are ways of enrolling a skeptic in your plan.

This section contains a step-by-step process for neutralizing the objections of a "skeptic," and even for converting a "skeptic" into an enthusiastic supporter. I've put "skeptic" in quotes, because I hope that by the end of the discussion, I will have persuaded you that a skeptic is only a person with a commitment.

ENROLLING OTHERS

The engine behind your breakthrough project is your commitment. The people closest to you will sense its power immediately. When you declare, you're detonating a little bomb that has a tremor effect. These tremors—the perceived impacts of your declaration—can sometimes provoke people to hold on tight, the way they would during an earthquake, regardless of whether they're actually committed to defending the status quo. Or, the tremors of your declaration can provoke others to shift their commitments and drop bombs of their own.

The first step toward enrolling others is to choose an empowering interpretation—which is that your skeptics are not simply operating out of a commitment to sabotage you. Rather, they have—and may discover—valid commitments that are as important to them as yours are to you.

Perhaps the most common commitment that provokes people to object to your declaration is *a commitment to know who you are*. Declarations are often frightening, even upsetting, to family, friends, and colleagues. So when you declare, you announce a reality that's radically different from the past, and sometimes even *a person* who may be radically different from the one your loved ones know! This can frighten people, especially those who know you best.

Keep in mind that, for them, watching you declare a new reality can be like the moment in the movie *Close Encounters of the Third Kind* when Teri Garr watches her husband build a mud mountain in the middle of their living room. The people close to you want to think they know you; completely apart from the content of what you declare, the first thing your declaration implies is that they don't know you as well as they thought. And the human tendency to try to keep things the way they are—that is, safe—means that the people close to you often resist your ability to declare in an immediate, knee-jerk sort of way. In some ways, the more radical your declaration, the more likely it is that you'll encounter resistance—and the less likely it is that your husband will jump on board and say, "Of course you can put a man on the moon, honey!"

These sorts of objections are relatively easy to recognize. Their identifying characteristic is that they deny permission to declare. "You can't just say something and have it come true! Who do you think you are?" Or, in other words: "Hey, wait a second! Who are you? You're changing identity on me!"

When Leslie announced that she was leaving her consulting firm to start a soul food restaurant, her father said, "You can't just start from scratch anytime you want to!"

And when Elinor declared to her company that she was working up and instituting a flex-time policy, her boss said, "What? I thought you were on our side!"

A second big category of objections, closely related to the first, are those that arise out of *a commitment to stay connected*. If your skeptics are objecting in a quick, knee-jerk way, it's often not because they object to the new reality itself, but because they're terrified that the strength of your new vision means you'll leave them behind. This can be difficult for loved ones, who care a great deal about remaining connected to you. Your skeptics sense that your new reality is a true break from the past— a past that includes them, and are afraid of the separation they anticipate between who they are now and who you intend to be.

Very often, you can recognize these objections because they overtly or covertly predict failure. "You're not cut out to be an entrepreneur," a friend might say. "You'll be working fifteen hours a day." The subtext of these objections goes something like: You'll never do that, because if you do, then we'll be apart. "You won't exercise every day," they say, and the subtext is: If you do, and I don't, you won't be attracted to me anymore. Your skeptic, then, is attempting to preserve a connection that he feels is threatened by your announcement of how things are now going to be from now on.

Another variation on objections that arise out of a commitment to stay connected are those that arise from *a commitment to preserve autonomy*. We all know what it's like when a boss comes in with a big smile and says, "Team, we're about to embark on a wonderful new project!" You cringe because you feel you'll have to do something you might not want to do; you raise your hackles and your resistance before you take in what your boss is saying. Similarly, when your loved ones and colleagues react to you this way, they're taking their connection to you as a premise. At the same time, the strength of your declaration is enormous; so they feel they'll have no choice but to go along with your declaration. Their two commitments—to stay connected and to preserve their autonomy—seem to conflict.

These objections usually assume a duty. "So now I have to weed the garden on my weekends?" your husband may ask. Or, if you want to have an art exhibit in Cincinnati: "I hate Cincinnati." The logic behind these sorts of objections goes beyond the assumption that You can't train for the marathon, because if you do, and I don't, you won't be attracted to me anymore. Because remaining connected is taken for granted, a conclusion develops: Therefore I'll have to train for the marathon, too—and I don't know if I want to! In other words, your skeptic is reacting to the authority that his connection with you implies.

In all three cases you will need to listen carefully for the commitment underlying the objection, and identify what your skeptic is committed to. Once your skeptic has expressed an objection, give the permission to declare themselves by offering a rough draft of your guess. So, for example:

- If, when you announce that you want to start your own divorce coaching business, and your brother says, "How do you expect us to run things?" you could respond by saying: "What

I'm hearing is that you're committed to keeping our family business profitable. Is this accurate?"

- If your sister says, "You can't take over Dad's business! That's a bad idea!" you can reply: "What I'm hearing is that you're concerned about protecting what Dad has built over the years. Is that accurate?"
- If your boss says, "And when would you manage to work up a child care policy? On your coffee break?" you can reply: "What I'm hearing is that you're committed to keeping me productive in the company. Is that accurate?"

If your skeptic is being difficult, she may reply, "No, it's not accurate!" but not volunteer what her actual concern is. In this case, you need to ask directly: "So what are you committed to?"

This simple process of taking the time to identify your skeptic's commitment will make their objection feel a lot less threatening!

Once you've identified the commitment beneath your skeptic's objection, the next step is to validate it. If the objection's coming out of a commitment to know you, for example, you may need to help your skeptic see your declaration as a discovery, not a betrayal. The easiest way to do that is simply to acknowledge its newness. Affirm your own surprise at your discovery. "Yes, this is new," you may want to say. "It's new to me, too." Amy Jo told her family that although she'd thought that she could be committed to the business for life, and had gotten an M.B.A. etcetera toward that end, she now knew that she could not. And that she knew it would be a big change for them to adjust to.

An alternative is to establish a continuity between your past commitments and the ones you've just declared. "This may seem new," you may want to say, "but it's a version of what you already know about me." Elinor told her boss that although she'd previously shared his view on the child care issue as one primarily about remaining close to one's children, she now saw it as a productivity issue for the company, because she realized how much more it would cost them, in time and labor, to train replacement employees. Her new commitment, she explained, was springing out of her old commitment to keep the company productive.

Because fear of separation is a universal, objections that come out of a commitment to stay connected are in some ways the easiest to neutralize. We all understand that in many ways the bonds we have with others are fragile; one reason we don't declare our dreams is that we, too, are afraid of separation. In nearly every workshop, there's one participant who, like Jenny, comes back on the second day convinced that she needs to leave her husband because he isn't supportive. While there may be cases where women do need to leave, my own feeling is that the urgent "need" to separate comes from a seemingly unresolvable conflict: On the one hand, we know we can't create a new reality alone; at the same time, the drive to fulfill our commitment, to become more of who we really are, is irresistibly compelling. If our loved ones don't jump on board immediately, we sometimes panic. We think we need to find other, more supportive people—*now!*—before our determination and vision dissipate.

One way to create a bridge to your skeptics is simply to state your commitment to stay connected. If you're wary about how your new reality might cause alienation, say so. This doesn't mean backing off what you declare, but rather reassuring your skeptics that you realize your declaration impacts them, and that you care about their reaction. In other words, invite your skeptics to your party. For example, when Page announced that she would do an art exhibit of her nature paintings, she invited her husband and children to accompany her on her visits to various museums and galleries she thought might be interested in her work. Their outings became a once-a-week ritual that enabled them to participate in her dream, even though she was spending more time alone, painting.

Keep in mind, though, that inviting doesn't mean demanding that your skeptic jump on board immediately. If what you're hearing are two commitments—one to preserve the connection to you, the other to preserve your skeptic's autonomy—you will need to validate both. We tend to think that support for our breakthrough project means the full participation of those around us; this may not be the case. One of the things I hope Chapter 10 will accomplish is to enable you to see the many possible pathways for how to create your new reality. Keeping this in mind may enable you to validate your skeptic's right not to participate. After Jenny went home on the second day of the workshop, she told her husband that she was committed to running the New York City Marathon. In her words, he immediately began "grumbling" about how his knees were "shot." Jenny then asked her husband how he'd feel about handing her paper cups of water along the route. She affirmed, in other words, both that she wanted to stay connected *and* that her husband had the choice not to run the marathon with her. Her husband jumped on board and bought her a subscription to *Runner's World* the next week, because Jenny gave him the freedom not to.

If you're experiencing repeated, strenuous expressions of negativity directed at your new reality, and the objections are specific in nature, chances are, your skeptic is committed not just to knowing who you are, or staying connected, or preserving their autonomy, but to having an actual impact on your new reality. If this is the case, you will want to ask, within the context of your declaration, what your skeptic would like to see happen; how he or she would like to create that reality, and, specifically, how he or she would like you to contribute. Asking these questions gives your skeptic a chance to discover his or her actual commitment. In addition, the questions include them in the building process by helping them to see that their underlying commitment requires them to take some responsibility for creating what they want. Sometimes you will be able to spur the objector into a declaration about what they're going to do to realize what they want; in other cases, the objector will discover that they're not committed to taking any action. Either way, having to take responsibility neutralizes the objection.

These sorts of strenuous objections may be the ones we need to listen to most carefully of all. The vehemence behind them reflects a strong passion, longing, or hope that needs to be respected. When someone objects this strenuously, they always have a commitment, and may even be seeing a worm in the apple that you don't see.

The beauty of enabling others to discover their true commitments is that it actually gives you the opportunity to establish a deeper relationship with the skeptics, based on their deeply held, and newly discovered, commitments. You may even find you're able to align yourself with people you've historically been at odds with, because you discover commitments of theirs that you may be able to get behind. When you ask these questions, you and your complainers may discover that beneath their complaining, they're committed to something great.

This technique of listening for the underlying commitments of others, and enrolling them by accepting those commitments, forms the basis for how to deal with even the strongest resistance to your new reality. A story one of my consultants told me illustrates how this might work. According to my consultant, when J.F.K. announced that we'd put a man on the moon, and began to assemble a team of scientists to do it, one after another came to him with objections. One engineer said he couldn't do it because the capsule would burn up as it fell through the atmosphere. Another said the astronauts would never survive, because there was no way to provide sustainable, breathable air for them. Kennedy was able to see that these scientists weren't objecting because they were committed to maintaining a reality in which no one ever walked on the moon. Rather, they were committed to protecting the astronauts from a real danger they perceived, which they felt stood in the way of the project's success. What Kennedy essentially did was to identify the commitment behind the objection and enroll each person according to their commitment. As the story goes, he put the person concerned with the capsule burning up in charge of inventing the Teflon coating for the outside of the capsule. And he assigned the scientist concerned with the oxygen the task of inventing a system to enable the astronauts to breathe.

The more committed your skeptic is to her or his objection, the more effective this tactic is. When you treat your objector's objection as a valid commitment—even if he expresses it as, "That's impossible because . . ."—you neutralize the potential fight. Once you stop fighting with the "that's impossible" and start focusing on resolving the valid concern that follows the "because . . . ," you jump over the wall between you and your skeptic, and start looking at the problem from where he or she stands. By leveraging the energy your skeptic is using to resist, you can convert it into energy he will use to fulfill his own commitment—the commitment your listening enabled him to discover.

One last note: Occasionally, your skeptic will affirm a commitment you can't affirm. You may be committed to rearranging the workload at the office to enable your company to allow for flex-time for mothers. Your colleague objects because he likes his dependable schedule and is committed to knowing when he's going to come and go every day. He doesn't care about the women in the office. The thing to do in this case is simply to validate your skeptic's right to hold a commitment you don't share. Your interest in what your skeptic is committed to can help build the bridge you need to get even a hardened skeptic on board.

EXERCISE: ENROLLING OTHERS

In this exercise, you will practice putting yourself into the line of fire.

1. Choose your skeptic. For the purpose of this exercise, practice on a person whose opinion matters less to you than your nearest and dearest—your office's resident pessimist, for example, but not your boss or your husband. This way, you can develop your enrolling skills in a less dangerous context.

2. Declare your breakthrough project. Say what you're going to do, and when you're going to do it by.

3. Help your skeptic identify the commitment behind his or her objection by articulating a rough draft of it. Use the phrase "What I'm hearing is that you're committed to . . ." and follow up with "Is that accurate?"

4. Ask your skeptic the following questions.

   • So, what are you committed to in this situation?

   • What would you like to see happen?

   • How would you like to create that reality?

   • And, specifically, how would you like me to contribute?

5. Once you've accurately identified the commitment beneath the objection, validate it, if you can, in one or more of the following ways.

   • If the commitment is to know you, either admit that your declaration is a new discovery even to you, or point out the ways in which it's not so new.

   • If the objection is to remain connected, reiterate your own desire to stay connected.

   • If the commitment is to preserve autonomy, affirm that your loved one isn't compelled to feel the way you feel, or do what you do.

   • If the commitment is to affect your new reality, affirm that you value his input. If you think you might modify your plan in a way that takes his concern into account, tell him so.

   • Even if you can't affirm a commitment to what your

skeptic is committed to, validate his or her freedom to think differently.

6. After the conversation is concluded, register your accomplishment! On a page in your notebook, write down what your skeptic said. Note a part of her objection that you could have taken personally, but didn't. List the areas in which you might have approached her from a stance of already knowing, but didn't. And record what you think you did differently.

7. Take your ground by telling someone close to you about your experience.

Congratulations!

REGISTERING YOUR ACCOMPLISHMENTS

In preparation for registering your own accomplishments, I'll offer what our participants said about their achievements. They had the advantage of registering their accomplishments in front of a group; I encourage you to do the same with your friends and family.

"In the last few months," said Mary Scott, "my frustration has been that I save everybody else's kid, but don't have time for my own. This project will allow me to do the same kind of work I do but integrate the people who are most important to me."

"I found out that I was the source of my own anger," said Elinor. "For the first time I've set a goal that's totally opposite to what I'm 'supposed' to do. And I own it, and I can see it happening. It's only a matter of time. In addition, I've really been beating myself up thinking I don't have balance, etcetera. Turning forty, realizing I've put so much into my work, realizing that's what I wanted to do. Now realized that balance can be in cycles."

"I took the Bar," said Amy Jo, "but hadn't come up with a group of women to support me. Now I believe I can pick any woman here and call and say, I know I have to, but I need somebody to say it's okay to be scared but you know you have to do it."

"I've made a commitment to my overall personal growth," said Alane, "which I think I was waiting for something to break on the outside, to allow it. And to pulling back from work. I'm realizing that I'm responsible for achieving my potential. This will allow for more creative expression, and allow me to be more energetic, and then give more quality—rather than just quantity—hours at my work. What would have been pre-dictable would be just to keep up the manic pace at work and not ask myself where I was going, and never get to Italy."

"I've gained the courage to face what I know I've needed for a long time," said Shelly, "which is to leave my job. I have lots of great friends now, a kick-start to a new life, and more aware-ness of my talents. If I get a job I get gratification out of, I think I'll be more confident. I will no longer continue in the mode of perpetual procrastination and fogginess. And I have already thrown off my conservative demeanor! Even this pathway exer-cise made me realize that I clam up and shy away from things that are going to lead me where I want to be. I will start every race at the starting line, not in the back of the pack anymore. And in all my work I will continue to believe that I add value, I have value, and what I have is valuable. I'm not doing the turtle anymore when I get out in the world!"

"I guess I've had a major, major shift," said Helene. She is speaking loudly and clearly, as if she's ready to take over leading the workshop. "Before, I was living to die. Now I'm living to live. I see, now, how I'll help others to live—and that there's no limit to where I can go. If I hadn't come I would have contin-ued to sink and die. Impact on career: I will be a much more productive and committed person. I now don't see any limits. I've got a new smile and a new voice!"

"I realized that I'm in control of my life," said Debra. "I need to let the past be the past, and I've acknowledged what drives me. Hearing the others' stories made me stop wallowing in my own self-pity and realize that I need to be more sensitive to other people's feelings and more selective in the things I get in-volved in. I'm going to deliberately plan my personal goals, as I do my professional goals. I'm going to stop watching myself on TV, like an actress, waiting for whatever happens. I think I know why I've been alienating others. I'm going to make a refuge for us rather than simply decorate a home for me, and overall, have a healthier mental attitude. You are all invited to my new home for a house blessing on October 15!"

"Unlike most of you, I didn't plan to be here," said Josie. "My boss took the workshop, and yesterday afternoon, she made me come. I'm so glad she did. I thought this was a workshop for me to learn how to motivate others, but now I realize that it's not the other people who have been stopping my growth. It's me. Whenever I hit a problem that's too overwhelming, I just shut down, and then I lose ground, and when I come back up I've lost all this time. So I've had small successes, but never a big one. Now I realize that I don't have to stay committed to all that junk that minimizes me in comparison to other people. I'm through with that. I'm just going to walk away! I have a new attitude, and can de-stress. I can relax my shoulders now instead of being tense. I'm free. In addition, I needed to take half-steps," she continued. "I need to focus on me for a while. I never thought it was a valid goal to spend time pampering myself, but now I know that if I don't, I'll never be able to nurture anybody else."

"I guess the biggest thing I got," said Jenny, "was the ability to make myself vulnerable. It's safe. Amy Jo pointed out to me at the break yesterday that she thought that was the real me: I had a lot of walls, and barriers, and layers. And I'm excited to take care of my body, and spend a lot of time, which I would have called wasted time before, valuing it."

"I hope you will acknowledge and celebrate each layer peeling off," said Hafeezah.

"When I read about this workshop," said Leslie, "I thought it would be a fun thing to do. But what has always been an issue is that I'm not really being true to my own success, the success I want with my kids. To thine own self be true, you know? Now I have the freedom to author my own success rather than having to set an example or break any more barriers. And I've gotten the encouragement to smile more!"

"If my life had a theme song," said Lauren, "it would be 'When You Wish Upon a Star.' I've wished and wished. Now, for the first time, I've created a concrete plan to risk. I learned to nail down a dream. And I think I've finally gotten complete on not being a doctor."

"So much has happened for me," said Lynda. "I gained the courage. I heard courage but I didn't know what it felt like, or what confidence felt like. Going through the fact and interpretations got to the angers I've been feeling. I was angry for my mom, that she had to be a single mother, and that I ended up on public assistance. As I listened to different women share their angers, I was able to name mine. I need to have the courage to face them. I just haven't been able to show it with family, because I've been too angry with my mom and my dad, whom I didn't meet until I was thirty-five years old. I'm going to deal with that so I can be finished and complete with them. I now feel I can make the connections that everybody else sees, and connect to my family in the now. I'm energized, and most of all, I'm going to listen for the first time in my life."

"This group released the power in me, and made me not afraid," Jane said. "I'm going on the air, and I'm going to write a book."

"I came here to get unstuck personally and professionally," said Sara. "I set out to do it many times before, but this time, I have a solid plan of things I'm going to be accountable to. I feel a connection to a lot of inspirational women and a lot of role models. And I'm going to forge a connection to a child without giving up on having a man in my life!"

"Yesterday I said that I wanted to be self-expressed," said Zully, "and I accomplished that without reservation or resistance or being embarrassed. I've been designing my life throughout, but always thinking I wasn't capable or that it wasn't enough. I've gotten a lot of confidence from you all, realizing how much I am valued by others. Plus, I loved making two separate declarations: one for my artistic expression; one for doing philanthropic work. I thought I had to have one thing, yet I've always been involved with so much it's always been hard to answer the question, when people ask me what I do. Now I will answer by talking about whatever I'm committed to do in the moment!"

"When people ask me, 'What do you do?'" said Hafeezah, "I say, 'When?' So, Mary Scott?"

"I got clarity," Mary Scott said. "And I got a way to integrate lots of visions and people into one goal. I created a way to help other girls and also to do it with my own girls, and my son. This is the first time I think I'll ever have integrated personal and professional!"

"I've realized I need to be doing what I'm committed to," said Julie. "I realized how important the social mission of whatever I do is. Also, how creative I am in a group, how comfortable I can feel when I don't have to prove myself. And how terrifically uncomfortable I am with my own achievements."

"I got that my biggest obligation to others," said Page, "for the rest of my life, is to be doing what I love."

....

EXERCISE: TAKING YOUR GROUND
1. To register your accomplishments, turn to a fresh page in your notebook and answer the following questions.
   • What perspective do you have now that you didn't have when you began reading this book?
   • What skills have you practiced and developed?
   • What do you know about yourself that you didn't know before?
   • And what now seems possible that didn't before?
2. Declare the ground you've gained to your loved ones, and anyone else who will listen!

....

CREATING CONTINUING SUPPORT FOR YOUR DREAMS

Committed support structures are there to remind you of your commitments when the world intervenes. They help you take actions consistent with your commitments, rather than consistent with your immediate circumstances. The people in these support structures, once you tell them what it is you want, will be listening for a bigger you than your (sometimes collapsible) listening allows for. And they will be returning you to your commitments when you forget or get distracted from them by the needs of the moment.

So, in answer to the question you may have had at the beginning of the chapter—Where do these supporters come from?—the answer is: They are people who share your commitments.

They can consist of a structured group, gathered from the group you assembled for your brainstorming, designing, and pathway mapping. You can ask these women to reconvene in about three weeks, giving yourself time to have done something but still feel a bit of pressure. Again, if you've engaged them in the design process, this will be something they will want to do as much as you do.

You can also, as the enrollment section suggests, rely on your loved ones—anybody who loves you enough to share your commitment to create a life you love. Your colleagues may share your commitment to the policy reforms you're trying to bring about, or they may simply hold a commitment to create a less stressful work environment. Women you meet at your hair salon, though they may not be committed to your cause, may be committed to sharing information between women. And this one commitment may motivate them to put you in touch with someone who can help you more specifically.

I believe in having as many people as possible know what you're looking to create in your life. That perpetual declaring is what connects you, over and over, to new people and possibilities. The technique Amanda suggested for creating an alternate conversation for possibility—telling everyone you talk to the dream you're currently trying to build—is a terrific habit to develop. Reach out, in every way you can. In the time it took me to write this book, by the way, we created the Lifedesigns website—www.lifedesigns.com—which is dedicated to connecting women looking to gather possibilities with those who want to offer resources. So use it, and us—either on the Internet, using out tapes, or via our newsletter. Or come to a workshop! We'll be there for you.

Throughout our lives, we change almost without noticing. And periodically we need to create breakthroughs to catch up with who we've become. So the process you have practiced here is one I know you will use over and over. No matter where you are in your life's journey, I trust I have convinced you of a few crucial concepts. First, that the greatest gift you can give anyone is to live a life that lights you up. Second, that no matter how "absurd" or "impossible" you think the life of your dreams is, a pathway to it does exists in your current life. Finally, that your ability to reach out and declare your dreams connects you in a way you may never have connected before. And continuing to declare them to anyone who'll listen means that you never again have to pursue them alone.

EXERCISE: DECLARING THE LIFE OF YOUR DREAMS

1. What I'd like you to do, for the last exercise in the book, is simply to describe a day in the life of your dreams. That life may contain many elements you haven't yet worked on. Whatever your ideal day consists of, each of those elements is an area in which you can define a breakthrough project and bring it to completion. So now write down, in order of priority, the areas in which you'd like to design breakthroughs.

2. Speak about the life of your dreams, what you have accomplished by reading and doing and being in this book, to a person you love!

About the Author

Gail Blanke is president and founder of Lifedesigns, a motivational consulting firm whose mission is to empower women worldwide to live the life of their dreams. She is former senior vice president of Avon Products, Inc., where she spearheaded its Breast Cancer Awareness Crusade and initiated the Women of Enterprise Awards. She is the author of *Taking Control of Your Life: The Secrets of Successful Enterprising Women*. *Mirabella* magazine listed her in their tribute to "1,000 Women for the Nineties." She currently serves as president of the New York Women's Forum, and has received numerous leadership awards. A graduate of Sweet Briar College who studied at the Yale University graduate school of drama, Gail lives in New York City with her husband, Jim Cusick, and their daughters, Kate and Abigail.